The Untold History of the United States

Young Readers Edition, Volume 2, 1945–1962

Also written by Oliver Stone

On History: Tariq Ali and Oliver Stone in Conversation

A Child's Night Dream

Also Written by Peter Kuznick

*Rethinking the Atomic Bombings of Hiroshima and Nagasaki:
Japanese and American Perspectives* (in Japanese, with Akira Kimura)

*Nuclear Power and Hiroshima:
The Truth Behind the Peaceful Use of Nuclear
Power* (in Japanese, with Yuki Tanaka)

Beyond the Laboratory: Scientists as Political Activists in 1930s America

Rethinking Cold War Culture (with James Gilbert)

Also written by Oliver Stone and Peter Kuznick

The Untold History of the United States

Let's Talk About War: Let's Talk About What War Really Is
(in Japanese, with Satoko Oka Norimatsu)

The Untold History of the United States

Young Readers Edition, Volume 2, 1945–1962

Written by
OLIVER STONE and PETER KUZNICK

Adapted by
ERIC SINGER

atheneum

ATHENEUM BOOKS FOR YOUNG READERS

New York   London   Toronto   Sydney   New Delhi

𝒜
atheneum

ATHENEUM BOOKS FOR YOUNG READERS

An imprint of Simon & Schuster Children's Publishing Division

1230 Avenue of the Americas, New York, New York 10020

Text copyright © 2019 by Secret History, LLC and Eric Singer

Jacket illustration copyright © 2019 by Sugio Yamazaki

ATHENEUM BOOKS FOR YOUNG READERS is a registered trademark of

Simon & Schuster, Inc. Atheneum logo is a trademark of Simon & Schuster, Inc.

For information about special discounts for bulk purchases, please contact Simon & Schuster

Special Sales at 1-866-506-1949 or business@simonandschuster.com.

The Simon & Schuster Speakers Bureau can bring authors to your live event.

For more information or to book an event, contact the Simon & Schuster Speakers Bureau

at 1-866-248-3049 or visit our website at www.simonspeakers.com.

Book design by Sonia Chaghatzbanian

The text for this book was set in Bembo.

Manufactured in the United States of America

1218 FFG

First Edition

10 9 8 7 6 5 4 3 2 1

CIP data for this book is available from the Library of Congress.

ISBN 978-1-4814-2176-8

ISBN 978-1-4814-2178-2 (eBook)

For Rachel and Evie
—E. S.

Contents

Foreword by D. Watkins

I thought I hated history.

That idea makes me cringe. What makes me cringe even more is that I know thousands of children in this country probably feel the same way because of the way we were educated. I'm Black. I grew up in Baltimore, which is a Black city. I attended Black schools where the history of *all* Americans wasn't properly taught or acknowledged.

For example, this is how Black history was taught back when I was coming up: We started as slaves, and then Lincoln freed us, so that Rosa Parks could sit and then get kicked out the "white only" section of a bus, which made Dr. King march, and then Michael Jackson moonwalked on TV, setting up Michael Jordan for the free throw dunk that ended racism.

The few Black accomplishments mentioned are sparsely sprinkled throughout twelve years of schooling that beat you over the head with a curriculum about how Christopher Columbus discovered America, even though people were already there, the brave earlier settlers, and how amazing the Founding Fathers were. Some students bought into the rhetoric and even grew to be mildly patriotic, mainly because our teachers always forgot to explain how racist the Founding Fathers were whom they praised. I'm sure our classes would have been a lot more interesting if we knew what our Founders really thought about people of color. A few examples in their own words:

- "[Indians and wolves are] both being beasts of prey tho' they differ in shape."   —*George Washington*

- "[Blacks are] inhabitants, but as debased by servitude below the equal level of free inhabitants, which regards the slave as divested of two-fifths of the man."   —*James Madison*

- "Blacks smelled bad and were physically unattractive, required less sleep, were dumb, cowardly and incapable of feeling grief, advance it therefore as a suspicion only; that blacks whether originally a distinct race or made distinct by time and circumstances are inferior to the whites in the endowments of body and mind."   —*Thomas Jefferson*

Our current system and culture allows these guys to be heroes. Many public schools don't dive that deep into history, so I never got to learn about the toxic racism of people like James Madison and Thomas Jefferson. The same system also never taught me that enslaved Africans and African Americans went on to become just as, if not more, important than the Founders. My people have done so much for this country, only to be reduced to mere footnotes on the heel of history. That's why so many of us thought the subject wasn't important. Luckily, rap music exposed us to heroic figures like Malcom X, Angela Davis, Assata Shakur, and the Black Panthers, challenging many listeners to do our own research and learn what this country is truly about.

The Untold History of the United States teaches lessons, as the title implies, that have not been so much "untold" as "untaught." America has a funny way of muffling important parts of our country's development—important figures and events that all citizens and prospective citizens need to know about. I could have benefited tremendously from this series when I was a child. It would have given me a better understanding of my country; how it began and how it still operates. We had nothing like this growing up, but I'm thankful that we have this tool to pass on now.

Had I read books like this when I was in school, I might have learned that America would not be America without Black people and how free slave labor allowed this country to rise to power. I might have learned about how Blacks were used as guinea pigs in experiments that led to many of the advancements in modern medicine. Or about how for years, ignorant people have run home on the weekends to watch their favorite Negroes score touchdowns and dunk basketballs without knowing or caring much for their history of oppression.

America needed people like me. I never knew it. Only years later, after reading and studying history, did I learn that without my people there would be no Elvis, Beatles, or Beach Boys, since they stole and mimicked Black music. Then there's the traffic light, potato chips, the gas mask, the mailbox, the blood bank, the carbon filament for light bulbs, the pacemaker control unit, the fireproof safe, the telegraph, the home video game console, the imaging X-ray spectrometer, mobile refrigeration, the elevator, the mop, the almanac, the car phone, ice cream, the lawn mower, the fire extinguisher, the ironing board, and air-conditioning units—all of which wouldn't exist without African Americans. The list goes on and on. When I discovered these secrets, I felt different. I realized that I didn't hate history at all because I was included. My people were a part of the story.

Winston Churchill said, "History is written by the victors." And for too long those powerful victors have been snuffing out our history. This volume speaks truth to their power and goes far beyond, giving voice to all of us who were impacted by the Cold War's oppressive policies and culture. It is a model for how our history should be written in these uncertain and perilous times.

D. Watkins is an editor at large for Salon. He is also a professor at the University of Baltimore and founder of the BMORE Writers Project. Watkins is the author of the New York Times *bestsellers* The Beast Side: Living (and Dying) While Black in America *and* The Cook Up: A Crack Rock Memoir.

Introduction

In 1945, the world changed dramatically. With the end of World War II, the bloodiest war in human history, people around the world reflected on new realities. The war had claimed at least 60 million lives, left much of Europe and Asia in tatters, and forever changed the global balance of power. Twenty-seven million perished in the Soviet Union alone and well over 10 million in China. While Europeans and Asians dug out of the rubble and struggled to repair unimaginable physical, psychological, and social wounds, Americans buried 415,000 soldiers and pondered their country's new role as a global superpower. How would the United States handle the grave responsibilities associated with that new role? And how would Americans grapple with the burden of being the first country in history to use atomic weapons?

At the time, Americans were divided between two fundamentally different visions of the role the United States should play in the postwar world. Some Americans believed in US *hegemony*—that is, they believed the United States should lead and dominate the world. Henry Luce, the wealthy publisher of *Time*, *Life*, and *Fortune* magazines, was one of those Americans. He called the twentieth century the "American Century."

In 1941, Luce wrote, "We must accept whole-heartedly our duty and our opportunity as the most powerful and vital nation in the world, and in consequence to exert upon the world the full impact of our new influence, for such purposes as we see fit and by such means we see fit."

President Franklin Roosevelt's former vice president Henry Wallace, who served as President Harry Truman's secretary of commerce until Truman fired him in September 1946, sharply disagreed with Luce. In 1942, he spoke out against Luce's nationalist vision: "No nation will have the God-given right to exploit other nations," Wallace declared. "There must be neither military nor economic imperialism."

Many Americans agreed with Wallace. They shared his utopian vision for a "Century of the Common Man." They didn't believe that one nation should dominate the world. They believed in independence, freedom, equality, and peaceful coexistence for all people, regardless of nationality. They also believed that an international body should control and soon abolish atomic weapons so that they would never again be used.

On September 2, 1945, Japan formally surrendered to the Allied forces on the deck of the USS *Missouri* in Tokyo Bay. Americans cheered Japan's surrender. Headlines blared the news. PEACE! IT'S OVER! screamed the *Charlotte Observer*. The *Saipan Beacon* announced, JAPS QUIT—WAR ENDS! Ticker-tape parades cascaded down the avenues of American cities. Bells tolled and music played as people danced in the streets.

In the middle of New York City's Times Square, a jubilant sailor dipped a young nurse into a kiss. "You can imagine how people felt," recalled the nurse, Edith Shain, sixty years later. "They were just elated. Someone grabbed me and kissed me, and I let him because he fought for his country."

All of the excitement, though, masked a strange pall hanging over the nation. Thoughts of the burned-out ruins of Hiroshima and Nagasaki had become seared in people's minds. Many wondered what the next war might look like now that humans had developed and unleashed atomic power. They were concerned that other countries might build similar weapons and use them against the United States. CBS newsman Edward R. Murrow observed, "Seldom, if ever, has a war ended leaving the victors with such a sense of uncertainty and fear, with such a realization that the future is obscure and that survival is not assured." In such an uncertain world, at such a crucial time, would Henry Luce's vision for American dominance of the world win out? Or would the world heed Henry Wallace's call for international cooperation and peaceful coexistence?

The Cold War

When President Roosevelt died on April 12, 1945, tension and distrust that had existed between the United States and the Soviet Union before World War II reemerged. During the war, Roosevelt had been committed to a friendly relationship between the two countries. Now, President Truman's decision to drop atomic bombs on Hiroshima and Nagasaki convinced Soviet premier Joseph Stalin that the United States would do anything to get its way. The Soviet Union then sped up the construction of its own atomic bombs. The race to build bigger and more powerful nuclear weapons became known as the "nuclear arms race."

From 1945 to 1991, both the United States and the Soviet Union convinced, coerced, or bullied other countries to join sides. They spied on each other, supported and paid for wars against their enemies, and threatened each other repeatedly with nuclear war. This period, the most dangerous in human history, became known as the "Cold War."

This book is about the Cold War. But the story that it tells is very different from what you might read in a typical American history textbook. Most textbooks explain that the Cold War was a struggle between the United States, with its system of free-market capitalism, and the Soviet Union, with its system of communism. This is certainly true, but it doesn't come close to telling the whole story. Decisions made and actions taken by the United States and the Soviet Union between 1945 and 1962 forever altered the world in which we all live. Those decisions impacted people's lives from the centers of Moscow and Washington, DC, to the farthest reaches of the globe. Countries, cities, communities, villages, and tiny islands forever changed as a result of the Cold War.

Some textbooks focus only on the political conflicts between the two nations while glossing over the impact that the Cold War had on ordinary men, women, and children. This book tells their stories. It focuses specifically on how the decisions made by the United States during the Cold War impacted people's lives around the world. How did decisions made in Washington change the ways children played, the ways families lived, and the ways people interacted with one another across the globe?

To be sure, the Soviet Union also ruthlessly imposed its will upon Eastern Europe throughout the Cold War. Those accounts have been written about in many other books, and we encourage you to read them. One of the most important lessons we hope you will learn from this book is that in order to even begin to understand history, we should understand as many different perspectives as we can.

During the Cold War, the United States was responsible for contaminating remote Pacific islands with radiation from nuclear testing. It supported dictatorships that grievously oppressed their citizens. It waged wars against its communist foes. It transferred vast amounts of wealth from the poor of the earth to the rich. It also planned and attempted assassinations against leaders like Cuba's Fidel Castro, who stood firmly in the way of American objectives. Were those decisions the best ones that could have been made?

By 1962, the United States and the Soviet Union and the rest of the world came to the utter brink of nuclear war during the Cuban Missile Crisis—a confrontation that included what historian Arthur M. Schlesinger Jr. called "the most dangerous moment in human history." If leaders had made different decisions between 1945 and 1962—if they had made an effort to understand and empathize with their adversaries—might the world have avoided that most dangerous of moments?

This book prompts us all to ask many hard questions about the actions taken in our names and the decisions made by the elected officials of prior generations. Armed with knowledge about those leaders and their actions, along with stories of how those in prior generations resisted destructive behaviors and sought to make a better world, young Americans can correct the mistakes of the past and create a more peaceful, equitable future for all.

Note: This book is roughly chronological. It runs from 1945 to 1962. However, so that we can tell these stories thoroughly, you will notice that at some points the narrative seems to go "back in time" to other periods before 1945. This approach allows us to explore how people and ideas evolve over many years.

PART ONE

Atomic Fallout

1

Hiroshima:
Imagination and Reality

When Americans found out that the United States had dropped atomic bombs on Hiroshima and Nagasaki in August 1945, many recoiled in horror. Others made light of the atomic bomb and its destructive power. Since photos and film footage from Hiroshima were still censored by the government, most Americans could not visualize the destruction that atomic bombs could do. As American cities had never been bombed, it was incredibly difficult for people to imagine what such devastation would look like. Americans read newspaper stories that described the bomb as the biggest ever dropped, more powerful than 20,000 tons of TNT.

Without actual photos depicting the damage at Hiroshima and Nagasaki, comedians, journalists, artists, and even bartenders let their imaginations run wild. Referring to Hiroshima, one radio announcer remarked that after the atomic bomb, the city "looked like Ebbets Field after a game between the Giants and the Dodgers." Bartenders in Washington, DC, invented the "Atomic Cocktail," an incredibly strong green-tinted drink that went "boom" when you drank it. General Mills sold "Atomic 'Bomb' Rings" for a breakfast cereal box top and fifteen cents. Ads for the rings urged people to "look into the 'sealed atom chamber' in 'the gleaming aluminum warhead . . . [and] see genuine atoms SPLIT to smithereens!'"[1] General Mills was bombarded with orders from 750,000 kids. Atomic pistols, atomic robots, atomic chemistry sets, uranium board games, PEZ candy space guns, and model nuclear reactors lined toy store shelves across the country.[2] Royal Tot Manufacturing Company of New York produced a "safe, harmless, cap shooting, giant atomic bomb." Children could buy just one bomb or an entire arsenal.[3]

Influenced by toy companies, radio shows, and conversations at the dinner table, kids across the country played atomic cops and robbers, pretended they were pilots of atomic spaceships, played atomic arcade games, and threw radioactive snowballs at their friends. At the playground in New York's Washington Square, *Life* magazine observed that children were making up new atomic games:

> We watched a military man of seven or eight [years old] climb onto a seesaw, gather a number of his staff officers around him, and explain the changed situation. "Look," he said, "I'm an atomic bomb. I just go 'boom.' Once. Like this." He raised his arms, puffed out his cheeks, jumped down from the seesaw, and went "Boom!" Then he led his army away, leaving Manhattan in ruins behind them.

While the kids played, their parents worried. A distressed mother in Pelham Manor, New York, wrote a letter to radio commentator H. V. Kaltenborn:

> Since [Hiroshima] I have hardly been able to smile, the future seems so utterly grim for our two boys. Most of the time I have been in tears or near-tears, and fleeting but torturing regrets that

I have brought children into the world to face such a dreadful thing as this have shivered through me. It seems that it will be for them all their lives like living on a keg of dynamite which may go off at any moment, and which undoubtedly will go off before their lives have progressed very far.[4]

As many in the United States wondered and fretted about what it might be like to experience an atomic blast, those in Hiroshima and Nagasaki were living through an actual nuclear nightmare. Americans were about to learn much more about that hell.

John Hersey's *Hiroshima*

Subscribers to *New Yorker* magazine woke up on Saturday morning, August 31, 1946, to find in their mailboxes what would become the twentieth century's most important work of journalism. The cover illustration featured the delights of everyday life: people strolling through a beautiful park, a relaxing game of badminton, swimmers splashing in a lake while others danced on the beach.[5] But it masked the painful truths inside, revealed in just one long article simply titled "Hiroshima."

The article's young author, John Hersey, was born in Tianjin (formerly known as Tientsin), China, to missionary parents who worked for the YMCA. He learned Chinese before he learned English. In 1924, Hersey moved with his family back to the United States, and they settled in Briarcliff Manor,

John Hersey, Pulitzer Prize-winning investigative journalist and author of *Hiroshima*.

New York. After graduating from Yale and traveling to study at Clare College in England, he was sure he wanted to be a journalist.

Eight years of working with talented authors like the legendary Sinclair Lewis made Hersey an incredibly gifted writer. He wrote extensively about World War II as it unfolded for *Time* and *Life* magazines, and he won a Pulitzer Prize in 1945 for his novel *A Bell for Adano*. Hersey had realized his dream, to become a well-respected journalist and write stories that would change the world. Now, he would tackle Hiroshima for the *New Yorker*.

In August 1946, when Hersey's *Hiroshima* was published, most Americans still could not relate to the horrors that the Japanese had faced just a year earlier. Hersey decided that his role as a journalist was to tell the whole story about what really happened there in a steady, matter-of-fact way. Recalling the detailed research Lewis had conducted on each of his characters, Hersey knew that his writing would be much more powerful if it described what happened to the actual victims. What did Hiroshima look like through their eyes?

August 6, 1945

Hersey spent three months in the devastated city listening, learning, and observing. He saw people's shadows permanently emblazoned on concrete by the blast. He visited hospitals and interviewed doctors and nurses who had seen the most horrific injuries. He talked to children who were dying of leukemia and other radiation-related diseases. Hersey admitted that while he was there, he was "terrified all the time. If I felt [terrified] coming there eight months later, what must the feelings of the people who were there at the time have been?"[6] Gazing out over the Ota River, Hersey wondered: How could one bomb possibly cause such unimaginable death and destruction?

After interviewing close to forty survivors, Hersey chose to write about six of them: Miss Toshiko Sasaki, a secretary at the East Asia Tin Works; Masakazu

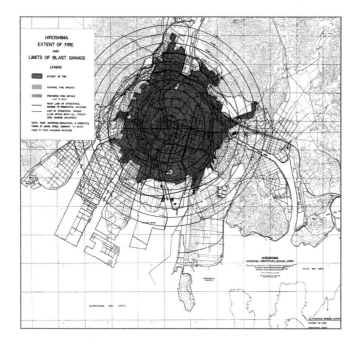

This map shows the horrific destruction caused by the atomic bomb in Hiroshima. The bomb detonated directly above the city's center, igniting a firestorm that extended roughly 1.5 miles in every direction.

Fujii and Terufumi Sasaki, two doctors; Father William Kleinsorge, a German priest; Mrs. Hatsuyo Nakamura, a seamstress; and Kiyoshi Tanimoto, pastor of Hiroshima's Methodist Church.[7] His writing was as a journalist's should be—sober, unemotional, and very detailed.

Hersey painstakingly described how each of his subjects experienced August 6, 1945. At 8:15 a.m., as Mrs. Nakamura gazed out her window at her neighbor's house, suddenly:

> Everything flashed whiter than any white she had ever seen. She did not notice what happened to the man next door; the reflex of a mother set her in motion toward her children. She had taken a single step . . . when something picked her up and she seemed to fly into the next room over the raised sleeping platform, pursued by parts of her house. Timbers fell around her as she landed, and

a shower of tiles pommelled her; everything became dark, for she was buried. The debris did not cover her deeply. She rose up and freed herself. She heard a child cry, "Mother, help me!," and saw her youngest—Myeko, the five-year-old—buried up to her breast and unable to move.

As Dr. Fujii read the morning paper on the front porch of his small hospital, he saw the atomic flash.

Startled, he began to rise to his feet. In that moment . . . the hospital leaned behind his rising and, with a terrible ripping noise, toppled into the river. The Doctor, still in the act of getting to his feet, was thrown forward and around and over; he was buffeted and gripped; he lost track of everything, because things were so speeded up; he felt the water.

Father Kleinsorge saw the atomic flash as he ate breakfast with the other priests in their mission. Stunned and confused, he "had time for [only] one thought: A bomb had fallen directly on us. Then, for a few seconds, he went out of his mind."

He never knew how he got out of the house. The next things he was conscious of were that he was wandering around in the mission's vegetable garden in his underwear, bleeding slightly from small cuts along his left flank; that all the buildings round about had fallen down except the Jesuits' mission house, which had long before been braced and double-braced by a priest named Gropper, who was terrified of earthquakes; that the day had turned dark; and that Murata-*san*, the housekeeper, was nearby, crying over and over, *"Shi Jesusu, awaremi tamai!"* Our Lord Jesus, have pity on us.[8]

Hersey ended his article with the testimony of ten-year-old Toshio Nakamura:

> "The day before the bomb, I went for a swim. In the morning, I was eating peanuts. I saw a light. I was knocked to little sister's sleeping place. When we were saved, I could only see as far as the tram. My mother and I started to pack our things. The neighbors were walking around burned and bleeding. Hataya-*san* told me to run away with her. I said I wanted to wait for my mother. We went to the park. A whirlwind came. At night a gas tank burned and I saw the reflection in the river. We stayed in the park one night. Next day I went to Taiko Bridge and met my girl friends Kikuki and Murakami. They were looking for their mothers. But Kikuki's mother was wounded and Murakami's mother, alas, was dead."

Once word got out about Hersey's article, copies of the *New Yorker* flew off newsstand shelves. The ABC network broadcast it over the radio. For four straight nights, Americans sat in their living rooms and listened to the gut-wrenching stories narrated by Paul Robeson and three other prominent actors. Albert Einstein requested a thousand copies to share with his friends and colleagues. A college student wrote to the *New Yorker*, "I had never thought of the people in the bombed cities as individuals."[9]

Sadako's Cranes[10]

Over 200,000 individuals died when the United States dropped atomic bombs on Hiroshima and Nagasaki. Many more suffered long after from exposure to the devastating radiation. Sadako Sasaki was one of them.

Sadako was two years old in 1945 when the *Enola Gay* flew over

Sadako.

Hiroshima. She grew up as the city struggled to rebuild. By 1955, Sadako had become an outgoing and creative twelve-year-old. She was very athletic— one of the strongest members of her school's track team. She routinely won races against her classmates. On race days, she forgot about everything else and gave each race her all.

One bitter cold day, Sadako was practicing sprints on the field behind the school. All of a sudden, a strange and disorienting sensation came over her. She fell to the grass, unable to move any further. A teacher ran over to help. Sadako tried to get back on her feet, but her legs would not support her body.

Her father took her to the Red Cross Hospital. Sadako's whole family was there waiting for her. After the doctor examined her, he asked to speak to her parents in private. From outside the room, Sadako heard her mother's anguished cry, "Leukemia! But that's impossible!" Sadako covered her ears in denial. She couldn't possibly have leukemia. She was perfectly healthy.

Over the next few months, Sadako became weaker and weaker. The radiation from the atomic bomb had caused her disease, which sapped all of her energy and caused terrible headaches. Her bones felt like they were knives, cutting her from within. Eventually, she was confined to her bed in the hospital.

One day, Sadako's friend Chizuko visited her in the hospital. Chizuko was determined to cheer up her friend and make her feel better. She pulled a piece of origami paper out of her bag and began folding it again and again. Finally, Chizuko had contorted the single piece of paper into a beautiful crane. Sadako asked Chizuko how the crane was supposed to make her well again. Chizuko responded, "Don't you remember that old story about the crane? It's supposed to live for a thousand years. If a sick person folds one thousand paper cranes, the gods will grant her wish and make her healthy again."

The two friends sat together on Sadako's bed, folding crane after crane. Maybe, just maybe, the gods would listen and make her healthy again. At first, the cranes were uneven, but as the girls practiced, they became more and more precise. Chizuko lined up the cranes on a small table. Ultimately, they made so many that Sadako's brother offered to hang them on strings from the ceiling.

Kokeshi

By July 1955, Sadako had made over 600 paper cranes. But she was not getting better. As she drifted in and out of sleep, she asked her parents, "When I die, will you put my favorite bean cakes on the altar for my spirit?" Her mother couldn't answer. She just reached out and held her daughter's hand. Her father insisted, "That will not happen for many, many years. Don't give up now, Sadako chan. You have to make only a few hundred more cranes."

In mid-October, Sadako couldn't remember if it was day or night. She couldn't talk, she could only listen. She heard her mother cry and desperately wanted to comfort her, but she could not seem to muster the strength. She tried to fold another crane, but her fingers couldn't make the motions. Her doctor came in and told her, "It's time to rest. You can make more birds tomorrow." Seeing the hundreds of colorful paper cranes floating above her head gave her comfort. Sadako nodded and fell asleep.

Sadako passed away on October 25, 1955. She had made 644 cranes. Her friends folded another 356 and buried them with her. They gathered up Sadako's journal entries and compiled them into a book called *Kokeshi*, which made its way around Japan. Children across the country read Sadako's story and raised money to build a statue in her honor.

In 1958, a statue of Sadako Sasaki
was unveiled in Hiroshima's
Peace Memorial Park. Children
across Japan raised money for its
construction. Every year, people
from around the world drape the
statue in bands of paper cranes to
remember Sadako and her bravery.

In 1958, three years after her death, the statue was erected in Hiroshima's
Peace Memorial Park. Today, Sadako stands proudly and strongly on a pin-
nacle of stone. In her hands is a wide golden crane, which she appears to be
releasing into the world. Perhaps the world, sick with the disease of war, will
learn from Sadako's example. As countries raced to build bigger and more
powerful nuclear weapons in history's bloodiest century, how many more
Sadakos would there be before people woke up to the terrible human consequences of war from the air?

Maiden Voyage[1]

Through such unimaginable pain and suffering, many in Hiroshima and Nagasaki believed that their lives would improve and their cities would emerge from the ashes of war.

On a hot and humid day in August 1953, a train pulled into Hiroshima station carrying Norman Cousins, an American journalist and antiwar activist. Waiting for him was Reverend Kiyoshi Tanimoto, one of the people John Hersey had spotlighted in the *New Yorker*. Since 1949, Tanimoto and Cousins had been writing letters back and forth about the people of Hiroshima and how they were coping with such an unimaginable situation.

Tanimoto earnestly grabbed his visitor's bag and led Cousins to his hotel. On the way there, Tanimoto told Cousins about the "Hiroshima Maidens," a group of sixty young women his church had been supporting since that fateful day eight years earlier.

Young children at the time of the bombing in 1945, the Maidens had all been badly burned, disfigured, or otherwise disabled by the atomic bomb's blast and heat. As they grew into their preteen and teenage years, they became alienated from their peers who had not

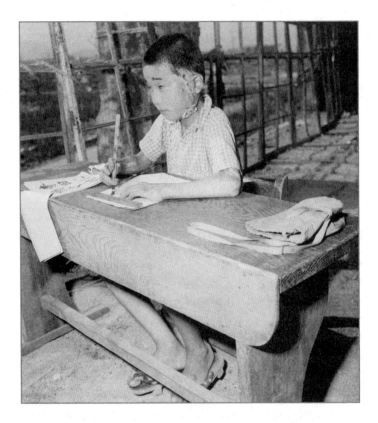

This girl sits at her school desk in July 1946. She will bear the scars of the atom bombing of Hiroshima as long as she lives.

suffered such horrible injuries. Many people in Hiroshima and across Japan shunned and resented those with physical disabilities. While others their age were going out on dates and spending time with friends, the Maidens became lonelier and lonelier. Some of them even found it difficult to go outside during daylight hours for fear of being judged or ridiculed. Though some of them had part-time jobs, most of them spent the majority of their time at home.

The young women found friends in one another. They laughed together, dreamed together, confided in one another. They fantasized about being born into a world with no war, a world that did not have the capability to cause such human anguish. They thought wistfully about what it might be like to have their skin swept clean of deformities once again.

At Nagarekawa Church, Reverend Tanimoto gave the Maidens a space free from all of the anxiety and the pain of the outside world. The building itself was a small structure made out of brick and cement plaster. It had suffered great blast damage from the bomb. Tanimoto worked with his parishioners for years to rebuild it. As for so many other construction projects under way across the city, the goal was to rebuild the church stronger and safer than before. A new city's spirit of hopefulness rose from the ashes.

Doctors' Donations

Cousins accompanied Tanimoto to Nagarekawa. They walked through the church's simple wood doors, descended a flight of stairs, and entered a large basement multipurpose room. Waiting for them on rows of wooden benches were the Maidens, who had been anticipating the American journalist's visit with conflicted emotions. Most of them had never met an American before. What would he be like? Why was he coming to visit them? Were all Americans as vicious as the ones who had dropped the bomb on their city?

Gradually, the young women warmed up to Cousins once they realized he was there to listen to their stories. Through an interpreter, they told Cousins about their experiences and their dreams. They had read in magazines and newspapers about new American developments in plastic surgery. During World War II, nine military plastic surgery clinics opened in the United States to help treat the facial burns of disfigured veterans.[2] No such clinics existed at the time in Japan. The Maidens shared their biggest hope with Cousins: that one day, they might travel to the United States to undergo facial reconstructive surgery. To them, surgery was the only hope of being able to lead normal lives.

As the Maidens spoke passionately about their dreams of traveling to the United States, Cousins listened with excitement, but also with caution. Could he figure out a way to bring them? He would have to involve others.

Plastic surgery was expensive. Where would the money come from? Bursting with emotion, Cousins told them that he had no idea if what they were asking for could happen. However, he promised to look into the possibility when he returned home and to write to Tanimoto with his findings.

Cousins was incredibly moved by the stories he heard in the basement of Nagarekawa Church. Immediately upon his return to the United States, he began contacting people about the Maidens' dream. He asked everyone he knew for ideas. The young women would need funds for travel, lodging, hospital stays, and, of course, the surgeries themselves. Cousins went from foundation to foundation asking for money. Foundation after foundation turned him down. They worried about who might be responsible if one of the Maidens died in surgery. They wondered why they should help one small group of Hiroshima victims when there were so many others in need. They worried that their help might be perceived as giving comfort to the Japanese, who were still thought of as the enemy by millions of Americans.

After six months, Cousins was exhausted and dejected. What would he tell the Maidens? He had made it his mission to bring them to the United States. He couldn't just throw in the towel and tell them that he'd failed. In desperation, he shared the idea with his personal doctor, William M. Hitzig. Dr. Hitzig happened to be on the board of New York's Mount Sinai Hospital. At Mount Sinai, Dr. Hitzig shared the Maidens' story with Dr. Arthur Barsky, one of the country's most accomplished plastic surgeons. To Cousins's great joy, Dr. Barsky and his staff agreed to take responsibility for the operations. Even more, the hospital agreed to donate the operating rooms and beds completely free of charge. This was no small expense, for some young women had to endure four or five operations, which caused them to be in the hospital for four to six months. The entire group would need to live in the United States for at least a year.

To work out living arrangements for the Maidens when they weren't in the hospital, Cousins contacted the American Friends Service Committee, a Quaker group whose members work for social justice, human rights, and peace around the world. The committee arranged for the Maidens to stay with American families. There, they would participate in family activities, share household chores, and learn skills that would help them take control over their lives when they returned to Hiroshima.

The Maidens waited in anticipation as Cousins arranged for their travel, the surgeons cleared their schedules, and the families prepared their homes. Finally, in April 1955, Dr. Barsky and Dr. Hitzig flew to Tokyo to meet with a group of Japanese surgeons, who would also be traveling to the United States. The Japanese doctors were eager to learn more about American plastic surgery practices. Barsky and Hitzig each gave up a month's salary so that they could visit the Maidens and determine which ones would benefit the most from surgery.

Barsky and Hitzig were not prepared for the barrage of Japanese press waiting for them upon landing in the Japanese capital. Why did American surgeons care about these deformed children from Hiroshima? Who was paying for the trip? Was the United States bringing the Maidens over as a propaganda tool? Would they be paraded across the country so Americans could gawk at them, as people would at animals in a zoo? Cousins explained that he, along with the doctors, happened to be in a position to help and wanted to do so. Then the doctors explained that they were doing it out of the goodness of their hearts and that it was not paid for in any way by the government. The reporters seemed satisfied and eventually wrote positive articles about the trip.

Cousins and the doctors traveled from Tokyo to Hiroshima. They met with the Maidens and immediately explained that of the forty-three who were eligible for the trip, only twenty-five could go. Sadly, the others would remain in Hiroshima. The men felt terribly guilty about that. They knew they needed to be up front with the Maidens—to treat them with dignity, respect, and honesty. They feared that the young women would be resentful or that they would pit themselves in competition with the others. Instead, the Maidens were positive, mature, strong, and hopeful. Regardless of whether or not they were going to be able to go themselves, they were happy for the entire group.

The American and Japanese doctors examined all forty-three Maidens in local hospitals. They then met with one another to determine which girls would make the best surgery candidates.

The night before the doctors made their final decisions, the Maidens attended a special service at Nagarekawa Church. The air was thick with great anticipation, hope, and anxiety. The young women stepped to the altar, one by one, to offer prayers. They prayed that Cousins and the doctors would feel no guilt over having to decide among them. Then they prayed that their friends who couldn't go would feel no anguish about being left behind.

The doctors wrote personal letters to all forty-three Maidens. Some of them found out that they were about to embark on the journey of a lifetime. Others received the news that they would be left behind. The doctors asked those who were chosen to make a special effort to lift the spirits of the others—and to comfort them with the knowledge that the American doctors would not forget about them.

Repentance Rather Than Hatred

Just after 9:00 a.m. on May 8, 1955, a US Air Force C-34 transport plane descended through the clouds as it made its final approach to Travis Air Force Base near San Francisco. The plane landed gently and taxied to a stop near a large hangar. Ground crews pushed a heavy wheeled staircase up to the plane. The door opened, and down the stairs came the twenty-five Hiroshima Maidens, looking remarkably fresh for having just traveled all the way from Japan by way of Hawaii. Michiko Sako, who represented the entire group of young women, told the reporters who had congregated next to the plane that the "stunning effect of the Hiroshima bombing must have been similar to that felt by the survivors of Japan's attack on Pearl Harbor."[3]

Later that day, after the Maidens had an opportunity to eat and freshen up at the base, they headed back up the staircase into the plane and eagerly anticipated the final leg of their fantastic 6,700-mile journey to Long Island's Mitchel Air Force Base. They had made it all the way across the world, completing a journey that few people their age had ever taken.

Though they were exhausted, a few of the young women shared their impressions with newspaper reporters who wanted to write stories about the remark-

The Hiroshima Maidens pose for a photograph shortly after they arrive in Hawaii.

able trip. Toyoko Minowa, sporting a wide smile, declared, "I feel at home here in New York and don't feel like I came to a foreign country. People are so nice and friendly to us. I feel that the people with whom we fought in war ten years ago are now our friends." Michiko Sako told *New York Times* reporters, "We in Hiroshima had a terrible destruction upon us, but we should have repentance rather than hatred . . . [When the city was bombed], we began to hate war."

Their Quaker hosts met the Maidens at the base and drove

Hiroshima Maiden Shigeko Sasamori exchanges gifts with her American host and newfound friend.

them to their homes away from home, where they rested for two weeks before their operations began. During those two weeks, they had the opportunity to sightsee, meet friends, and adjust to life in the United States. Their hosts were afraid that their guests would become homesick or have trouble adjusting, but the opposite happened—the Maidens soaked up every moment. They adapted remarkably well to exotic American foods, routines, and rhythms of life. One host father reflected, "So far, no home-sickness. And they love American food, especially frankfurters. We've gone sight-seeing together—to the United Nations, to the museums, and to places in New England. We've gone to concerts and baseball games. My wife and I couldn't be more grateful. I don't know how we're going to part with them." Another host father echoed those feelings: "The girls couldn't be more cheerful or more delightful as guests. 'Guests' really isn't the word for it. They're really members of the family."

Full Hearts

The young women brought hope and joy into their new homes. "If you asked me what I expect to remember most about their visit to our home," a host mother remarked, "I should say it was the laughter they brought with them and shared with us. We had feared we might have to make a special effort to keep things from becoming too grim or restrained in the presence of disfigured persons. But these girls have a warmth about them and a gift for laughter that created an entirely different and certainly much more welcome atmosphere than the one we anticipated." The strong bond that developed between the Maidens and their host families resulted in lifelong friendships.

The surgeries were complicated and intense. Doctors couldn't simply cut out the burned sections of skin and sew them up again. They had to spend many hours taking skin from healthy parts of the body and transplanting it to the parts that had been burned or disfigured. Together, the Maidens endured 129 operations in just the first six months of their visit. They endured hundreds more over the next year. Doctors tried the best they could to get rid of wide facial scars and to rebuild their hands, arms, and legs.

Most of the Maidens handled the operations very well and went on to live productive and inspiring lives. After ten surgeries, Suzue Oshima still exhibited a few facial scars. However, her fingers and hands were no longer disfigured. She was now able to move them freely. On the plane back to Hiroshima, Suzue set her hair in curlers and helped others style theirs. With money that her Quaker hosts donated, Suzue went on to open her own beauty shop named Darien, after the Connecticut town where she lived for eighteen months.

After their surgeries, a group of maidens smile for a
newspaper photograph.

Michiyo Zomen could barely move her hands when she arrived at Mount
Sinai. Now, on the flight home, she used them to write thank-you letters to
her host family in English. Not only were her hands repaired; she arrived
back in Japan with the ability to speak a new language and the confidence
to go on with the rest of her life. She also returned home with a brand-new
typewriter.

When she got off the plane in Tokyo, Michiyo, who barely had the confidence to speak in public before the trip, stood up in front of hundreds of
reporters, government officials, and religious and business leaders and spoke
about what it was like to live with an American family, attending school

in the United States and going through such a painful and lengthy healing process. She told the crowd, "I hold out my arm to you. This is not a simple thing. It means much to me to be able to do this. For years my arm was bent . . . they gave my arm back to me." She continued, "This is what you see. What you do not see is the heart that is so full. If the heart could speak, it would tell you about this feeling that we girls all now know."[4]

This Is Your Life

Reverend Tanimoto had accompanied the Maidens to the United States. Amid all the publicity surrounding the Maidens' story, a television reporter invited Tanimoto to appear on a show called *This Is Your Life*. The show, which ran from 1952 to 1961, was one of the very first reality TV programs and one of the most popular in America. Ralph Edwards, the host, invited guests onto the stage and told emotional stories about them. Then, often as a complete surprise to his guests, significant people in their lives would appear from behind a curtain: teachers, long-lost friends, former coworkers, estranged family members. *Time* magazine once called it "the most sickeningly sentimental show on the air." People at home laughed, cried, and gasped right along with the participants.[5]

On May 11, 1955, Americans sat down in front of their television sets to watch what would become one of the most talked about shows of the year. A loud, symphonic introduction with trumpets blaring announced the beginning of the program, as the words "THIS IS YOUR LIFE" appeared from behind black-and-white clouds. Edwards appeared next, with perfectly groomed hair and sparkling white teeth. The crowd cheered enthusiastically as the music died down. The camera panned wider to reveal Kiyoshi Tanimoto, nattily dressed in a suit and tie. Edwards introduced him as "a gentleman whose life was changed as the hands of the clock reached the hour of eight fifteen one summer morning."[6] The dapper host then asked the reverend a few questions about when he arrived in the United States and what he was doing, but when Tanimoto attempted to describe the Maidens and their plight, Edwards quickly cut him off. It was clear that he was only concerned with the Tanimoto family.

Edwards described the morning of August 6 in greater detail. When he got to the moment just before the bomb fell, a piercing air-raid siren engulfed the studio, momentarily startling Tanimoto and the audience. Edwards asked Tanimoto what he remembered doing at the moment the siren sounded: "Did you run for cover?"

Tanimoto's Story

On August 6, 1945, Reverend Tanimoto did not run for cover. Instead, immediately after the bomb exploded over Hiroshima, he ran toward the city center. Dazed victims of all ages limped past, some carrying the dead bodies of their loved ones. As he crossed Koi Bridge, Tanimoto heard the screams of people trapped beneath their burning homes. The screams grew louder and louder. Fire was everywhere. Realizing that he could not help them, Tanimoto was overcome by a feeling of deep shame. As he ran toward his own family, he prayed, "God help them and take them out of the fire."

Flames blocked the streets. Tanimoto couldn't get through. He realized that he would need to find another way to his family. After running seven miles, he turned toward the Ota River. The side he was on was mostly ablaze, but the other side was free of fire. He shed his shirt and took off his shoes. He then threw himself into the water.

The current in the middle of the river was fierce. It began to move him swiftly downstream. Tanimoto thought he was about to drown, so he used every last ounce of energy to fight out of the current and onto the opposite side. When he reached land, he began running along the riverbank until he encountered more fire. How would he get around it?

He chose to go left, around a Shinto shrine. As he came out from behind the ornate wooden structure, his eyes fell immediately upon his wife, carrying their infant daughter. What a stroke of luck! Strangely, Tanimoto did not embrace them. After what he had seen on his trip into town, he found himself incapable of much emotion. Instead, he declared matter-of-factly, "Oh, you are safe."[7]

Mrs. Tanimoto told her husband that she had been buried underneath their home with the baby in her arms. The debris weighed down on them. She was nearly unconscious but was jolted awake by the baby's anxious cries. She quickly became worried that the entire structure would collapse. Through the wreckage, she saw a glint of light. She reached up frantically, stretching the hole wider, inch by inch. After thirty minutes, the hole was big enough for her to thrust the baby through. Then she made her own way out.

Once he knew that his wife and daughter were safe, Tanimoto turned his attention to his church and his parishioners. He once again parted from his family and headed back into the burning city.

Kiyoshi Tanimoto's daughter was named Koko. Miraculously, Koko escaped major bodily injury, but many of her friends grew up disfigured by the bomb's horrific fire. "Some of them," Koko recalled, their "mouth[s] could not close because the lips were together with the chin. As a child, I didn't know where to look. I thought about it, why these girls are so ugly looking? And I learned and found out they were other survivors of Hiroshima. They were burnt by the fire. And I said to myself when I grow up I am really going to give a big punch to whoever was on the B-29 *Enola Gay*, to take revenge."

As a young girl, Koko simply could not forgive the men who dropped the atomic bomb on her city. She couldn't imagine why human beings would do such atrocious things to other human beings. As she grew up, she became more aware of people dying around her. Leukemia and other radiation-related illnesses claimed the lives of many children like her. Growing up in an environment where death and disease took many of her friends' lives, the passionate, headstrong girl made a pledge to herself over and over again: "Someday in the future I'm going to do something about this."[8]

Big Surprises

Back in the television studio, Tanimoto, who did not run for cover when the siren blew, didn't want to offend his host by telling the truth. Sensing Tanimoto's hesitance, Edwards interjected another statement: "Not when the siren blew. You were used to that. Every morning it went off, didn't it?" Tanimoto nodded.

Suddenly, a man's silhouette appeared behind a curtain. A voice echoed across the studio, "At zero six hundred on the morning of August the sixth, 1945, I was in a B-29 flying over the Pacific, destination Hiroshima." The voice was that of Captain Robert Lewis, the copilot of the *Enola Gay*, the plane that dropped the atomic bomb, forever altering the course of Tanimoto's life. Lewis later reappeared, still behind the curtain. This time, his voice shook: "Looking down from thousands of feet over Hiroshima, all I could think of was, 'My God, what have we done?'"

The copilot emerged from behind the curtain and reached out to shake Tanimoto's hand. Tanimoto extended his hand in kind, then backed away, not quite knowing how to react, as Lewis gave his jumbled version of what had happened on that fateful day. The captain struggled to make eye contact with Tanimoto. Edwards, perhaps not understanding the gravity of what was taking place, sought to cut the tension between the two men: "And so, Reverend Tanimoto, you on the ground, and you on your military mission, Captain Lewis, in the air, both appealed to a power greater than your own." Next, the host dismissed the bewildered and possibly drunk captain from the stage. At that moment, Tanimoto smiled warmly, extended his hand, and shook Lewis's.

Never before on American television, and perhaps never since, has a bomber come face-to-face with someone he has bombed. It was an incredibly powerful moment. What Tanimoto didn't know was that there was still one more surprise to come. Waiting backstage were his wife, his ten-year-old daughter, Koko, and her three siblings. Koko, dressed in a kimono, whispered quietly to her mother as Lewis emerged from behind the curtain, "Who is that man?" Her mother responded that it was the copilot of the *Enola Gay*.

A Change of Heart

Koko had been waiting for this moment her entire life. She had always vowed that if she met the man who dropped the bomb, who caused so much misery and so much pain for her friends and her family, she would punch and kick and scream at him. After all those years of thinking about what that would be like, the moment was finally upon her. While she waited to be introduced, she stared sharply into Lewis's eyes. She decided that if she got the chance, she would confront him directly. She would share with him her feelings of pain and hatred.

Koko's eyes were still fixated on Lewis. She wanted so badly to hate him, but all she could see were the tears in his eyes. The ten-year-old girl who for years harbored such hatred and venom, having grown up with the Maidens, anguished over their deformities, and been lavished in their kindness, suddenly realized that war was bigger than any one person. The true enemy, Koko realized, was war itself.

Edwards finally called the family out onstage. Tanimoto, who had expected to be away from his family for quite some time, embraced his wife and children warmly, then stood with them at the center of the stage. Captain Lewis reemerged along with the rest of the show's guests and stood behind them. Edwards then presented the family with jewelry and a home movie camera so they could watch the show at home.

Koko's experience on *This Is Your Life* changed her entire perspective on what happened in Hiroshima. All of the hate escaped her soul and was replaced with the burning desire to bring peace to the globe. She grasped Lewis's hand and stood there by his side. She went on to devote her entire life to that objective. Today, she still travels the world giving speeches to many audiences about how dangerous nuclear weapons are and how human beings must work together to eliminate them from the face of the earth.

Bikini Atoll[1]

For four years after the end of World War II, the United States was the only country in the world with atomic weapons. However, many politicians, scientists, and military personnel knew that America's monopoly would end one day. Inevitably, other countries would develop their own bombs. To make sure it stayed ahead in the nuclear arms race, the United States began making and testing bigger and more powerful bombs.

In order to understand how the new bombs would work, American officials decided to test them in a part of the world far from major population centers. They chose Bikini Atoll, a chain of islands in the middle of the Pacific Ocean. However, though sparsely populated, people did live on Bikini.

Because the atoll was so remote, Bikini's inhabitants had very little contact with the rest of the world until the early twentieth century, when Japanese fishermen, explorers, and merchants discovered the atoll and the rest of the Marshall Islands. Before World War II, the Japanese decided that the islands would be an important base in their fight to control the wider Pacific Ocean. The arrival of a world war

Soldiers watch in awe as an atomic bomb is detonated at the Nevada Test Site, 1951. Before the United States began testing nuclear weapons in the South Pacific, it tested them on American soil.

to Bikini jolted the islanders, who had never even seen a gun before the Japanese arrived. After Japan's defeat, the United States asserted control over the Marshall Islands. Though the islanders had already been through a lot, nothing prepared them for what lay in store.

Good-bye, Bikini

In early 1946, Commodore Ben Wyatt arrived at Bikini to serve as the new American military governor. *Time* magazine described him as a "softspoken" and "sensitive" man who "may have wondered why progress had to sacrifice this lovely coral atoll, instead of an empty wasteland [or] a dismal slum." After church services on a Sunday afternoon, Wyatt gathered the Bikinians together and asked them if they would temporarily leave the atoll their people had been living on for thousands of years so that the United States could test new atomic bombs. The American soldier told the islanders that they would be testing the bombs "for the good of mankind and to end all world wars."

The Bikinians were cautious. They doubted Wyatt. After years of Japanese occupation and war, could they trust their new occupier, the United States? Their meeting with Wyatt was the first time that many of them had met an American. And now that American was asking them to gather all of their belongings, leave their homes, and move to Rongerik Atoll, 125 miles away. What would life be like there? Would they ever be able to move back home?

The distressed Bikinians discussed Wyatt's proposal. They thought about what it would mean to themselves, their families, and their ancestral homeland. Finally, Bikinian leader King Juda stood up. He looked into the worried eyes of his people and told them, "We will go believing that everything is in the hands of God." Emso Leviticus, a young Bikini woman, remembered that "no one dissented in front of the Americans when they asked us if we would be willing to go to another island so they could test their bombs. . . . It had been decided that we would all stand behind Juda when he gave our answer to the man with the stars on his hat and clothes."

As Bikinians packed their belongings and prepared for their journey, 242 American naval ships and 156 planes arrived on their atoll, carrying 42,000 Americans. The US Navy also brought 5,400 pigs, goats, and rats. American scientists wanted to test the impact of atomic blast and radiation on the animals. Botanists, geologists, oceanographers, and zoologists from the Smithsonian Institution and various American universities also arrived on the island. They wanted to learn more about how the atomic bomb affected sea life and plant life. They wanted to observe plants and animals before and after the test to determine what effect the atomic bomb's blast, heat, and radiation had on bodies and ecosystems.

Rongerik

In March 1946, the Bikinians left on a US Navy tank landing ship, bound for Rongerik, an island that many believed was inhabited by evil spirits. The trip was fun for Emso, a curious young girl:

> [I had] never . . . seen anything like this before, I had fun on the ship. We finally arrived at Rongerik Atoll, and after we unloaded all of our belongings onto the beach, the Council immediately began to decide on which families would live in the various

houses that had been prepared for us. We started dividing up the food that the Navy men had given us and we tried to fall back into the daily routines of our lives. Routine was difficult now though because there were many newsmen on Rongerik taking pictures of us. I guess it was all exciting in a way, but it was also a little scary. Those people who were looking at us were strange. The island itself looked so different from Bikini. It was smaller. And, from the beginning, we had reason to lack confidence in our abilities to provide for our future on that tiny place. We could only remain hopeful and keep thinking that one day soon we would be returned to Bikini.

Less than four months later, on July 1, 1946, an American B-29 plane dropped one atomic bomb over the Bikini lagoon. The *Washington Post* described the explosion as "an unearthly brilliance that petrified observers . . . a man-made atomic monster." Twenty seconds later, a "fearsome blaze of light was followed by a giant rumble which reached [the] command ship 18 miles from the Bikini target area." Pink-outlined clouds billowed and curled five miles up into the atmosphere as the island disappeared entirely from view. Next, a strong shock wave created a heavy rush of wind, popping the ears of those observing. One of the observers exclaimed in amazement, "Hosanna, Lord, I'm still alive."

On Rongerik, the Bikinians suffered terribly. Lore Kessibuki, a Bikinian storyteller, remembered how his people starved. A mysterious illness infected people when they ate fish from the surrounding waters. Kessibuki explained, "In Rongerik you just shouldn't eat the fish. The fish have a history of being poisoned by the food that they ate from the reef—even though they were the exact same kind of fish that we used to eat on Bikini." Kessibuki believed that the disease was caused by evil demons that inhabited Rongerik long ago. "Even after these bad spirits finally left the island," he recalled, "it was believed that if a tree started to grow there it would eventually mature and create a fire on its own because the demons had planted evil spirits within the seeds of the young trees. All remaining food on the island was later ruined by [a spirit] who came from the south and cast magic spells over the entire atoll."

King Juda's oldest son, Rubon, remembered that when he and his fellow islanders ate fish, "[our] bodies would change back and forth from being real cold to having our heads feel hot and feverish. Sometimes we would build a big fire and stand beside it to get the blood flowing into our arms and legs—thus reducing the coldness—and that relieved the pain a bit." When asked why the Bikinians continued to eat the fish, Rubon replied, "I must remind you that we were

Once Bikinians arrived on Rongerik, they had to build new homes. Here, men haul leaves from the pandanus plant across the beach toward a new village site. They used the pandan leaves to thatch roofs.

hungry. It is amazing what we were willing to endure when we found ourselves in this state. There were times when we were able to sail to nearby Rongelap Atoll and bring back coconuts and pandanus for our families to eat, but upon our return everything would be divided up among all of our people, so the food never lasted very long." After two years of unimaginable misery, the US Navy moved the Bikinians to a camp on Kwajalein Island, then again to Kili Island. The Bikinians continued to suffer. Finally, the United States paid them $25,000 for aid and promised to pay each Bikinian $15 per person every year. Bikinians, who were used to fishing for their own food and building their own homes, now ironically depended upon the US government to keep them alive.

Bikini Atoll, July 25, 1946. This photo was taken 3.5 miles from the center of the *Baker* underwater nuclear explosion. Between 1946 and 1958, the United States tested sixty-eight such weapons at Bikini.

Between 1946 and 1958, the US Navy tested sixty-eight atomic and hydrogen bombs at Bikini, leaving the atoll "hopelessly contaminated." The radiation from all of those bombs led to the deaths and illnesses of many people in the Marshall Islands. It made people commit suicide to escape the suffering. Babies were born with defects.[2] Some were called "jellyfish babies" because they looked like blobs of jelly, not human beings. Most died within hours. The radiation is still killing islanders today.

Bombshell

On July 5, 1946, four days after the first Bikini atomic bomb test and half a world away, the sun shone brightly at the Piscine Molitor swimming pool in Paris. It was a perfect day for a beauty contest. In front of a packed audience, French clothing designer Louis Réard was to unveil his latest garment.

Some in the crowd observed how one of the women next to the pool was wearing a smaller swimsuit than the rest of the contestants. She posed and winked as photographers snapped picture after picture. As the contest entered its final round, the judges called the woman, Micheline Bernardini, onstage and declared her a finalist for the "most beautiful swimmer" award.

The audience buzzed with shock and excitement. Never before had they seen such a small and shapely bathing suit. From some angles, it looked as if Bernardini was more naked than dressed. Her upper body was barely hidden beneath patches of fabric supported by a strap fastened around her neck. Another triangular patch of fabric covered her lower abdomen but revealed her thighs and hips.

Many in the audience had never seen a woman dressed in such a way, at least not in public.[1]

Réard was fascinated by newspaper articles about the July 1 Bikini test. Images of the mushroom cloud over the atoll with windswept palm trees in the foreground dazzled readers who could hardly imagine how powerful the bomb actually was. Sensing how captivated people had become with the atomic bomb test, Réard decided to name his new explosive bathing suit the "bikini," after the now-evacuated and contaminated atoll.

The Bikini Effect

In many ways, Réard's bikini had the same effect on people as the atomic bomb did. The swimsuit excited and terrified people at the same time. Young, single, unmarried women who wore such clothing were exciting, blasting apart gender expectations. These blond and brunette "bombshells" endangered the accepted role of women being in the home to cook and care for children. How could women possibly pack lunches and iron sheets while they strutted around the pool in a bikini? In the same way that the atomic bomb exploded cities and islands, women outside the home threatened to shatter traditional marriage and family. Indeed, other male fashion designers throughout the 1950s answered Réard's bikini with more conservative bathing suits and underwear, designed to keep women off-limits to anyone except their husbands at home.[2]

The bikini also revealed another trend. After World War II, especially in America, it seemed as if anything was possible. The Allies had freed Europe from Nazi horrors. Hitler had committed suicide in a bunker. Japan was beaten and coming under American control. Fascism had been vanquished. To some, every possible horror had been obliterated.

But to others, the atomic bomb ushered in an era of great uncertainty, a future that could easily be wiped out the next time countries decided to fight one another. Many people who grew up during this time knew that they had to live life for the present. If atomic war could destroy the world tomorrow, why not have as much fun as possible today? The bikini symbolized a time of greater freedom and joy among young people against a backdrop of great anxiety and doom.

Yellow Cake

Of course, to the people in Hiroshima and Nagasaki and those struggling to survive in the Marshall Islands, such joy and freedom were barely imaginable. Many Americans, including Unitarian minister A. Powell Davies, read newspaper headlines from Bikini with horror. How could the United States defend the bombing of innocent people in cities? How could it move people from their ancestral homelands and then blow up those homelands? Davies gave sermon after sermon from his pulpit at All Souls Unitarian Church, a brick-faced colonial building with grand columns and a massive steeple in the heart of Washington, DC.

The church's congregants loved Davies. He championed African-American civil rights and stood against anti-Semitism. He believed that the United States should send postwar aid to starving Europeans. He believed that the public should control the construction and storage of nuclear weapons, not the military. Davies defended the rights of all people to practice their religion—or *not* practice a religion at all. The *Washington Post* called him "the most resolute and indomitable champion of righteousness as he saw it and the brotherhood of man."[3]

On November 7, 1946, while reading the society column of the *Washington Post*, Davies nearly choked on his coffee in disbelief. Two nights before, at a meeting of the Officers' Club of the Army War College, army and navy officers had thrown a party to celebrate the official end of the first two atomic tests at Bikini. A large photograph in the *Post* showed Vice

Admiral William H. P. Blandy, the commander at Bikini, his wife, and Rear Admiral Frank J. Lowry smiling widely as they cut into a large cake shaped like an atomic bomb's mushroom cloud. A bakery in East St. Louis, Illinois, had baked the bizarre cake. It was then driven over 800 miles to the nation's capital. Davies found it obscene that while Bikinians suffered and died on Rongerik, American military commanders feasted on a cake that celebrated "the most cruel, pitiless, revolting instrument of death ever invented by man."[4]

Three days later, Davies delivered a powerful sermon called "Lest the Living Forget." In front of his packed audience, the troubled minister asked:

> How would it seem in Hiroshima, or Nagasaki, to know that Americans make cakes—of angel food puffs—in the image of that terrible, diabolical thing that brought sudden death to thousands of their friends, and a lingering, loathsome death to thousands of others? It is a crime—a crime against whatever may be left of decency here in America—to do this incredible thing. It is the most corrupt and rotten thing I have seen in eighteen years of living in this land that I love—and which, to me, is the only hope for the human future on this globe. The naval officers concerned should apologize to the armed service of which they are a part, and to the American people. No apology would be sufficient to efface what it may mean to the people of the world.[5]

Davies ended by saying that he "only [hoped] to God [the photo] is not printed in Russia—to confirm everything the Soviet government is telling the Russian people about . . . 'American degenerates.'"

In fact, Russian papers did report about the cake. According to the Associated Press, "one [newspaper] commented that American 'atomists' would 'like to stew a big atomic kasha and make millions of peaceful people bear the consequences.'" Another paper made fun of the American soldiers by publishing a cartoon photo of a fat American man dressed in an overcoat cutting into a cake.

Letters to the editor, both supporting the officers and condemning them, flooded the newsroom of the *Post*. One ex-infantryman suggested that, for Memorial Day, "we could have darling little cakes made in the shape of coffins, and the cutest little crosses pressed of angel-puffs. And a few drops of cherry extract could be—you guessed it—drops of blood. . . . I think the entire episode was a monument to poor taste, and the *Post* shares the guilt by printing such obscenities." After reading about Davies's sermon, *Post* reader Lieutenant Commander J. N. Talbott declared:

> Utter astonishment could not describe my feelings when I read the tirade let loose by a Washington minister at two men who contributed such a large part in the defeat of our enemies. . . . This minister might just as well damn every Air Corps officer, every bombardier, every flame-throwing private, every machine gunner and every rifleman to everlasting hell for using a weapon as destructive as the one he carried in defense of his country. . . . God grant that this nation have such a weapon as this if & when our enemies feel the time is ripe to strike another blow at freedom and mankind.[6]

Elementary Art

Other newspapers and magazines across the country reported on Davies's fiery sermon. His thoughts about the atomic bomb cake soon reached Japan. In Hiroshima, Dr. Howard Bell read about Davies. Dr. Bell was an American education expert who was helping Japan rebuild its schools after

World War II. He worked with Japanese teachers at Hiroshima's Honkawa Elementary School to update textbooks and write new lessons.

The situation for children at Honkawa was incredibly sad. Four hundred of the school's teachers and children had been killed in the bombing. Others were suffering terribly from leukemia and other deadly illnesses caused by radiation. Some children had lost their entire families and were now orphans. Teachers at the school were the only family they had.

Bell had never seen such human misery. He admired the strength of the children and teachers and felt that he needed to support them in any way possible. Bell noticed that the children were drawing pictures of what had happened to their families, their friends, and their city. Their pictures were windows into what life was like for them before the bombing, and after. Surprisingly, some of their pictures were full of hope for the future. The children dreamed of a peaceful world free from bombs, war, and death. They knew that the world could be a better place and that their city would rise from the ashes.

However, there were not enough art supplies in the devastated school for the children to continue their artwork. Dr. Bell, knowing that Davies would understand, sent him a letter about the children and teachers of Honkawa. He told Davies that the school had very few supplies for the children to continue their artwork and their healing. Bell asked Davies if American children could help by sending their used pencils and old crayons to schools in Hiroshima.

Davies swung into action. He gave a passionate sermon on February 13, 1947, titled "In Reply to a Letter from Japan," asking the children at All Souls to collect and donate their used art supplies. In response, the church collected a half ton of crayons, glue, erasers, paper fasteners, and pencils. Davies sent the supplies to Hiroshima, and shortly thereafter, Bell distributed the supplies to three schools: Honkawa, Fukuromachi Elementary, and Ninoshimakisen Orphanage.

A few months later, the children of Honkawa sent two portfolios to All Souls. Each portfolio held forty-eight drawings the children had completed

Zyunko Hotta's drawing.

Hiroko Nakajima's drawing.

Misako Simomura's drawing.

Yoshiko Itoo's drawing.

Yasuko Nagakawa's drawing.

with their new art materials. Twelve-year-old Hiroko Nakajima drew a picture of herself wearing a detailed pink kimono. Nine-year-old Yoshiko Itoo drew a vibrant scene of her friends playing on Honkawa's playground. Eight-year-old Zyunko Hotta drew a colorful and very true-to-life portrait of herself, her classmates, and her teachers taking a walk among Hiroshima's hills and cherry blossom trees. Misako Simomura showed the infamous atomic bomb dome next to new buildings that had been built since the bombing. Fishermen rowed their boats on a tributary of the Ota River while new streetcars ran on a bridge above. In her drawing, she passes by a small market with freshly stocked fruits. And in a gesture of unbelievable graciousness, eleven-year-old Yasuko Nagakawa sent a stencil of the words "America Is Our Friend" in Japanese calligraphy. Rather than feeling anger toward Americans, the schoolchildren embraced the hope that there would be "no more Hiroshimas."

PART TWO

The Cold War
Comes Home

5

Truman to Wallace: You're Fired

Two weeks after John Hersey's *Hiroshima* essay came out in 1946, Secretary of Commerce Henry Wallace gave a major speech at New York's Madison Square Garden. Twenty-thousand people filled the stands. Tensions between the United States and the Soviet Union had been building ever since President Truman took office in April 1945. Wallace, still believing that the twentieth century could be the Century of the Common Man, pleaded with the world for peace. The crowd roared in approval. He suggested that instead of distrusting each other, the United States and the Soviet Union should compete peacefully with each other. He then declared that no nation should be allowed to spend more than 15 percent of its overall budget on the military.

At first, Truman told reporters that he had read the whole speech and agreed entirely with what Wallace said. This angered Secretary of State James Byrnes. He, along with Truman's adviser Bernard Baruch, threatened to resign. The president became worried that Secretary of War Robert Patterson and Secretary of the Navy James Forrestal would too. In a knee-jerk reaction, Truman sided with Byrnes and

Henry Wallace, President
Roosevelt's former vice president
and President Truman's secretary
of commerce. An outspoken critic
of Truman's decision to drop
atomic bombs on Hiroshima and
Nagasaki, Wallace imagined a
world in which people could be
independent, free, and peaceful,
regardless of nationality.

Baruch, who wanted the United States to be much more forceful against the Soviet Union. Truman wrote Wallace a fiery letter demanding his resignation.

That night, Truman wrote in his diary, "[Wallace] wants us to disband our armed forces, give Russia our atomic secrets and trust a bunch of adventurers in the Kremlin . . . I do not understand a 'dreamer' like that." This was a fateful moment in history. With Wallace gone, the final chance to avoid the Cold War and nuclear arms race disappeared.

After his departure, Wallace's vision for a Century of the Common Man crumbled within two years. Instead of urging cooperation with the Soviets, Truman hinted that communists might threaten the very fabric of the United States. He continued his diary entry: "The Reds [communists], phonies and 'parlor pinks' seem to be banded together and are becoming a national danger." Then he turned out the lights. Truman didn't seem to lose much sleep over the increasingly dangerous state of the world or the role that he played in creating it.

Old Man River

Onstage with Wallace at Madison Square Garden was African-American singer, scholar, athlete, actor, and peace activist Paul Leroy Robeson. Like

Wallace, Robeson also wanted peace with the Soviet Union. However, despite his accomplishments, this talented and celebrated man would eventually fall victim to growing American Cold War hysteria.

Like Truman, many Americans believed that communism was spreading around the world. What might happen if communists showed up in American cities, neighborhoods, or even next door? Would their foreign ideas destroy the American way of life? In many cases, people of color were the first to be labeled communists, especially if they spoke out against the United States in any meaningful way. Robeson was both black and outspoken, a dangerous combination in the early days of the Cold War.

Robeson was born in 1898. He came of age in Princeton, New Jersey. His dad, a runaway slave, was pastor at the city's African Methodist Episcopal Church. Not able to gain admission to all-white Princeton University, Robeson attended nearby Rutgers. Getting into Rutgers was no small feat. At the time, only fifty African Americans attended white colleges in the entire country.

Robeson enrolled in 1915 as a wave of racism and xenophobia swept the nation. That year, D. W. Griffith's *The Birth of a Nation* premiered in theaters. The film, wildly popular across the country, portrayed the Ku Klux Klan (KKK), a white supremacist terrorist organization, as heroes and African Americans as scoundrels and rapists.

Despite the racial climate, Robeson shot to the top of his class. One of his classmates recalled, "[Paul] was always in the library studying. It was clear right away he was going to be a good student, or die trying." With a beautiful mind and a kind soul, he became very popular with his classmates. Upon graduation, they elected him Rutgers valedictorian.

In addition to his incredible thirst for knowledge, Robeson was also an extraordinary athlete. At the time, most Americans could not imagine a black athlete playing on a white college team. In fact, it was almost unheard of. Only fourteen African Americans played on white teams between 1915 and 1919.

Many of Robeson's Rutgers football teammates couldn't imagine it either. He recalled that on his first day of scrimmage, his teammates "slugged [him] on the face and smashed [his] nose, just smashed it." When he returned to the field after ten days recovering from his brutal injuries, the determined seventeen-year-old ignored his tormenters and began running plays again. His dad had had the courage to run away from slavery. Surely he could handle a little rough-and-tumble on the field.

In spite of the beatings and his teammates' racism, Robeson went on to become one of the best football players in Rutgers history. Sportswriter Walter Camp called him "the greatest defensive end ever to trod the gridiron" and deemed him All-American, one of the sport's all-time best. Robeson also soared above his peers in other sports. He threw the javelin on the Rutgers track team, played catcher on the baseball team, and filled any position on the basketball team.

Of his academic performance, one of Robeson's classmates remembered on the eve of graduation that he was "the most brilliant student at the college." Another recalled, "He led his class. None of us could hold a candle to him. He was pure black and proved beyond any doubt that a black man can have the highest intelligence."

On June 10, 1919, a beautiful day in New Brunswick, Paul Robeson strode to the front of his class to deliver his valedictory speech, titled "The New Idealism." After years of global despair and racial unrest, Robeson's classmates looked to the future, to a world free from the horrors of World War I. This would be the first of many major public addresses he would give throughout his life. He gazed out at an ocean of white students, professors, and parents, and in his hauntingly beautiful voice, he described his vision for America.

He told the polite audience that the same positive attitude and national commitment that had led to the end of World War I would spill over to "a restructuring of American life" on the home front. A "new spirit" would finally sweep away racism and bring all Americans together. It would be a long, difficult journey, but one that could be accomplished together.

White Americans, he proclaimed, should adhere to Christian principles and never forget the new postwar spirit. Black Americans should elevate themselves and their families by embracing the most American of values, "self-reliance, self-respect, industry, perseverance, and economy." The "new idealism" would be realized when "black and white . . . clasp friendly hands in the consciousness of the fact that we are brethren and that God is the father of us all."[1]

Walking in Dignity

As great an athlete and a scholar as Paul Robeson was, it was his amazing voice and his talent as an actor that made him famous. In 1923, he began acting with the hugely popular Provincetown Players. The Players put on shows that dealt with subjects Broadway wouldn't touch—chiefly the struggle of the working class.[2] They welcomed Robeson with open arms.

After three successful years of acting, Robeson and his wife moved to London, where he became the first African-American actor to play the role of Shakespeare's Othello with a white Desdemona. For ten years, he traveled the world on tour. He performed in almost every European capital, making more money than many white actors. He soaked up the cosmopolitan culture. He met many people and had many conversations about politics and justice.

When Robeson performed in the Soviet Union, he had an epiphany, marveling at how people viewed him first as a talented human being and second as a black man. In Moscow, he was able to dine at any restaurant, sleep in any hotel, and enter any public place. This was so different from the way he was treated in the United States. In many places in the United States, African Americans had to use separate washrooms, drink from separate water fountains, sleep in separate hotels, and dine in different restaurants than whites. Horrifically, 281 African Americans were lynched in the United States between 1920 and 1930. The KKK controlled a major wing of the Democratic Party.

For years, Robeson had experienced deep racism. Princeton wouldn't consider him. His Rutgers teammates beat him. His law colleagues kept him from practicing. Now here he was, in the heart of communist Moscow, enjoying opportunities that he never could on his home soil. He recalled of the Soviet Union, "Here I am not a Negro but a human being for the first time in my life . . . I walk in dignity." To Robeson, that was true freedom.

Paul Robeson signs autographs for grateful fans at a Russian war anniversary fund-raiser in June 1942.

When he returned home, Robeson introduced many white Americans to African-American spirituals and folk songs that echoed "the rhythmic cry of the slave." Honoring the legacy of his father, he sang songs like "Joshua Fit de Battle of Jericho" and "Ev'ry Time I Feel the Spirit" in front of packed audiences. His tortured but tender cadence moved critic after critic, compelling one to write that his voice projected a "universal humanism that touches the heart."[3] Another wrote that "the voice of Paul Robeson is the embodiment of the aspirations of the New Negro who pleads best the race's progress by adhering strictly to the true endowment of his ancestors."[4] In 1936, his deep, baritone version of the *Showboat* ballad "Ol'

Man River" boomed over American phonographs. It became one of the most popular songs of its time.

Robeson began to speak out against segregation at home and injustice around the world. It angered him that African diplomats, some of the smartest people in the world, could not even use the restrooms at gas stations as they traveled to meetings in Washington, DC. How did that look to the rest of the world? How did it look when white policemen killed seventeen African Americans in the 1943 Detroit race riot? How was it possible that the armed forces, about to fight a war to free many around the world from the terrors of fascism, were themselves segregated on the basis of race?

Many African Americans fought abroad for their country and for the freedom of so many people

Paul Robeson reaches for actress Uta Hagen's hand as Shakespeare's Othello, a role he reprised on Broadway in 1943. Robeson was the first black actor to play the role in close to a century.

around the world. They returned to a country that had no laws against lynching. That was unacceptable to Robeson. He formed a delegation, and together, they visited Truman at the White House in 1946. At the time, civil rights activist W. E. B. Du Bois remarked that Robeson "was the best known American on earth, to the largest number of human beings. His voice [was] known in Europe, Asia and Africa, in the West Indies and South America and in the islands of the seas. . . . Only in his native land [was] he without honor and rights."[5]

Truman greeted the delegation in the Oval Office. Robeson told the president, "Negro war veterans who fought for freedom want to know that they can have freedom in their own country." He asked Truman, "How can Secretary [of State] Byrnes stand up in the Council of Nations as a representative of a land of freedom, when lynchings and discrimination are common occurrences in that land?" Truman felt threatened by Robeson's direct manner. Instead of listening to Robeson, the president questioned his loyalty to America and dismissed the world-renowned actor as a communist. He told Robeson not to mix domestic and foreign policy.[6]

Silencing Americans

Fear of the Soviet Union abroad translated into fear of communists at home. Would the Soviet Union send agents in disguise to steal atomic secrets? Destroy American companies? Poison American food and water supplies? Though Truman warned Robeson not to mix domestic and foreign policy, the president and the Federal Bureau of Investigation (FBI) did just that when they accused American citizens of being communists or Soviet agents.

Robeson visited Truman just as the president and FBI director J. Edgar Hoover began cracking down on "subversives," or troublemakers, in the federal government. Though Truman feared that the FBI under Hoover could become an "American Gestapo," the president still made all government employees take loyalty tests. The government organized large meetings during which employees sang "God Bless America" and took freedom pledges. If they had the wrong views about religion, foreign policy, or race, they risked losing their jobs and having their lives destroyed.

Speaking out against American injustices at home and around the world, as Robeson was doing, became a dangerous activity with terrible consequences. Those who spoke out were often accused of disloyalty to the country. Between 1947 and 1951, loyalty boards fired 300 government employees and forced 3,000 to resign.

The Hollywood Ten

In 1947, the House Un-American Activities Committee (HUAC) accused many Hollywood actors and artists of being members of the Communist Party. The committee called nineteen witnesses before Congress, including famous writers and directors. Several witnesses—Alvah Bessie, Herbert Biberman, Lester Cole, Edward Dmytryk, Ring Lardner Jr., John Howard Lawson, Albert Maltz, Samuel Ornitz, Adrian Scott, and Dalton Trumbo—became known as the "Hollywood Ten." The eleventh, playwright Bertolt Brecht, had escaped Nazi Germany by moving to Hollywood. He force-fully denied being a communist. Under enormous pressure from the committee, he ended up returning to East Germany. For Brecht, America was the "land of the free" no more.

Oscar-nominated film director Edward Dmytryk, one of the Hollywood Ten, testifies in front of the House Un-American Activities Committee in 1947.

The studios that employed the Hollywood Ten would not support them. Studio executives would not hire anyone they suspected of being communists or knowing communists, even though they were some of the biggest names in Hollywood. Many Hollywood celebrities spoke out in support of their friends and coworkers. Among the most vocal were Humphrey Bogart, Gregory Peck, Gene Kelly, William Wyler,

Charged with contempt of Congress, nine of the Hollywood men gave themselves up to US marshals. From left to right: Robert Adrian Scott, Edward Dmytryk, Samuel Ornitz, Lester Cole, Herbert Biberman, Albert Maltz, Alvah Bessie, John Howard Lawson, and Ring Lardner Jr.

Lucille Ball, Frank Sinatra, Burt Lancaster, Edward G. Robinson, Lauren Bacall, Orson Welles, Katharine Hepburn, Pete Seeger, Henry Fonda, Ethel Barrymore, Benny Goodman, and Groucho Marx.

Sadly, HUAC did not listen. The Hollywood Ten were sentenced to prison terms in 1948.

Henry Wallace, who had just thrown his hat in the ring to run against Truman as a Progressive in the 1948 presidential election, spoke out against HUAC and what the committee was doing to the Hollywood Ten. In December 1947, Wallace had told a crowd in Tulsa, Oklahoma, "The House Committee has taken the offensive against truth. It is trying to silence the writers and artists and political leaders who are most adept at carrying truth to the people. It is trying to intimidate into silence the professors, teachers, scientists and ordinary citizens who like to speak the truth." Wallace believed that truth and peace would "usher in the century of the common man." Unfortunately, by the late 1940s, the forces of distrust and fear severely tested the strength of American democracy. Many incredibly talented people like Paul Robeson became the victims of such hysteria.

It's America. I Have a Right to Sing

In late August 1949, Harlem's chapter of the Civil Rights Congress asked Robeson to sing at a benefit concert near Peekskill, New York. Violent protesters followed him, determined to disrupt the event. The protesters resented how Robeson praised the Soviet Union. They also hated how Robeson criticized the United States for discriminating against African Americans and other people of color. To many fearful Americans, Robeson represented a threat to white supremacy and American dominance over the rest of the world. For those reasons, he would soon find himself labeled a communist and shunned from American public life.

Before the Peekskill concert, many white residents, fearful of African-American concertgoers, called the police and asked for protection. Before the concert was to begin, a group of World War II veterans lined up shoulder to shoulder at the entrance, blocking fans from entering. Singer Pete Seeger recalled that a federal officer or representative arrived to spread the message that "this man Robeson loves the Russians. He doesn't love America. And he's coming to sing. I think you know what to do about it." Even though the police had been called, only four deputy sheriffs arrived on the scene.

As the sun went down over the Hudson River, fistfights broke out between concertgoers and protesters. Those setting up chairs inside were beaten and concert flyers were burned. The police officers stood by and did next to nothing. Organizers finally canceled the concert after two and a half hours of violence. Robeson himself was never able to get near the concert grounds.

Robeson was not about to let burning fires and racial violence deter him from singing. Instead, he went on the radio and announced, "It's America. I have a right to sing. I'm going to sing."

Civil rights activists, Robeson fans, and veterans all listened intently to Robeson's words. The Civil Rights Congress then announced that it would reschedule the concert for September 4. This time, it would be much bigger.

Organizers planned for a crowd of 20,000 people. They had learned their lesson. This time, they would enlist union members and veterans sympathetic to Robeson for security.

The union members and veterans formed a circle around the concert grounds. As the concert drew near, a crowd of 1,000 protesters once again arrived at the entrance. Many held rocks and sticks. Local and state police arrived to keep order. They made sure that protesters stayed away from the crowds of concertgoers arriving for the event.

Inside, Paul Robeson and Pete Seeger relaxed. They took comfort that so many people turned out to attend and secure the concert. Seeger remarked, "We congratulated ourselves on how it's America, and [protesters] didn't break up the stage or anything." As 2,000 union members and veterans joined hands peacefully to keep protesters at bay, Seeger, Robeson, and others belted out song after song. Robeson himself sang for well over an hour.[7]

When the concert ended, the ring of security broke up to let people out to the parking lot. At that moment, the gang of protesters stormed the entrance to the concert, blocking those trying to exit. Author Howard Fast, the concert's chairperson, reported that local and state police officers joined together with the protesters, throwing rocks and hurling racial epithets. Fast recalled, "It was a battle, not a concert."[8]

Some of the protesters, yelling ugly names like "nigger" and "nigger lovers," followed concert-goers out of the parking lot and onto local roads. They stoned buses full of African-American and white passengers and overturned sixteen cars. Some bus drivers, fearful for their lives, abandoned their passengers and ran. The passengers themselves had to drive the buses out of the danger zone. All told, 150 people were injured in the riot.[9]

After being under siege inside the concert grounds, Seeger, his wife, and his two babies finally made it to their car. He noticed some glass on the pavement. He told his

Pete Seeger, who was featured at the 1949 Civil Rights Congress concert in New York, plays banjo and belts out a song in 1955.

family to duck. "Around the corner was a pile of stones, each about as big as a baseball, and a young man heaving them with all his force at every car that came by. And around the corner was another pile of stones and another young fella heaving them. There must have been 15 or 20 piles of stones before we got into Peekskill."[10]

Media Spin

Rather than blame the protesters for disrupting the concert, many newspapers, including the *New York Times*, blamed Robeson and the concertgoers for provoking the riot. *Times* editors blamed Robeson for rescheduling. They argued that by doing so, he and the concert organizers were asking for violence. They called the concert "a calculated display of Communist organizational strength." Then they insisted that the protesting veterans were not racist, even though crosses were burned on the concert grounds, a form of intimidation introduced by the KKK. Rather, protesters were trying to prevent Robeson and communist concertgoers from infiltrating a small New York community.

Vincent Boyle, leader of the protesters, remarked, "We are being plagued by . . . Paul Robeson and his communistic followers. . . . It is an epidemic because they are coming here to induce others to join their ranks and it is unfortunate that some of the weaker minded are susceptible to their fallacious teachings unless something is done by the loyal Americans of this area."

Four years of anti-communist rhetoric had finally boiled over into violence in Peekskill. The *New York Times* and other newspapers stopped reporting regularly on Robeson's accomplishments. When they did report about him, they referred to him as "the baritone and Communist Singer," "the left-wing singer," and the "pro-Communist singer." The government took away his passport. He was no longer allowed to travel outside the country.

Robeson continued to perform at churches and union gatherings throughout the 1950s. No white newspapers would review his performances. In 1958, he published an autobiography called *Here I Stand*. No mainstream American newspaper would review it, though African-American and foreign newspapers raved about it.[11]

Robeson lived out the rest of his life in isolation and sadness. The All-American football player, brilliant actor, speaker of fifteen languages, and human rights activist fell victim to American Cold War hysteria. Mainstream textbooks don't tell his story. Very few monuments commemorate his achievements. Paul Robeson and many others like him have been largely lost to history.

6

Two Can Play at That Game

As the Peekskill concert exploded into violence at home, a different kind of blast took place nearly 6,000 miles away in the Soviet Union. At the Semipalatinsk Test Site, the morning of August 29, 1949, was cold and gray. Sagebrush, plume thistles, and yellow wildflowers bristled as stiff winds blew across the desolate ground.

Suddenly, the earth began to quake violently. The sky turned an ominous shade of red. Seconds later, a mushroom-shaped cloud blossomed over the horizon. It quickly grew taller and wider, replacing the red in the sky with massive amounts of billowing smoke. Semey, the closest town to the explosion, disappeared entirely from view.

The predictions of American scientists and officials like Arthur Holly Compton, J. Robert Oppenheimer, and Henry Stimson had come true. Just four years after Hiroshima, the Soviet Union exploded its first atomic bomb, more powerful than the one dropped on Nagasaki. As predicted, the American monopoly of atomic weapons was over.

Soviet Development

On September 3, an American RB-29 flying from Yokota Air Base in Japan to Eielson Air Force Base in Fairbanks, Alaska, detected dust from the Semipalatinsk explosion. The federal government kept the news secret from Americans for twenty days, at which point President Truman shocked the nation by reporting: "We have evidence that within recent weeks an atomic explosion occurred in the U.S.S.R."

The public was stunned. Many American scientists were furious. Truman, who had told Oppenheimer that he believed the Soviets would never build one, still didn't believe it. After all, even the US Air Force had predicted that the Soviets would not test a bomb for years.

Americans were scared. Many wondered why Truman hadn't acted on the Acheson-Lilienthal Report (officially titled the "Report on the International Control of Atomic Energy"), which was written by a committee chaired by politicians Dean Acheson and David Lilienthal in 1946. The report proposed controlling the spread of nuclear arms and warned against future nuclear

Russian officials observe an early Soviet nuclear test at Semipalatinsk.

Hungarian scientist Leo Szilard, discoverer of the nuclear chain reaction. He became an advocate for international arms control and improved relations between the United States and the Soviet Union.

warfare. It also recommended that the world set up an Atomic Development Authority, a group that would supervise the mining and use of uranium and plutonium, the main substances used to create the weapons. The authority would then make those materials available for peaceful use.

Critically, the report, which could have prevented a nuclear arms race, asked the United States to destroy its existing bombs within three months. The United States would not agree to do so.

If Truman had followed the original report, the United States and the Soviet Union could have used the four years between 1945 and 1949 to figure out a way to stop the madness. Instead, the mistrust between the two nations finally boiled over into a public race for nuclear weapons, a race that could still lead to the end of life on the planet.

After the bomb test, Soviet scientists breathed a huge sigh of relief. Russian physicist Yuli Khariton remarked, "In possessing such a weapon, we had removed the possibility of its being used against the USSR." The bomb, he felt, allowed "our country . . . to defend itself from really threatening mortal danger." Physicist Igor Golovin wrote that their sleepless nights and Herculean efforts had been worth it because "they had knocked the trump card from the hands of the American atomic diplomats."

Built on Bones

The explosion at Semipalatinsk startled a young Kazakh couple. They viewed the mushroom cloud from the window of their home and instinctively went outside to get a better view. Never before had they seen such a spectacle. It seemed like they were living in another world.

Two years later, the Kazakh woman gave birth to a baby girl, Yeerkish. Yeerkish was born with dwarfism and a severe hip deformity. She never grew more than three and a half feet tall. Forty years later, Susan Reed, a reporter for the *New Republic*, interviewed Yeerkish and described her condition: "[Yeerkish] sits on a suitcase on the floor near her bed because it is the most convenient height for her bowed and misshapen legs. Movement for her is difficult. She ambles around the house, stiffly shifting her weight from one knobby knee to the other, stretching her long arms to reach the table."[1]

Between 1949 and 1989, roughly one nuclear test per month took place at Semipalatinsk. Like Yeerkish, one in every twenty children from that region was born with serious deformities. More than 50 percent of the region's residents have died before the age of sixty. "Almost all my classmates and friends have died," reflected Aiken Akimbekov. "When the wind blows [from the direction of the test grounds], it makes people feel sick. It causes high blood pressure in some, and it also brings a very strange smell."

The Soviet government kept the dangers of radiation secret from its citizens. During the first atomic test, one village was completely covered by the atomic cloud. Ninety percent of those who lived in that village were poisoned by radiation over the next year. Cancer rates in the Semipalatinsk region are still 25 to 30 percent higher than anywhere else in Kazakhstan. At least 220,000 people were exposed to extremely high levels of radiation during the period of nuclear testing.

Rather than admitting the truth, Soviet officials explained that the diseases were caused by genetic defects or poor sanitation. Like the atomic bomb victims in Hiroshima and Bikini Atoll, people like Akimbekov had no idea how terrible radiation could be until it was too late.[2] Yuriy Strilchuk, director of training for the National Nuclear Center of Kazakhstan, defended Soviet atomic testing by citing the American threat: "The Soviet Union had to do this. . . . The buildup of nuclear weapons on one side led to the buildup on the other side.[3]

Citizens of the villages near Semipalatinsk were not the only Soviet victims of the atomic bomb. Prisoners at the Norilsk gulag, a political labor camp, mined and treated uranium ore. Political figures whom Stalin suspected of being disloyal to the Soviet Union often ended up in a gulag. In many cases, their families, friends, and employees did too. Famous actors, authors, and scientists sometimes disappeared out of the blue, kidnapped by Stalin's secret police. Most victims of the "Great Terror" were ordinary citizens. Overall, during Stalin's reign, at least 12 to 14 million prisoners ended up in gulag camps like Norilsk, performing hard labor and dying horrific deaths.[4]

One female prisoner remembered that she had to dig forty-foot foundations for buildings at Norilsk with her bare hands: "When you had finished

Mine workers labor at Kolyma gulag, Siberia.

you would get into the bucket for the earth, like in a well, and they would pull you out. More than once the rope broke. And that was that. The bodies were left at the bottom. Norilsk is built on bones." In the uranium mining camps, prisoners also mined uranium with their bare hands. Their life expectancy once they began mining was three months.[5]

7

Survival Is a Choice

Two days after Truman told Americans that the United States no longer held a monopoly on atomic bombs, Billy Graham, the thirty-year-old Baptist preacher, remarked in a sermon, "An arms race unprecedented in the history of the world is driving us madly toward destruction!" He continued anxiously, "Do you know the area that is marked out for the enemy's first atomic bomb? New York! Secondly, Chicago; and thirdly, the city of Los Angeles!"[1]

It was becoming clear to many Americans that the next war would probably be fought with atomic weapons. To those who had lived through two world wars in just over thirty years, World War III was a very real prospect. The Soviet Union built and tested an atomic bomb in just four years. It was just a matter of time before other countries did too. What would an atomic war look like? Could anyone survive?

The United States was at a far greater risk of attack from the air than ever before. While European cities had suffered massive destruction in both world wars, American cities had not been bombed. Though many Americans had read John Hersey's article and subsequent book, most couldn't imagine an attack from the air. What would happen to New York, Chicago, or Los Angeles if those cities were attacked in the same manner as Hiroshima?

The FCDA

Under pressure to do something about the threat, President Truman established a new federal office. His administration called it the Federal Civil Defense Administration (FCDA). The objective of the FCDA was to teach Americans about the dangers of nuclear weapons and the things they could do to protect themselves if the bombs fell on their towns. Most important, in order to address the fear many people had of a nuclear attack, the FCDA tried to convince Americans that they could survive one. In fact, not only could the country survive, it could be even stronger afterward. Schools would still function and factories would still produce goods. Life would go on.

The FCDA educated Americans through the public school system. If teachers could convince children that they could survive an atomic attack, they would go home in the evenings and teach their parents. After all, many parents trusted their own children more than they did government officials.

To convince kids that they could survive an atomic attack, the FCDA told local school districts to conduct bomb drills. In many schools, these were not just drills. They were full-scale dress rehearsals. If a bomb exploded while kids were in school, students would know just what to do.

Prepping for the Bomb

In Baltimore, Maryland, students at General Vocation School #198 stood silently on the morning of February 27, 1953, as Psalm 140 echoed throughout the school's auditorium:

Deliver me, Lord, from the wicked; preserve me from the violent,
    From those who plan evil in their hearts, who stir up conflicts
every day,
    Who sharpen their tongues like serpents, venom of asps upon
their lips.

When the psalm concluded, everyone remained standing for the singing of the Lord's Prayer. Next, they saluted the flag and sang "America the Beautiful."

Principal Hottes then introduced the assembly's speaker, Schuyler C. Blackburn, deputy director of the city's Civil Defense Organization. Blackburn stepped to the podium purposefully. He told students that survival was a *choice*. Their teachers, parents, or other adults might not be around to help out. They could survive a nuclear attack only if they took necessary steps to save themselves.

After Blackburn's speech, students viewed the civil defense film *Duck and Cover*. Like those at school #198, millions of kids across the country watched as friendly Bert the Turtle walked confidently through town while a catchy theme song played in the background. Then, out of the blue, a monkey dropped down from a tree, grasping a branch tied to a stick of dynamite. Bert immediately recognized the danger and collapsed to the ground, covering himself with his shell.

A narrated voice explained that Bert was always ready for danger. He has his shell that will protect him—"Sometimes it even saves his life!" If kids wanted to survive a nuclear attack, they needed to protect themselves with whatever they could find around them. Even if a teacher couldn't reach them, they should know what to do:

Now, we must be ready for a new danger, the atomic bomb. . . .
You will know when it comes. We hope it never comes, but we
must be ready. It looks something like this: there is a bright flash!

Brighter than the Sun! Brighter than anything you have ever seen! If you are not ready and did not know what to do, it could hurt you in different ways. It could knock you down hard, or throw you against a tree or wall. It is such a big explosion it can smash in buildings and knock signboards over and break windows all over town. But, if you duck and cover like Bert, you will be much safer. You know how bad sunburn can feel. An atomic bomb flash can burn you worse than a terrible sunburn.[2]

On the screen, confident children ducked and covered in the school corridor, ducked and covered on the street, ducked and covered next to a wall. They obediently fell to the ground, covered their heads with their arms, and shielded themselves with whatever materials they could.

Next, Paul and Patty, brother and sister, stood in their suburban living room, ready to go to school. Their mom took them by their hands and kissed them good-bye. They were happy and confident as they strode out the door, ready to conquer any dangers that might befall them. They were prepared for a Soviet attack. Then a massive flash filled the screen as the narrator excitedly declared, "It's a bomb! Duck and cover!"

The film repeatedly warned that kids might be alone when the attack came, but they could still survive. The safe world in which they lived might be gone at any moment. One minute, they might be playing with their friends on the playground. The next minute, they would be fighting for survival. In the dangerous world the adults created, it would be up to kids to save themselves.

If You Grow Up

Schools were not the only places where children learned how dangerous the Cold War world had become. One of the most popular baseball card

Students at P.S. 58 in Brooklyn, New York, take Bert the Turtle's advice and duck under their desks during an air-raid drill.

companies, Philadelphia's Bowman Gum Company, released a collection of "Wild Man Picture Cards." Corner stores sold them in thin foil packages next to the checkout counter. One of the cards was called "Atomic Doom." It asked, "What will a war be like—if it comes? Science is constantly increasing the destructive power of the atomic bomb. In a future war, not one or two but many of these weapons could be let loose on target areas." The outcome? "Explosions might cause a chain reaction destroying the earth or rendering it so barren that it could not support human or animal life." An image on the card showed the earth blowing up.

The 1952 movie *The Atomic City* depicted a child, Tommy, playing at his house with a friend. His mom was in the kitchen making dinner. Tommy asked his playmate, "What do you want to be if you grow up?" Tommy's mother, shaken by her son's disturbing question, responded, "*When* you grow up, not *if*, *when!*"

Children who grew up in the early 1950s learned from their parents, their teachers, and their government that nuclear war could end their lives. They also learned that they could protect themselves and *do* something about it. Robert Musil, who was a child in the early 1950s, remembered, "It was with that awful knowledge—we were not safe at all—that I experienced duck and cover drills, and developed an early disillusionment with, even disdain for, authority."[3] Another child of that era recalled, "The thought of a building bursting into flames . . . is kind of startling. . . . It undercuts the sense of reality. You kind of grow up knowing that certain things are stable . . . that certain presuppositions about the way things are remain constant. Namely, buildings stand. They may burn down or let's say in an earthquake, they might collapse, but reality is fairly stable. When you suddenly see a picture like that, it's kind of like getting the rug pulled out." Sociologist Todd Gitlin recounted from elementary school: "Every so often, out of the blue, a teacher would pause in the middle of class and call out, 'Take cover!' We knew, then, to scramble under our miniature desks and to stay there, cramped, heads folded under our arms, until the teacher called out, 'All clear!'"

One adult remembered about the earlier drills, "You could feel the tension in the air, fear. The kids are fidgety and jumpy and talking—whispering—but then there would be an absolute silence. You never knew if it was a drill—a test—or the real thing."

In *Born on the Fourth of July*, Ron Kovic wrote of his atomic childhood, "We joined the cub scouts and marched in parades on Memorial Day. We made contingency plays for the cold war and built fallout shelters out of milk cartons."

Parents became concerned about how they could identify lost or wounded children in the event of an attack. In response, school officials in New York,

San Francisco, and Seattle made identification tags that students were to wear around their necks at all times. Some officials in Milwaukee even considered tattooing children with their names and telephone numbers, but the district rejected that idea. Tattooing reminded too many people of what the Nazis did to Jews and other persecuted groups during the Holocaust. Plus, tattoos would be of no help if skin was burned off, which is what happened to many atomic bomb victims in Hiroshima and Nagasaki.[4]

Soviet schools also conducted civil defense drills. Vladislav Zubok and Constantine Pleshakov recalled, "We learned to look for an *Enola Gay* in the skies even before we learned to brush our teeth. Soviet middle schools would hold civil defense classes in which ludicrous survival skills were taught in preparation for all-out war. Although still half believing in Santa Claus, we were already very skeptical of gas masks and bomb shelters."[5]

What to Do If a Bomb Falls on the Fourth of July

On Independence Day, 1951, radio news broadcasters in Baltimore reported on a tremendous flash of light that cut sharply across the sky. A horrific roar and loud "bang" could be heard more than seventy-five miles away. At ground zero, children who had been playing baseball just seconds before the blinding flash ran around in dazed confusion while their mothers and fathers who had been doing yard work and chatting with neighbors rushed away from their burning homes. Flames shot up from broken gas mains and water gushed from mangled pipes.

Through a thick haze of smoke, scores of volunteer stretcher-bearers arrived on the scene along with teams of rescue workers from the Red Cross. Radiological and reconnaissance teams, highway clearance teams, park rangers, and police squads descended upon the rubble, frantically trying to pull burned and maimed victims from the fires that now consumed many of the city's neighborhoods. As a band played patriotic songs, local civil defense authorities, police officers, and firefighters swiftly executed evacuation procedures that they had developed only one year earlier. Their efforts paid off as the fires were extinguished, the smoke cleared, and the crowd breathed a collective sigh.

Thankfully, this "disaster" was only a drill. It was one of the Baltimore Civil Defense Organization's "mock" atomic bombings. Tens of thousands of people watched in earnest from the stands of Memorial Stadium.

Immediately following the "attack," the crowd was treated to a massive fireworks display followed by an equally massive traffic jam. A newspaper article noted that many of the spectators caught in the gridlock must have wondered what traffic would be like after an *actual* atomic attack.

The roar of mock enemy aircraft and the "bang" of the explosion were broadcast over the radio. People listening thought the attack was real. Switchboards at local radio stations and newspapers were flooded with calls from frantic listeners who, after listening to the drill, believed that Baltimore was under enemy attack. One panicked caller to a local radio station exclaimed, "I was scared to death. To tell you the truth, I thought the Reds were here."[6]

8

We Refuse to Cooperate

The Baltimore drill was not an isolated one. Events just like it were taking place all across the country. In the early 1950s, the FCDA began forcing American citizens to take part in an annual drill called Operation Alert. When the air-raid sirens sounded, residents of sixty cities had to stop what they were doing and take cover for fifteen minutes. While they ducked under desks and crammed into basements, local civil defense officials rehearsed the preparations they had made for nuclear war.

Operation Alert was the biggest dress rehearsal for nuclear war that ever occurred in the United States. Citizens and civil defense officials took it very seriously. When sirens began to wail, most Americans listened to instructions they heard on the radio and read in pamphlets to do whatever they could do to get out of harm's way.

Officials at Mercy Hospital in Canton, Ohio, didn't take any chances. They evacuated all patients, employees, and medical equipment to a makeshift hospital twenty miles from downtown. Of course, they didn't actually move real patients. Instead, they enlisted

In 1953, students and teachers calmly evacuate Highland View School in Oak Ridge, Tennessee, during a bomb drill.

Boy Scout and Girl Scout volunteers to act as patients. Hospital personnel moved them out of the hospital on stretchers and in wheelchairs, then carried them to waiting buses, which transported them to the remote hospital. As time went on, hospital staff became so good at evacuation that they were able to accomplish the entire move within ninety minutes of the siren's sounding.

What would happen if the Soviets dropped a hydrogen bomb on St. Louis? People would evacuate in an orderly manner to Wright City, forty miles west of town. Wright City was ready for them. Huge signs pointed the westward evacuees down US Route 40 to the town's largest public

Local officials call out instructions from a civil defense vehicle to make sure Highland View students and faculty follow evacuation procedures.

park. There, civil defense auxiliary police registered evacuees. Each registrant received an identification number, which made it easier for them to be identified for medical care and housing assignments. The head of the Wright City school lunch program and representatives from local community groups cooked up a hearty meal of stew, corn flakes, and coffee, which those playing the part of nuclear refugees happily consumed. In a tent nearby, first aid crews treated those who were wounded.[1]

Similar scenes played out all across the country during Operation Alert. Cars ground to a halt; streets cleared of people; children ducked under their

Once evacuated to a wooded area, students sit down and wait for the "all clear" as their teachers make sure they are all accounted for.

desks. In New York City, calm traffic cops directed drivers out of Times Square and toward the Lincoln Tunnel. There were no breakdowns, accidents, or disruptions of any kind. Traffic flowed much easier than on regular days at rush hour. In most cities, everything went smoothly and according to plan. Those injured were treated; those who lost their families were reunited; and all were eventually able to return home. Civil defense officials went out of their way to convince Americans that they could survive a nuclear attack. Not only would they survive, they would rebuild a better and more perfect society afterward.

Operation Alert 1955

By the end of the 1950s, these drills had become a routine part of American life, especially as hydrogen bombs got bigger and bigger. Most Americans obeyed the government's orders to take shelter and follow commands when the sirens blew. At the same time, some Americans began questioning the reasons why they had to "duck and cover" when they knew that drills like Operation Alert would never save them in the event of an attack. What good was ducking under a desk or driving in an orderly fashion toward the Lincoln Tunnel when buildings and tunnels would be pulverized? Would people even be able to reach their cars before the massive blast and subsequent firestorm vaporized them? From John Hersey's *Hiroshima*, many Americans knew that such drills were hopelessly unrealistic. In an actual attack, bridges would be destroyed, communications would be knocked out, rivers would boil, and radioactive fallout would likely poison those who weren't killed instantly.

Operation Alert and other drills sent people the message that they could survive nuclear war. This greatly alarmed peace activists who knew that the only true defense against nuclear weapons was to eliminate them from the face of the earth. Operation Alert suggested that nuclear war was inevitable and that the human race needed to live with it.

Pacifist Dorothy Day was not prepared to "live with" nuclear weapons or nuclear war. In 1955, New York State passed a law directing citizens to obey Operation Alert. If they didn't obey orders and take shelter, they could face a $500 fine and a year in jail. Day, upset with the government for spreading false information about the true effects of a nuclear attack, decided to confront authorities with civil disobedience.

Day printed flyers and handed them out to New Yorkers on the day of Operation Alert 1955. The flyers read: "We will not obey this order to pretend, to evacuate, to hide. In view of the certain knowledge . . . that there is no defense in atomic warfare, we know this drill to be a military act in a

Pacifist and activist Dorothy Day. She was not prepared to "live with" nuclear weapons or nuclear war.

cold war to instill fear, to prepare the collective mind for war. We refuse to cooperate."[2]

At 2:00 p.m. on June 15, 1955, air-raid sirens echoed across the concrete canyons of New York City. Civil defense officials corralled harried office workers out of buildings and down subway steps. Central Park became a manicured wilderness, as those enjoying an urban hike or visiting the zoo with their children took shelter inside the closest buildings. Benches and phone booths emptied. President Dwight Eisenhower and 15,000 government personnel fled Washington to secret bunkers, where they would carry on the business of government as the public dealt with the horrors of a Soviet hydrogen bomb.[3]

While the melee played out, Dorothy Day and a handful of other protesters sat calmly on benches outside city hall. They prayed and meditated as television and newspaper reporters swarmed around them. Many of the reporters could not understand why they refused to take shelter. They asked question after question. Calmly, Day and the others replied that they believed the government was not being truthful about the effects of nuclear weapons and that it was ridiculous to convince people that they could survive an atomic attack. Better to spend those resources on getting rid of nuclear weapons.

The police moved in. They handcuffed Day and twenty-seven others and pushed them into police vans. As New York City returned to normal after the drill, the vans sped away to the city jail. That evening, Day and the others came before Judge Louis Kaplan. Judge

Kaplan called them murderers, blaming them for the fake deaths of close to three million people who the fake H-bomb would have killed. He ordered each protester to pay a high bail of $1,500. Then he ordered one of the female protesters, twenty-nine-year-old Judith Malina, to Bellevue Hospital for psychiatric treatment.

We Shall Not Be Moved

Newspaper and television coverage of the Operation Alert protest inspired others to disobey the drills. Mary Sharmat, a young mother, was one of them. When she read in the *New York Times* that Operation Alert 1959 would take place the next day, Mary told her husband that she would refuse to take shelter. She recalled, "I felt that nuclear air-raid drills taught fear and hate towards an enemy. No enemy was coming to attack New York City, and I could not hate an unknown enemy in a nuclear age. I would disobey a bad law."

Mary thought that she would be arrested. She and her husband withdrew $500 from their bank account to be used for bail. They packed an overnight bag with baby food and diapers for their young son, Jimmy, whom she took with her. At 11:30 a.m., Mary strolled Jimmy out of their apartment building and walked north to Eighty-Sixth Street and Broadway. She sat down on a bench in Broadway's median strip, right next to a civil defense van. Pushing the stroller back and forth, Mary tried to keep Jimmy from crying as she debated whether to stand her ground or abandon her plan. When the siren wailed at noon, she made her final decision: She would stay put and face the consequences.

All around her, civil defense officers in white helmets streamed about like ants on an anthill. They directed pedestrians into buildings, under awnings, and onto subways. Cars, buses, and trucks came to a standstill. And then there was Mary, sitting out in the open, calmly pushing Jimmy back and forth.

Americans protest against the use of their tax dollars for the building of nuclear weapons in the 1950s.

An officer's scream pierced the calm: "Operation Alert! You must take cover immediately!" He demanded that Mary take shelter. She refused. He threatened to call the police. Mary replied, "Then call them." Another officer came over to see what was going on. The sirens wailed above. Jimmy began to cry. Officers threatened to give her a ticket, but they eventually walked away in disbelief.

Hundreds of people milled about, under awnings, in doorways, and inside the glass doors of Broadway's shops, but none would join her. When the all clear sounded at 12:15, things returned to normal. Stores reopened; shopping resumed; traffic began to flow once again. Mary got up off the bench, ran a few errands, then headed home.

Later that day, Mary's husband brought home the early edition of the *New York Times*. Right smack in the middle of the front page was a photo of another young mother and her two kids. They, too, had disobeyed orders to take cover while sitting on a bench outside city hall, just as Day and the other activists had done before them. Unlike Mary, the other woman, Janice Smith, was arrested. As police took her into custody, she told them, "All these drills do are scare birds, babies and old ladies. I will not raise my children to go underground." In addition to the *New York Times*, Smith's photo appeared on the front pages of four other New York newspapers.[4]

Mary knew that she had to connect with Janice. She called every single Smith in the telephone book. Finally, she found the right one. The two women talked for hours and hours. At the end of the call, they agreed to talk on the phone for at least an hour per day going forward. Together, they set a goal of finding other women who would join in their protest the following year.

May 3, 1960

Through the fall and winter, Mary and Janice did indeed talk every day. On a trip to the playground with Jimmy, Mary met Pat McMahon, a mom with four children. McMahon was a follower of Gandhi and a member of the War Resisters League. The three women then met Adrianne Winograd, another activist who strolled her child to the Central Park playgrounds each day. While their children played, Winograd recruited. Within six months, the group numbered fifty women.

The young mothers decided on a name for their group, the Civil Defense Protest Committee. Though they were all extremely busy running their households, they donated all of their extra time to planning the protest against the next Operation Alert. They reached out to the New York chapter of the Women's International League for Peace and Freedom, which helped them raise thousands of dollars in donations from across the city. Together, they organized seminars on the true dangers of atomic weapons and recruited another 250 volunteers. Then they distributed hundreds of flyers. One read that the only goal of civil defense was "to frighten children and to fool the public into thinking there is protection against an H-bomb." By the time Operation Alert rolled around the following year, Mary and Janice had turned their own solitary protests into a movement 1,000 people strong.

May 3, 1960, was a beautiful spring day in New York City. The wind whistled gently through the huge oak trees between Broadway and the

Brooklyn Bridge. Suddenly, sirens rang out across City Hall Park. Protesters huddled together while brokers evacuated the nearby New York Stock Exchange; players left the field at Yankee Stadium; and hundreds of people packed themselves inside Grand Central station. There the mothers stood, surrounded by toys, strollers, playpens, tricycles, dolls, and, of course, their kids. They knew that the police would hesitate to be photographed arresting young, well-dressed mothers with their children and their belongings. Mary recalled:

> I was not alone, Janice was not alone, the two mothers from the Grand Concourse in the Bronx were not alone. Over five hundred friends gathered. . . . Many men came down. Our skirts gave them courage. We loaned out extra babies to bachelors who had the misfortune to be childless. Dozens of children played in an area designated "Stay Off the Grass." Some of the students brought their musical instruments and softly played folk songs such as "We Shall Overcome" and "We Shall Not be Moved." . . . The sirens sounded. We stood. Mothers with children, fathers with mutual deep concerns, bachelors who had hopes and a borrowed baby, maiden aunts who had no children but were taking care of the rest of us. We stood. There was dead silence through the park.[5]

Hundreds of curious onlookers jammed the sidewalks. Some of them joined the protesters. A civil defense officer pushed through the crowd, waved his arms, and shouted, "You are all under arrest!" The crowd cheered and clapped wildly. As police carted away twenty-six protesters, they chanted "Gandhi is our leader. We shall not be moved" and sang "America the Beautiful," "Battle Hymn of the Republic," and "The Star-Spangled Banner." Newspaper and TV reporters began to show up in earnest. Mary, Janice, and the others knew the newspapers would report their actions the next day.

A judge eventually sentenced fifteen men and eleven women to five days in jail. The protesters achieved their goal. They had brought wide attention to their movement against civil defense and their fight against nuclear weapons. Mary remarked triumphantly, "Civil defense at last became an issue. It was no longer ignored as an unimportant nothing to put up with because it's easier. . . . Voters back home at the polls began to care." A newspaper reporter observed, "We seem to be approaching a condition of sanity where within a year or so there'll be more people defying than complying with the Civil Defense drill."[6]

Infant Denise Davidson sleeps soundly as her mother marches to ban the bomb in front of the United Nations headquarters in New York City, 1962.

Indeed, civil defense protests broke out across the nation. They spread to New Jersey, Connecticut, Massachusetts, Pennsylvania, Minnesota, and Illinois. College students jumped on the bandwagon, refusing to participate in civil defense drills at City College, Columbia, Rutgers, Princeton, and Cornell. By 1962, under enormous pressure to eliminate civil defense, the federal government stopped funding Operation Alert. The civil defense protests proved that just a handful of concerned people—ordinary citizens—could make a huge difference. Mary, Janice, and thousands of others helped people across the country make a giant leap toward sanity in a world that was becoming more insane by the minute.

Children who grew up during the 1950s became antiwar activists in the 1960s and 1970s. Early years of rehearsing air-raid drills, viewing films like *Duck and Cover*, designing fallout shelters, and learning atomic first aid helped turn Cold War kids into passionate human rights activists. As high school and college students, they set out to save the world. They fought for African-American civil rights and women's rights. They marched against the US invasion of Vietnam. They demanded that the government stop producing nuclear weapons and threatening nuclear war. They felt that the fate of the world was in their hands and that they could do a much better job than their parents' generation had. They dreamed of a better future, one free from the world wars that had engulfed their parents' generation, bigotry, and poverty. Then they acted to turn their dreams into reality.

PART THREE

Culture of War

Losing Half a World

On the morning of Saturday, June 24, 1950, President Truman woke earlier than usual, as the early-morning light streamed through the front windows of Blair House, where he and his wife, Bess, were living while the White House underwent renovations. He sat up on the edge of his king-size bed, did his usual morning stretches, put on his bathrobe, and sat down to read the major newspapers. He glanced first at the entertainment pages. *Tarzan and the Slave Girl* had opened the night before at movie theaters in New York City. Richard Rodgers and Oscar Hammerstein were producing a musical titled *Anna and the King of Siam*. *Death of a Salesman*, *The Cocktail Party*, *South Pacific*, and *Kiss Me, Kate* were all showing on Broadway.

He flipped back to the front page. The day before, the Senate had started debating whether or not to arm American allies, including Great Britain and France. The cost was considerable, over $1.2 billion, but Texas politician John Connally told reluctant Republicans that it was the only way to prevent World War III.

Another article reported that the University of California had

Senator Joseph McCarthy in June 1954. That month, McCarthy accused the US armed forces of allowing communism to infiltrate their ranks.

decided to fire 157 staff members for not admitting they were members of the Communist Party. The National Association for the Advancement of Colored People (NAACP) announced that it would expel any suspected communists from its ranks, including civil rights pioneer W. E. B. Du Bois. Earlier in the year, physicist Klaus Fuchs had been arrested for stealing atomic secrets and passing them to the Russians. Joseph McCarthy, a Republican senator from Wisconsin, was also busy making headlines. He had been accusing State Department employees of being communists since February.

Following McCarthy's lead, many newspapers warned Americans that vicious, fanatical communists bent on destroying the American way of life lurked around every corner. Truman even read that a *Chicago Tribune* reporter had asked Norway's Trygve Lie, the secretary-general of the United Nations, if he was or had ever been a communist. Lie, shocked and amazed that an American reporter would dare to ask such a question, erupted in anger:

"Anyone who reads the record knows that I have always been a member of the Norwegian labor party, which is a Socialist, not a Communist party. . . . The only ideology I advocate is world peace and progress."

Truman had become used to McCarthy's paranoid attacks. The president didn't admit it, but his decision three years earlier to require federal employees to take loyalty oaths had fueled McCarthy's paranoid witch hunt. Now, scientists, writers, actors, directors, artists, teachers, and people from all walks of life were being hauled before Congress and persecuted for their political beliefs. The cat was out of the bag.

This all disturbed Truman, but it would have to wait. He was going on vacation. He put down the newspapers, got up from the red cushioned chair next to the window, got dressed, and left Blair House for National Airport. With great anticipation and a deep sigh of relief, the president settled into his cushy stateroom on the four-engine DC-6. The plane roared down the runway, took off into the humid, sultry Washington air, and turned westward, eventually landing at home in Independence, Missouri.

North Korea Invades South Korea

Independence, where Truman grew up, was a small midwestern town about ten miles east of Kansas City. It was so different from the bustling capital. On the drive to his childhood home from the airport, he gazed out the windows at people sitting on their front porches, pushing baby strollers, and hauling bales of hay to and from the fields. Truman looked forward to spending a few days with Bess and his daughter, Margaret, far away from the pressures of the presidency.

When he got home, the president changed out of his suit and tie and into a bathrobe. He settled into an all-weather chair on his screened-in porch. Bess and Margaret returned home from a wedding later in the evening, and the three had dinner together. At 9:20 p.m., the phone rang. It was Secretary

First Lady Bess Truman poses at Blair House with her daughter, Margaret, on December 14, 1948.

of State Dean Acheson. He told the president anxiously, "I have some very serious news. The North Koreans have invaded South Korea." Truman didn't know it then, but this would be the turning point in his presidency.

Japan had occupied and ruled Korea from 1910 to 1945. After World War II ended in 1945, Japan withdrew its remaining forces from Korea. American officials quickly divided the country into two parts. The northern part, above the 38th parallel, would be governed by the Soviet Union. The southern part would be governed by the United States. The division was meant to be temporary.

In the north, the Soviet Union appointed Korean general Kim Il Sung, the leader of guerrilla forces who had fought against the Japanese during the war. In the south, the Americans appointed Syngman Rhee, a Christian who had gone to school in the United States. Both were ruthless dictators who ruled with iron fists.

For five years, border skirmishes between North and South Korea erupted frequently. Thinking that Korea was of little strategic significance, the Joint Chiefs of Staff—the nation's top military leaders—recommended to the president that the United States should avoid getting involved in the conflict. At first, Truman listened to them.

Meanwhile, the Soviets watched nervously as the United States rebuilt Japan. After World War II, the United States rebuilt the Japanese economy, roads, railroads, and schools. Americans built military bases across the country and stationed ships in Japanese harbors. Why were the Soviets nervous? Because Japan's northernmost islands are very close to Sakhalin in Russia. With American air bases so close to the Soviet Union, the United States could launch atomic air raids on Russia. This was unacceptable to Joseph Stalin.

In 1950, Stalin felt a new burst of confidence. The Soviet Union had just exploded its first atomic bomb at Semipalatinsk. Stalin had also recently allied with Mao Zedong in China, the world's most populous country, which had experienced a communist revolution a year earlier. Believing that South Korea was about to invade North Korea, Stalin gave the green light to Kim to invade South Korea first. Kim promised a swift victory. The invasion occurred on June 25, 1950.

Communism Spreading

Standing there in his bathrobe, Truman was stunned. Immediately, he remembered a Central Intelligence Agency (CIA) report that described North Korea as "a tightly controlled Soviet satellite." If South Korea came under communist control, the president believed other countries would too. If the United States didn't respond aggressively, he and Acheson feared that the entire Asian continent might fall to the communists. Truman told the secretary of state that he thought he should cut short his vacation and fly back to Washington immediately. By then, it was 11:20 in Washington. A night flight back to the capital might arouse suspicion that something big was happening. Acheson told the president to stay in Independence and await his next call.

By the next morning, Acheson reported that 89,000 heavily armed North Korean soldiers had streamed south from North Korea. The South Korean capital city of Seoul was only thirty-six miles from the border. Many feared for the safety of the city's one million residents. Truman ate a quick lunch, kissed Bess and Margaret good-bye, and hurried back to the airport. He could not escape the weight of the presidency.

He arrived back in Washington to a storm of concern among congressional leaders and the media. Major newspapers like the *New York Times* urged the president to act or risk "los[ing] half a world." Republicans already blamed him for China's communist takeover. Now they worried that Truman would be soft on communism in Korea. The president told them that the United States would take a stand. Under a lot of pressure, he declared, "If we let Korea down, the Soviet[s] will keep right on going and swallow up one piece of Asia after another."

Western European governments were also panicking. They watched and waited anxiously to see what the United States would do. European empires that had plundered the world for riches and cheap labor now fretted about their very survival. The French were particularly alarmed. After World War II, they had moved to reestablish their colony in Vietnam, but they were being challenged by Ho Chi Minh's communist-led forces. The British were desperately hanging on to their colony in Malaya. If the United States didn't fight back in Korea, Truman feared, the entire continent could fall like dominoes to the communists. This fear became known as the "Domino Theory."

Truman was also worried that if the Soviet Union won in Korea, communists might invade other parts of the world, particularly Iran. Spinning a globe and pointing to the oil-rich country, he told staffers, "Here is where [the Soviet Union] will start trouble if we aren't careful. . . . If we are tough enough now, if we stand up to them, they won't take any next steps. But if we just stand by, they'll move into Iran and they'll take over the entire Middle East." The president asked the United Nations (UN) to intervene in Korea so that it wouldn't look like the United States was going to war with a small Asian country by itself.

The UN had been formed in 1945, made of up representatives from many countries around the world. Its job was to prevent minor conflicts between nations from becoming wider, more threatening wars. Truman convinced the UN to support military action against North Korea. He did so by refusing to call it a "war." Instead, he called it a "police action," which sounded more palatable. The UN agreed.

Although it was now a UN effort, the United States provided half the ground troops and almost all of the naval and air power. The main UN goal would be to push the communist forces back up into North Korea and to make sure they wouldn't threaten South Korea again. Crucially, since this was now a UN "police action," Truman did not have to ask Congress for permission to go to war. However, to the millions around the world who would be impacted, it *was* a war—one of the twentieth century's bloodiest.

Enter China

It became clear very quickly that the president's tough words were not working. In an unexpected attack, more than 100,000 Soviet-trained and -equipped North Korean troops overwhelmed US and South Korean forces. General Douglas MacArthur, leader of the UN forces, faced almost immediate defeat. The prickly general asked permission to push into North Korea. In a surprise attack, he landed 17,000 men at Incheon in September. Truman applauded MacArthur's "brilliant maneuver." He called the general's campaign one of the best military operations in history.

MacArthur was too cocky. He declared that UN troops would invade North Korea, defeat the communist forces, stop fighting by Thanksgiving, and return home in time for Christmas. He promised not to use American troops, only Koreans. However, there was one big problem with his plan. Foreign Minister Zhou Enlai of China had told the general more than once that the Chinese would enter the war if US troops moved north near China's borders. MacArthur ignored his warnings. The general simply did not believe that China would ever get involved.

Meanwhile, Stalin sent encouragement to Mao. He assured the Chinese leader that together, the Soviets and the Chinese were stronger than the United States and the United Nations. Stalin believed that launching the war was a way to get back at "the dishonest . . . and arrogant behavior of the United States."

MacArthur didn't care. He ignored the Joint Chiefs' demand that he not bomb within five miles of the border. Truman was becoming more and more concerned but was careful not to anger the well-respected general. MacArthur brushed off all of his critics, saying that to *not* bomb would result in disaster. He declared, "To give up any part of North Korea to the aggression of the Chinese Communists would be the greatest defeat of the free world in recent times."

Zhou Enlai's warning became reality on October 25. Chinese troops attacked UN positions at Unsan, well inside North Korea. Two weeks later, the Joint Chiefs cabled MacArthur. They asked him to reconsider his dangerous mission. MacArthur responded with his usual bluster. Reluctantly, the president and the Joint Chiefs decided to let MacArthur do what he had planned.

On November 24, the general launched a massive attack near the Chinese border. Suddenly, after dark, hundreds of thousands of Chinese troops stormed across the Yalu River, sending US and UN troops into frantic retreat. Korean War veteran Julius Becton Jr. recalled:

At about 8:00 p.m., the Chinese Communists attacked in massive force. They swarmed over the hills, blowing bugles and horns, shaking rattles and other noisemakers, and shooting flares in the sky. They came on foot, firing rifles and burp guns, hurling grenades, and shouting and chanting shrilly. The total surprise of this awesome ground attack shocked and paralyzed most Americans and panicked not a few.[1]

Thoroughly defeated and astonished at the ferocity of the Chinese attack, MacArthur solemnly announced, "We face an entirely new war." General Omar Bradley called it "the greatest military disaster in the history of the United States." *Time* magazine reported that it was the "worst defeat the U.S. had ever suffered." Acheson told Congress that the United States was now on the brink of World War III. Truman agreed. "It looks like World War III is here," he wrote in his diary.

10

MacArthur Goes Nuclear

The United States was now desperate. UN troops had been stunned on the ground. Truman considered using atomic bombs to attack Chinese targets from the air. In late 1950, the president publicly announced that the United States might use atomic bombs against both soldiers and civilians if necessary. He explained that General MacArthur, as the military commander in the field, would have control over their use.

There was a lot of pressure to use atomic bombs in Korea. Many Americans were becoming hysterical. The United States had never lost a battle like this overseas. A congressman from South Carolina declared, "If there ever was a time to use the A-bomb, it is now." A senator from Maine advocated using it against the Chinese. Representative Tom Steed of Oklahoma preferred hitting "The Kremlin." Representative Joseph Bryson of South Carolina just wanted to make sure it was dropped on somebody: "The hour is at hand when every known force, including the atomic bomb, should be promptly utilized." Lloyd Bentsen of Texas proposed that the president "advise the commander of the North Korean troops to withdraw [from South Korea] within one week or use that week to evacuate civilians from . . . cities that will be subjected to atomic attack by the United States Air Force." Overall, 52 percent of Americans believed that atomic bombs should be used in Korea.

On December 9, 1950, MacArthur asked for permission to use atomic bombs whenever he felt necessary. He requested eight bombs, but he decided that dropping thirty or fifty atomic bombs could produce "a belt of radioactive cobalt" that would win the war in ten days. The contamination would spread from the "Sea of Japan to the Yellow Sea." Therefore, he declared, "For at least 60 years there could [be] no land invasion of [South] Korea from the North."

Portrait of General Douglas MacArthur in 1945, just after the end of World War II.

In March 1951, servicemen at Kadena Air Base on Okinawa actively began assembling bombs. In April, the Joint Chiefs declared that the United States would use atomic bombs if faced with another invasion or bombing raids.[1] Then came what historians Mark Selden and Alvin Y. So termed "the most daunting and terrible nuclear project that the United States ran in Korea"—Operation Hudson Harbor. The goal of Operation Hudson Harbor was to figure out how to use atomic bombs on the battlefield. In September and October, in perhaps the most dangerous moment of the war, B-29s flew over North Korea on mock bombing raids. The operation called for dropping "dummy" atomic bombs and simulating "all activities which would be involved in an atomic strike, including weapons assembly and testing, leading, [and] ground control of bomb aiming."[2]

Old Soldiers Never Die

The situation was spiraling out of control. Many believed a nuclear World War III was about to take place. US, South Korean, and UN casualties mounted rapidly. Truman began urging for a cease-fire in March 1951. The president thought this would be a quick and tidy war. Now, MacArthur was pressing for all-out war with China. The belligerent general broadcast an ultimatum to China. Truman hadn't approved it. He bristled. "I'll show that son-of-a-bitch who's boss." MacArthur then issued a doomsday warning: "If we lose this war to Communism in Asia, the fall of Europe is inevitable." This was too much for the president and the Joint Chiefs. MacArthur risked lighting the world on fire. On April 11, Truman fired the out-of-control general.

Firing MacArthur would eventually spell the end of Truman's presidency. His approval rating sank below 30 percent for the first time. Most Americans held MacArthur in great esteem. Truman, less so. *Time* magazine noted, "Seldom has a more unpopular man fired a more popular one." Republican senators and congressmen wanted to impeach Truman. Senator William Jenner accused him of treason. Joseph McCarthy also wanted to impeach the "son of a bitch" for firing MacArthur. He said that Truman must have been drunk at the time. He accused Truman of signing "the death warrant of western civilization."

Meanwhile, seven and a half million onlookers cheered MacArthur at a parade in New York City. He received a hero's welcome in Washington, Boston, San Francisco, and Chicago. MacArthur stood in front of Congress and bade a final farewell. He told his mostly sympathetic audience that he was not a warmonger: "I know war as few other men now living know it, and nothing to me is more revolting." Then he got personal. "[From my time at West Point], I still remember the refrain of one of the most popular barrack ballads of the day which proclaimed most proudly that 'old soldiers never die; they just fade away.' And like the old soldier of that ballad, I now close my military career and just fade away, an old soldier who tried to do his duty as God gave him the light to see that duty. Good bye."[3]

Though MacArthur's luster faded over time, Truman's popularity never recovered. His approval rating sank to a record low of 22 percent. Secretary of State Acheson said that the war "was an incalculable defeat to U.S. foreign policy and destroyed the Truman administration." Truman seemed to come to the same conclusion. In March 1952, he announced to Americans that he would not run for a second full term.

A Nervous Chill

On Friday, July 11, 1952, Truman woke up with a sore throat and terrible stomach pain. He felt extremely tired and lethargic all day. Two days later, a "nervous chill" came over him as he emerged from a meeting with Democratic Party officials. He was exhausted; sweat poured down his hot skin. His heart was racing. He had to sit down. He had never felt like this before. He decided to call his doctor, General Wallace Graham. Then he called Bess in Independence and Margaret in London to tell them that he was ill. By evening, his temperature had risen to 103.6 degrees. The next morning, he was transported to Walter Reed Army Medical Center, where doctors examined him, took blood, and ran test after test.

Test results revealed that the president was very sick. He had strep throat, the flu, and a respiratory infection all at once. At one point, his lungs became so congested that one doctor didn't think he would be able to survive his term.

Truman remained in the hospital until July 19. He didn't return to his office until July 21, and even then, he only worked for a few days before he retired to Independence to rest up and fully recover. Meanwhile, the war in Korea raged, steelworkers were on strike, and a presidential election was in full swing. Though the sixty-eight-year-old president had already exceeded the life expectancy for an American male and though strep throat was a major cause of death at the time, the public was never made aware of the president's condition. Nobody can be entirely sure why Truman got so sick, but it is possible that extreme stress contributed to his illness. His firing of MacArthur and the public's strong disapproval of his Korean War policies weighed heavily on him. And such a thing had happened before. As a senator in 1937, he had checked himself into the Army-Navy Hospital in Hot Springs, Arkansas, complaining of nausea, headaches, and extreme exhaustion. When doctors examined him, they determined that his body was reacting to job-induced stress.[4]

The job had finally taken its toll. Harry Truman left office in January 1953 with only 32 percent of Americans approving of his performance.

11

Stalemate

Though MacArthur and Truman were gone, war from the air continued through the middle of 1953. American bombers burned almost every major city in North Korea to the ground. They bombed soldiers and civilians alike. The weapon of choice was napalm, a mixture of chemicals and gasoline that forms a gel. When the gel is lit on fire, it burns at a temperature of 1,800 degrees Fahrenheit. In contrast, water boils at a temperature of 212 degrees Fahrenheit. When napalm falls on cities, it creates instant firestorms. When it falls on people, it produces unimaginable pain, suffering, and death.

Out of a total population of 30 million, 3 to 4 million Koreans died during the war. Many of them died after napalm fell on their villages. *New York Times* reporter George Barrett described what happened at a village north of Anyang: "The inhabitants throughout the village and in the fields were caught and killed and kept the exact postures they had held when the napalm struck—a man about to get on his bicycle, fifty boys and girls playing in an orphanage, a housewife strangely unmarked, holding in her hand a page torn from the Sears-Roebuck catalogue."

Workers assemble napalm bombs at the Rocky Mountain Arsenal in Denver, Colorado, on August 2, 1951. US forces dropped approximately 250,000 pounds of napalm per day during the war, killing many thousands of Koreans.

When napalm hit the village of Tanyang, families who had escaped other attacks were clustered together in a cave. Eom Han Won, who was fifteen at the time, recalled, "When the napalm hit the entrance, the blast and smoke knocked out kerosene and castor-oil lamps we had in the cave. It was a pitch-black chaos—people shouting for each other, stampeding, choking. Some said we should crawl in deeper, covering our faces with wet cloth. Some said we should rush through the blaze. Those who were not burned to death suffocated."[1]

The war was hellish on both sides. Communist troops captured Eugene

Inman, a nineteen-year-old American soldier. He recalled that his captors led prisoners on a horrific death march. Each day, from the time the sun came up until it went down, they made Eugene and many others walk without food and water while civilians threw stones at them from the side of the road. If a prisoner collapsed or could not continue, he was shot, clubbed, or bayoneted to death. Men died of starvation and dehydration each day.[2] Eugene was one of the lucky ones. In August 1953, one month after North Korea, China, and the United Nations agreed to a cease-fire, Eugene was released after spending 1,004 days in captivity.

In all, over 36,000 young American servicemen died in Korea from 1950 through 1953, and 70 percent of US prisoners of war "collapsed" and

Women and children search through the rubble in Seoul.
During the war, 3 to 4 million Koreans died, out of a total
population of 30 million, as did more than a million Chinese
and 36,000 Americans.

collaborated with their captors. One army doctor who treated US prisoners reported, "The strong regularly took food from the weak. . . . Many men were sick, and these men, instead of being helped and nursed by the others, were ignored, or worse. . . . On winter nights, helpless men with dysentery were rolled outside the huts by their comrades and left to die in the cold." An astonishing 38 percent of US prisoners died. They died in a war that Congress did not declare.

Those who did return home were not greeted with ticker-tape parades and celebrations like the veterans of World War II or Douglas MacArthur.[3] After such terrible losses on both sides, the war had done nothing to ease tensions between the United States and the rest of the world.

The Korean War resulted in a stalemate. On July 27, 1953, UN representatives met North Korean leaders in Panmunjom, Korea, to sign a truce. South Korean leaders refused to attend the meeting. The truce agreement permanently divided North Korea from South Korea along the 38th parallel. It also said that there would be another meeting within three months to write a peace treaty. That meeting never occurred, so technically, the war still continues to this day.

Truman had sold the Korean War to Americans as necessary to defeat communism in Asia. If anything, the war did the opposite. It sent a message to the Soviet Union and China that the United States, even with the support of the United Nations and even with the threat of the atomic bomb, could lose wars. The rest of the twentieth century proved that to be true on many more occasions.

War Games

During the Korean War, the military became more and more a part of American life. Under Truman, the amount of money that the government spent on defense almost quadrupled, from $13.5 billion to $48.2 billion in

1951 alone. Within six months of the start of the war, defense spending soared to $54 billion. The government hired private companies called "defense contractors" to build airplanes, bombs, missiles, and helicopters. Companies like Dow Chemical used taxpayer money to produce napalm and other chemicals, including Agent Orange, which devastated many villages across the rest of the century. In 1952, the United States Patent and Trademark Office issued a patent for "Incendiary Gels," making the recipe for napalm available to the world. In Los Angeles County, 160,000 people worked to produce warplanes. Altogether, 55 percent of the county's residents worked in the defense industry.

Many people were concerned during the 1950s that American boys weren't being raised tough enough to fight off communist enemies. This attitude became more widespread after the Korean War ended in stalemate. Would the United States ever win a war again? What might happen if the Soviet Union attacked? Would American men be able to protect the homeland, or would they be too "soft" and insulated?

Toy companies, along with other manufacturers, used that idea to sell products. If boys became acquainted with powerful weapons of war from an early age, perhaps they would be able to powerfully defeat future enemies using skills and confidence acquired at an early age.

The companies sold war to children in the form of toy guns and military gear. The toys motivated young boys to imagine being manly soldiers when they grew up, fighting communism wherever it existed. In their suburban backyards, boys prepped earnestly for their roles as future soldiers. They built bunkers, fallout shelters, and makeshift first aid stations. On nice days, they burst out of their houses brandishing toys like the Sound-O-Power military rifle, a true-to-life model of the real M16. The company that made the Sound-O-Power claimed that it made sounds so realistic that even police would think it was a real gun when they heard it fire. Jimmy Jet was a model of an airplane cockpit, which contained a "moving picture screen" so kids could pretend they were actually flying a bomber over a city. The Gung Ho Commando Outfit contained in one package a grenade, a machine gun, terrain maps, a helmet, a canteen, and a cap pistol.

The Ideal Toy Company produced Count Down, a base from which air force missiles could be launched. The missiles were emblazoned with the initials USAF, making it clear that they belonged to the United States. A commercial for the toy showed a clean-cut boy wearing a plaid shirt, headphones on his ears, eagerly pressing the countdown button to initiate launch. The announcer then declared, "Yes, you can be in command of your own Ideal Count Down. It's a real electronic missile base. You sit at the controls and move missiles into place. You count down! You blast off! You track the flight!"[4]

There were nuclear-themed board games that enabled kids to mine for uranium and drop atomic bombs on enemies. There were "atomic guns," "space guns," and "atomic disintegrators." A commercial for an atomic bomb toy described it as a "safe, harmless giant atomic bomb."

An advertisement for a Lionel toy train featured an air force pilot speaking to viewers from his plane's cockpit. He told the eager boys listening that piloting a warplane takes time and patience and that by learning how to control the model train equipped with missile launchers, they could someday be just like him. He trotted out his son as an example.[5] The commercial was aimed not just at boys but at their fathers as well.

Presidential Militarism

Given how much the military influenced American culture during the early 1950s, it was only fitting that a five-star general run for president. Since Truman had announced that he would not run for a second term, the 1952 election pitted Illinois governor Adlai Stevenson against General Dwight D. Eisenhower. Initially, Eisenhower declined to run. As a military man, he did

Dwight Eisenhower waves to adoring crowds in New York's Times Square after returning from the war in Europe. Many of his fans and admirers pressed him to run for president in 1952.

not believe that his name should be associated with politics. As pressure mounted on him throughout 1951, the general maintained that he "[did] not feel that [he had] any duty to seek a political nomination." However, by early 1952, so many people called on him to run for president that he finally relented—he would run if called upon.

That call came quickly. On January 6, 1952, Senator Henry Cabot Lodge Jr., himself embroiled in a race for reelection in Massachusetts against the young John F. Kennedy, entered Eisenhower's name in the New Hampshire primary. He did so without even telling the general. However, even with his

Crowds gasp and a band plays as
Eisenhower's open-topped car passes
through Times Square.

name now officially in nomination, Eisenhower continued to insist well into February that he would not run unless a critical mass of people forced him to.[6]

One of Eisenhower's most ardent supporters was the legendary songwriter and composer Irving Berlin. Among 900 other songs, Berlin is known for composing "Anything You Can Do I Can Do Better," "There's No Business Like Show Business," "Puttin' on the Ritz," and "How Deep Is the Ocean." Despite being Jewish, he penned the classic ballad "White Christmas." Perhaps his most famous work is "God Bless America," an ode to the country that had welcomed him as a Russian immigrant in 1893.[7]

In early February 1952, Berlin found out that Eisenhower supporters, led by Henry Cabot Lodge, planned to "draft" him into the Oval Office. They were planning a political rally at New York's Madison Square Garden, which they named "Serenade to Ike." A political conservative, Berlin could hardly contain his excitement. He told the event's organizers that he would gladly entertain the crowd. That is, if there happened to be one at all. Eisenhower was in Europe at the time, and many reporters believed that in his absence, a very small number of people would attend. Shrugging off the naysayers, Berlin wrote an original song called "I Like Ike."

The event was scheduled for 11:30 p.m. in order to accommodate a boxing match beforehand. To the utter amazement of observers, thousands of people crushed into the Garden, cheering wildly for Eisenhower. Thundering chants of "I like Ike" echoed off the walls as throngs of frenzied supporters waved flags and banners.

The American Legion drum-and-bugle corps treated the crowd to a rousing performance of "Battle Hymn of the Republic." Then actress and singer Ethel Merman wowed the crowd with her rendition of Berlin's "There's No Business Like Show Business." Mary Martin and Richard Rogers belted out "I'm in Love with a Wonderful Guy." Actor Clark Gable gave a speech supporting Eisenhower. Finally, the song-writing genius himself, Irving Berlin, came up to the stage. Brandishing a silver microphone, he treated the adoring crowd to "I Like Ike." The frenzied crowd screamed in delight. Berlin brought the house down.[8] In the end, 25,000 people showed up for the event. It went until the wee hours of the morning. Police and fire marshals couldn't get them to leave.

Organizers of the Madison Square Garden show captured it on film. Then the famous businesswoman and aviator Jacqueline Cochran flew it to Paris to show to Eisenhower. If ever there was proof that a critical mass of Americans wanted him to run, this was

Young Irving Berlin, composer of "God Bless America" and staunch Eisenhower supporter, poses with his wife, Ellen Mackay.

it. Eisenhower responded emotionally to the film. He wrote in his diary, "I've never been so upset in years." After the screening, Cochran raised her glass and toasted: "To the President of the United States!" The general burst into tears.[9] It was now clear to him that he could stall no longer. He finally accepted that enough Americans trusted him to hold the highest office. He would run for president.

12

Eisenhower Answers America

The 1952 race between Dwight Eisenhower and Adlai Stevenson was the first presidential campaign to make use of television. That year, Republicans and Democrats spent between $4 million and $12 million on advertisements and televised speeches. Many middle-class Americans had only recently purchased their very first television set. They were enthralled by being able to take part in the political process right from their living rooms.

Before Eisenhower's campaign for president, many considered him to be a legendary war hero but one who was distant and out of touch with issues and people at home. Eisenhower's campaign managers knew that in order to get him elected, they needed to convince potential voters that he was familiar with and passionate about issues impacting American families. They needed to "sell" his presidency. To do so, they hired the advertising firm of Ted Bates to produce the first-ever televised political commercials. The campaign was called "Eisenhower Answers America."

Rosser Reeves created the advertisements. To find out what issues people cared about the most, he looked at polls conducted by

George Gallup. Gallup's polls routinely surveyed Americans to find out how they felt about a wide variety of topics. It turned out that in 1952, the most important issues facing people were high prices of goods, high taxes, political corruption, and the Korean War.

After World War II, the economy had gone through two recessions and was headed for a third. Americans were also grieving as thousands of young men were injured and killed half a world away in Korea, with no end in sight. Reeves's challenge was to convince Americans that Eisenhower would be able to address both problems. To accomplish this, he needed voters to get to know the general in the most intimate way possible. Reeves asked Eisenhower to appear personally in forty very short, twenty-second ads and answer questions from ordinary Americans.

One ad featured a middle-class housewife who was very concerned about the increased cost of living. She addressed Eisenhower: "You know what things cost today. High prices are just driving me crazy." The camera then shifted to the candidate, who replied in a comforting manner, "Yes, my Mamie gets after me about the high cost of living. It's another reason why I say, 'It's time for a change. Time to get back to an honest dollar and an honest dollar's worth.'"[1] By talking about his wife, Mamie, Eisenhower seemed to immediately relate to the concerned woman and concerned women everywhere.

Another ad featured a middle-class African-American man pitching Eisenhower a softball: "General, the Democrats are telling me I never had it so good." The determined candidate responded with a serious face and a stiff upper lip: "Can that be true when America is billions in debt, when prices have doubled, when taxes break our backs? And we are still fighting in Korea? It's tragic, and it's time for a change."[2]

The Democratic Party had been trying to convince voters that they "never had it so good." Now, Eisenhower called that idea into question. The economy, which had benefited so much from military spending during World

President Eisenhower waves to throngs of cheering onlookers during a ticker-tape parade in Rio de Janeiro, Brazil.

War II, was sputtering seven years later. Those in the middle class worried that the United States was spending too much on fighting a war abroad when many were struggling to pay bills at home. Eisenhower answered America with a conservative promise to stop unnecessary spending, lower taxes, and end the Korean War.

Reeves determined that the Eisenhower campaign would run "Eisenhower Answers America" ads in sixty-two specific counties in twelve specific states. The shrewd adman knew that if Eisenhower could merely convince 844,320 people to vote for him, he could achieve the 249 electoral votes needed to beat Adlai Stevenson.[3]

The campaign succeeded. With 442 electoral votes, Eisenhower destroyed Stevenson, who received only 89. Stevenson even lost his home state, Illinois, by almost 500,000 votes.[4] Eisenhower had successfully overcome his image

After his second inauguration, a triumphant Eisenhower takes his hat off to the crowd as his motorcade rolls down Pennsylvania Avenue toward the White House.

as an out-of-touch military man. On January 20, 1953, Chief Justice Frederick Vinson swore him in as the country's thirty-fourth president.

Humanity Hanging from a Cross of Iron

At the time, US-Soviet relations were extremely tense. During his campaign, Eisenhower helped fan the flames. He stood back while others, including Joseph McCarthy, attacked Stevenson for being a communist and questioned his patriotism. Eisenhower's running mate, Richard Nixon, was a fire-breathing anti-communist who belittled Stevenson as "Adlai the appeaser" who "carrie[d] a Ph.D. from Dean Acheson's cowardly college of Communist containment." Nixon didn't think it was enough to keep communism from spreading to other countries. He believed that the United States should "free" communist countries, by force if necessary.

Interestingly, though Eisenhower ran on an anti-communist platform, he hadn't seemed like such a strong anti-communist before he ran for president. In 1942, as a general during World War II, he had pushed hard for entering the war in Europe sooner, which could have helped the Soviets defeat the Nazis years earlier. He developed a friendly relationship with Soviet marshal Georgy

Zhukov. After the war, he believed the US-Soviet friendship would endure. Joseph Stalin was fond of Eisenhower. He told US ambassador W. Averell Harriman, "General Eisenhower is a very great man, not only because of his military accomplishments but because of his human, friendly, kind, and frank nature." In August 1945, Eisenhower went to Moscow and received a hero's welcome from the Soviet people. Stalin gave him the special honor of being the first foreigner to witness a parade in Red Square from atop the tomb of Vladimir Lenin.

Just before he took office, Eisenhower wrote that it wasn't necessary to build more weapons and a bigger military for the United States to be safe. He used Germany and Japan as examples. Both of those countries had built huge war machines before and during World War II, and both were soundly defeated. As a five-star general, he understood that atomic bombs had not been necessary to end World War II and that, by using them, the United States had set a very dangerous precedent for the future. In 1945, when he heard that an atomic bomb had been dropped on Hiroshima, he told a journalist, "Before the atom bomb was used, . . . I was sure we could keep the peace with Russia. Now, I don't know. I had hoped the bomb wouldn't figure in this war. Until now I would have said that we three, Britain . . . , America . . . , and Russia . . . , could have guaranteed the peace of the world for a long time to come. But now, I don't know. People are frightened and disturbed all over. Everyone feels insecure again." After the war, he supported efforts at international control. He wanted atomic bombs to be turned over to the United Nations and destroyed. He spoke regularly for civilian rather than military control of the bomb. And he continued to raise moral concerns about the use of such a weapon.

Winston Churchill, who had been reelected prime minister of England in 1951, had also grown more worried about the threat nuclear weapons posed to human life. When Stalin died in 1953, Churchill urged Eisenhower and others in Washington to take advantage of that incredible opportunity and end the Cold War once and for all. Churchill called for a summit with Soviet leaders. After six weeks, in his famous "Chance for Peace" speech, Eisenhower responded with one of his clearest and boldest statements about the toll the Cold War was taking on the nation:

> Every gun that is made, every warship launched, every rocket fired signifies a theft from those who hunger and are not fed, those who are cold and are not clothed. This world . . . is spending the sweat of its laborers, the genius of its scientists, the hopes of its children. The cost of one modern heavy bomber is . . . a modern brick school in more than 30 cities. It is two electric power plants, each serving a town of 60,000 population. It is two fine, fully equipped hospitals. It is some 50 miles of concrete pavement. We pay for a single fighter plane with a half-million bushels of wheat. We pay for a single destroyer with new homes that could have housed more than 8,000 people. . . . This is not a way of life at all. . . . Under the cloud of threatening war, it is humanity hanging from a cross of iron.

The *New York Times* called the speech "magnificent and deeply moving." The *Washington Post* hoped that the new president would reject Truman's "provocative words," "belligerent gesturings," and "militarization of policy." Eisenhower seemed to be calling for peace and disarmament. He also seemed to call for giving aid to countries around the world that were dealing with poverty, disease, and hunger. Many hoped that the new levelheaded president would solve problems by talking them out, not by threatening war, as Truman did. Eisenhower's speech was printed widely in Soviet newspapers. Some in the Soviet Union offered their own words of hope. Sadly, the window of optimism was short-lived.

Despite Eisenhower's lofty words, and despite the hopes of many

Americans and some Soviets that he would do something to put an end to the Cold War, he ended up leaving the world a far more dangerous place than when he first took office. During his two terms, he had multiple opportunities to roll back the Cold War and the arms race. He could have taken bold action that would have put the world on a different path. Instead, he presided over the largest military buildup in the history of mankind. When Eisenhower took office, the US atomic arsenal contained slightly over 1,000 nuclear weapons. When he left, it contained more than 22,000.

You Would Swear the Whole World Was on Fire

Eisenhower's election coincided with one of the most disturbing events in all of human history. Just three days before, on November 1, 1952, the United States wiped an entire island off the face of the earth with its first-ever hydrogen bomb test. The island of Elugelab burned for six hours under a mushroom cloud a hundred miles across. Then it disappeared. The blast, which was 700 times more powerful than the bomb dropped on Hiroshima, exceeded all expectations. One sailor commented, "You would swear the whole world was on fire." Physicist Harold Agnew, aboard a ship twenty-five miles away, observed, "Something I'll never forget was the heat. Not the blast . . . the heat just kept coming and coming on and on and on. And it was really scary."

Eisenhower acknowledged the new reality in his inaugural address. "Science," he warned, "seems ready to confer upon us . . . the power to erase human life from this planet." Many were now petrified: How long would it be before the Soviet Union developed a hydrogen bomb of its own? Eisenhower took comfort when he read a CIA report in summer 1953, which said that there was no evidence that the Soviets were working on a hydrogen bomb. He, along with the rest of the world, was in for another very rude awakening.

A New Bomb

On August 12, 1953, the sky lit up once again over the Semipalatinsk Test Site in Kazakhstan—this time, many times brighter than ever before. Soviet premier Georgy Malenkov addressed the world triumphantly. The Soviet Union had just successfully tested its first prototype hydrogen bomb.

The CIA report had been horribly wrong. The chief Soviet scientist's heart "beat wildly" as the tower upon which the bomb was placed vaporized in a flaming firestorm. When the dust settled, a huge crater appeared where the tower had stood only minutes before. The bomb's explosive yield was estimated to be roughly equivalent to 400,000 tons of TNT.[5]

If such a bomb had exploded over Washington, DC, the fireball would have extended farther than a mile in diameter and reached temperatures exceeding 200 million degrees Fahrenheit. That is, between four and five times greater than the temperature of the sun. If ground zero was the Pentagon, streets would have completely melted in front of the Pentagon City shopping mall, less than one mile away. Inside the mall, paint would have burned off walls and all metal surfaces would have turned to molten liquid while cars in the parking lot would have all exploded.

One second after detonation, a blast wave would have produced winds exceeding 750 miles per hour, three times greater than the strongest winds ever recorded on earth. The wind would propel burning cars, buses, trucks, and trains into the air with unimaginable force. Buildings would cave in and glass from windows would become airborne daggers, penetrating anything with which they came in contact. The firestorm would ignite all combustibles, including gas lines, fuel tanks, and airplanes parked or waiting to take off at National Airport. Much of Arlington, Virginia, and areas of Washington, DC, extending at least as far as the Lincoln and Jefferson Memorials, would endure more than fifteen times the heat energy that most people endured in Hiroshima. The corresponding ball of fire would flash over the Potomac

River, glowing 5,000 times brighter than a desert sun at midday.

The stone on the steps of the Jefferson and Lincoln Memorials would be pulverized into fine dust as grass and trees on the National Mall exploded into flames. Anyone out walking on the mall or visiting national park sites would be instantly vaporized. Then, as the blast contracted and the winds shifted, whatever buildings were left standing from the first unimaginable gust of wind would disintegrate for good. Anyone looking into the sky at the time of the flash for many miles around would be either temporarily or permanently blinded.[6]

Hot Fish

As the fear of atomic war played out at home, the United States continued to test bigger, more destructive nuclear weapons in the South Pacific. Those tests continued to poison and kill human beings.

On January 22, 1954, a crew of Japanese fishermen packed their gear for sea. They meticulously stacked supplies of food, drinking water, blankets, and clothing beneath the deck of their trawler, *Lucky Dragon 5*. Then they bid farewell to their families and turned their eyes to the sea. Tuna fishing in the winter was very dangerous and very solitary. The fishermen knew that they had to sail far out into the Pacific to catch the fish that would yield the highest prices at market. They also knew that, as with every journey, it was possible that they might not come back.

From the time *Lucky Dragon 5* left port, its voyage was anything but lucky. Almost immediately, the inexperienced twenty-two-year-old captain, Hisakicki Tsutsui, struggled with an engine that couldn't reach full power. It was only able to move the boat five knots, less than six miles per hour. Within three weeks of its five-week voyage, half of the trawler's 330 fishing lines had become lost or snagged on coral reefs.

Tsutsui knew that he and his crew could not return to Japan empty-handed.

Without a respectable catch, they would not be able to show their faces in their home port of Yaizu. The crew gathered to discuss their options. What if they sailed in a different direction, toward the untapped fishing grounds near the Marshall Islands? There, perhaps they could haul in a ton of fish quickly, turn around, and head for home with the prize they'd set out for. The fishermen agreed unanimously. Tsutsui pointed the ship away from Midway Island and steamed southwestward.

By the end of February, the crew had almost completely depleted their supplies. They had reached longitude 166°18' east, just west of the Marshall Islands. They could fish for only one more day. They barely had enough fuel for the return voyage.

While *Lucky Dragon 5* closed in on the Marshall Islands, its crew was unaware that the US government had advised the Japanese Maritime Safety Agency to tell ships not to sail anywhere near Bikini Atoll and to stay well east of longitude 166°18' east. The trawler was indeed east of 166°18' east, but barely. It was March 1, 1954.

At 6:45 a.m., the sun rose not in the east but in the west. It bathed the fishing trawler in a blinding flash of light. One of the crewmen, Matakichi Oishi, remembered, "A yellow flash poured through the porthole. Wondering what had happened, I jumped up from the bunk near the door, ran out on deck and was astonished. Bridge, sky and sea burst into view, painted in flaming sunset colors."

The United States had warned ships to stay east of 166°18' east because it was about to detonate a hydrogen bomb. Planners had prepared for the winds to blow fallout from the explosion westward and away from the Marshall Islands. However, on the morning of the blast, the winds shifted to the east. After warning American ships in the area that fallout might blow to the east, officials decided that the explosion would go ahead as planned. Of course, nobody alerted the crew of *Lucky Dragon 5*.

To make matters worse, the bomb exploded with twice the force predicted. At 15 megatons, it was 1,000 times more powerful than the bomb that destroyed Hiroshima. The cloud of radioactive coral drifted toward Rongelap, Rongerik, and Utrik Atolls, poisoning another 236 Marshall Islanders and 28 Americans. Unaware of the danger, children played in the radioactive fallout. Rescue ships did not arrive for three days. Meanwhile, radioactive dust and water made their way into victims' bodies, burning their skin and poisoning their blood.

As it was far enough east of the actual explosion, the trawler itself was not damaged. Soon, though, gray ash began to fall softly on the deck of the boat. It was atomized coral, containing the carbonized remains of fish and other sea creatures unlucky enough to have been within the blast range at the time of the explosion. Oishi described the scene as it unfolded: "The top of the cloud spread over us. . . . Two hours passed. . . . White particles were falling on us, just like sleet. The white particles penetrated mercilessly—eyes, nose, ears, mouth. We had no sense that it was dangerous."

That night, the crew of *Lucky Dragon 5* began vomiting. They felt lethargic, dazed, agitated. Fourteen days later, they arrived back in Yaizu covered in horrible burns. They bled from their mouths. They couldn't open their swollen eyes. Upon landing, they were quarantined on the outskirts of the city, unable to return home to their families. All of their clothing and personal effects were buried in a large pit. And the fish they had caught? By the time Japanese authorities understood what had happened, the fish had been shipped to Tokyo and sold to markets across the city.[7]

Nuclear Fallout

Lucky Dragon 5 was far from the only vessel that the American hydrogen bomb test had contaminated. In all, 856 Japanese ships had been exposed to varying amounts of radiation. In Japan, the fishing industry was devastated. Hysteria and panic set in. The Japanese people could not eat one of the most important foods in their diet for fear of being poisoned by radiation. A total of 457 tons of tuna were eventually destroyed. As a result, the bottom dropped out from the fish market, resulting in economic devastation.

Meanwhile, the American government denied any hazards from the test and blamed the fishermen for ignoring warnings to steer clear of the area, even though they were outside of the warning zone when they encountered the ash. Atomic Energy Commission (AEC) chair Lewis Strauss told the White House press secretary that *Lucky Dragon 5* had really been a "red spy outfit" conducting espionage for the Soviet Union, an obvious lie that the CIA quickly dismissed. Nevertheless, Strauss spoke at a press conference. He blamed the fishermen for ignoring AEC warnings and downplayed the damage to their health.

In September, Aikichi Kuboyama, the head radio engineer on *Lucky Dragon 5*, died at age forty. He became the first Japanese hydrogen bomb casualty, a new kind of *hibakusha* (the Japanese word for nuclear bomb victim). Many of the other crew members spent an entire year in the hospital. While recovering, one issued a poignant warning: "Our fate menaces all mankind. Tell that to those who are responsible. God grant that they may listen." In the Marshall Islands, the inhabitants of Rongelap did not return home until 1957. They remained in Rongelap until 1985, when scientists confirmed their suspicions that the island was still contaminated.

Eisenhower kept insisting that atomic energy could be used for peaceful purposes, but bomb tests were killing and sickening more and more people across the world. Indian prime minister Jawaharlal Nehru declared that US leaders were "dangerous self-centered lunatics" who would "blow up any people or country who came in the way of their policy." Privately, Eisenhower was worried about what the rest of the world thought. He told the National Security Council in May, "Everybody seems to think that we are skunks, saber-rattlers, and warmongers." Secretary of State John Foster Dulles went even further: "We are losing ground every day in . . . allied nations because they are all insisting we are so militaristic. Comparisons are now being made between ours and Hitler's military machine."

The *Lucky Dragon 5* incident fueled a worldwide movement against nuclear testing and made popular the term "fallout." Nowhere was the reaction stronger than in Japan, where people simply could not forget about Hiroshima and Nagasaki, no matter how effective US censorship had been. A petition circulated by Tokyo housewives called for banning hydrogen bombs. It collected 32 million signatures, an extraordinary total representing one third of the entire Japanese population.

13

Lunacy[1]

As the United States continued to test its weaponry, so did the Soviet Union. In August 1957, the Russians successfully tested the world's first intercontinental ballistic missile, or ICBM. ICBMs made it possible to launch nuclear weapons from afar without having to drop them from planes. They also made it possible to launch satellites into space. Amazingly, just two months later, on the afternoon of October 4, teletype machines sprang to life in Washington, DC, with a major Associated Press newsflash: MOSCOW RADIO SAID TONIGHT THAT THE SOVIET UNION HAS LAUNCHED AN EARTH SATELLITE.

Early October had already been an unbelievably busy time for news: The Milwaukee Braves and the New York Yankees were fighting it out in the World Series, a nasty flu outbreak was sweeping the nation, and *Leave It to Beaver* was about to make its television debut.

At 6:30 p.m. on Friday, October 4, news of the Soviet launch reached President Eisenhower. Eisenhower was busy trying to figure out how to respond to Arkansas governor Orval Faubus, who had refused the president's order to desegregate Central High School in

Little Rock. Through his press secretary, Eisenhower reacted to the stunning news by downplaying its significance: "The Soviet satellite, of course, is of great scientific interest . . . [but it does] not come as any surprise; we have never thought of our [space] program as in a race with the Soviets."

But a race it was! The United States was working furiously on its own satellite, Vanguard, which would be ready for launch in mid-1958. However, there was a design problem with the satellite and other defects with the rockets needed to send it into space.

The US Navy, which was building the satellite, had already published books about it in anticipation of its launch. Magazines had also written hundreds of articles detailing its potential. A popular book for space enthusiasts, *Discover the Stars,* was printed with a drawing of Vanguard on its cover and coached readers on how they could build a model of the satellite. According to *Discover the Stars*, the United States would dramatically open the space age launching a rocket into space before any other country.

After reading so much about Vanguard, most Americans could not imagine that the Soviet Union would beat the United States to space. Therefore, the humbling news came as a great shock. The Soviet satellite, Sputnik Zemlya, meaning "companion of Earth" or "fellow traveler," weighed 184 pounds and was 22.8 inches in diameter. It was roughly the size of a beach ball. It orbited the earth once every ninety-six minutes and seventeen seconds, transmitting a series of beeps to listeners on earth. Soviet officials crowed about the triumph of Soviet science and technology, which they claimed proved that the Soviet Union was superior to the United States.

Model of the Vanguard 1 satellite. The United States launched it into orbit on March 7, 1958, five months after the Soviet Union launched Sputnik.

Russians admire a model of Sputnik 3 at the USSR Exhibition in Sokolniki Park, Moscow, on August 5, 1959.

For over a decade, many Americans were comforted by the thought that the Soviet Union was nothing more than a backward country, no match for the United States with all of its superior technology. Writer John Gunther noted, "For a generation it had been part of the American folklore that the Russians were hardly capable of operating a tractor." Now, many of those Americans panicked. Would the Soviet Union suddenly be able to launch an ICBM at their cities? That fear was fueled by the Soviet Union's announcement, three days after Sputnik's launch, that it had successfully tested a new thermonuclear weapon that could be launched by a missile. Senator Lyndon Johnson hysterically warned that the Soviets would soon "be dropping bombs on us from space like kids dropping rocks onto cars from freeway overpasses."

Looking for Satellites

At 8:07 in the evening, a New York radio station picked up Sputnik's signal and broadcast it across the country to anyone who had a TV or a radio. *Beep, beep, beep.* The sound rang out across the world. Senator Johnson and his wife, Lady Bird, were at their ranch in Texas, hosting one of their famous cookouts, when they heard the news. Their dinner guests looked to the sky in silent awe. The senator later recalled, "As we stood on the lonely country road that runs between our house and the Pedernales River . . . I felt uneasy and apprehensive. In the open West, you learn to live with the sky. It is part of your life. But now, somehow, in some new way, the sky seemed almost alien."

Historian Doris Kearns Goodwin was a sophomore in high school when the Soviet Union launched the world into the space age. That Friday evening, she was at her boyfriend's house. The two amorous teenagers ran outside to see if they could locate Sputnik in the night sky. "We took a blanket," she recalled, "and we went to park nearby. And it was a very romantic setting, and we started to look for Sputnik. And then my boyfriend reached over and kissed me. . . . I didn't give Sputnik another thought."

The same evening, author James Michener was aboard a military DC-3 plane when it crash-landed in the Pacific Ocean. All of those aboard the plane floated to safety in a massive life raft. Their rescuers flew the disheveled group to Tokyo, where an ecstatic reporter hollered, "Have you heard the news?" Michener replied, "Yes. We ditched in the middle of the Pacific." Somewhat puzzled, the reporter responded, "No! The Russians have sent a spaceship into orbit around the world." Michener later reflected, "Within minutes we had forgotten our own adventure in the shadow of one so infinitely greater."

For millennia, human beings had dreamed about space. They mapped stars into constellations, determined how far planets were away from one another, and fantasized about slipping the surly bonds of earth toward unknown frontiers. Now, as people across the world looked to the sky on that remarkable

October evening, the fantasies seemed light-years closer to reality. After all the horrors that had unfolded throughout the twentieth century—the tens of millions killed in world wars and a nuclear arms race that was rapidly spiraling out of control—the Soviet launch of Sputnik gave people hope that some good might come out of the Cold War. Though that optimism proved to be short-lived, it motivated ordinary people to do extraordinary things with their lives.

Franklin Chang-Díaz

One of those people was Franklin Chang-Díaz. On the evening of October 4, the seven-year-old adventurer burst through the door of his home in San José, Costa Rica. He could not contain his excitement; he was fascinated by space and driven by his desire to go there one day. As a child, Franklin and his friends built pretend rockets by assembling chairs inside huge cardboard boxes outside his house. There, they sat in tense excitement with their backs to the ground as they went through launch checklists they learned about from radio reports. When the checklists were complete, one of the boys began counting down from ten. They were on their way to other planets, where they were certain to encounter exotic monsters and adventures beyond their wildest dreams.

Now that the Soviet Union had launched an actual satellite into that great unknown, Franklin knew that he had to be a part of it. He wrote a letter to Wernher von Braun, who was appointed director of the National Aeronautics and Space Administration (NASA) in 1960. He told von Braun about his appetite for adventure, his love for space, and his desire to go there one day. To his absolute amazement, von Braun wrote back. He suggested that Franklin come to the United States after he graduated high school to pursue a career as an astronaut.[2]

Over the next few years, Franklin watched as his friends, who had been his fellow adventurers, put their dreams of space on hold for more practical and secure careers. Franklin knew in his heart that he would be different. Throughout his childhood, he confidently told his friends and family that he would one day become a rocket scientist and work with von Braun at NASA. Most of them smiled and nodded, but they privately thought that one day Franklin would "grow up and join the real world."

Just after his eighteenth birthday, Franklin waved good-bye to his family at San José's airport and turned toward the gleaming silver Pan American Boeing 727 jet that was positioned on the tarmac. He stepped inside, feeling truly alone for the first time. He took

Astronaut Franklin Chang-Díaz smiles for his official NASA photo in 1980. He was the first Hispanic American to travel into space.

a seat next to the window on the plane's left side. Then he panicked. "I must be crazy," he remembered thinking, "fool enough to have talked myself into such an impossible plan." He grabbed his belongings and tried to run back to his family. However, by the time he reached the exit door, the flight attendants had closed it and he was unable to deplane. Franklin was on his way to Connecticut and the American relatives he would live with while he finished high school.[3]

In Connecticut, Franklin learned English quickly. The language came easily to him because he was so eager to converse with those around him. Within a year, he graduated from Hartford High School. Four years later, he received his undergraduate degree from the University of Connecticut, then went on to the Massachusetts Institute of Technology to study physics and thermonuclear fusion. Franklin completed his PhD in 1977, applied for and was granted US citizenship, and eventually got the job of his dreams in 1980. Through year after grinding year of tuning out the voices of those who told him it wasn't possible, his inner voice had guided him steadily toward this moment. He had made it to NASA's astronaut training program.

Thirty years after Sputnik compelled a seven-year-old boy to reach for the heavens, Franklin Chang-Díaz became the first Hispanic American to travel into space aboard the space shuttle *Columbia*. He recalled, "It wasn't that different from what I was thinking as a little kid, that that was how it was going to feel. But that was before the actual liftoff. Before that, the count-down and the procedures seemed very familiar to me. I was mentally totally ready." In July 1986, President Ronald Reagan awarded Franklin the Medal of Liberty, in recognition of his incredible journey from the box in his back-yard to the captivating wilderness of space.

Of the Cold War conflict on earth, Franklin reflected, "I think space is a great equalizer and I think you don't need to have a country that's rich in natural resources and territory to be able to work and do business in space. What you need is gray matter. That's the natural resource that you need and we've got plenty of that."[4]

Commonwealth of Satellites

Soviet leader and soon-to-be premier Nikita Khrushchev possessed some of the gray matter Franklin was referring to. After the Soviets launched another satellite, Sputnik 2, just one month after the first one, Khrushchev reached out to Eisenhower with a remarkable gesture of peace. Reflecting on twelve long years of increasing tensions between the United States and the Soviet Union, the Soviet leader believed that it was time for two former allies to come back together and end the Cold War once and for all. Buoyed by the triumph of Sputnik, Khrushchev suggested that the two countries "form a commonwealth of satellites" that would be "much better than competition in the race to manufacture lethal weapons." Furthermore, he suggested that leaders from both capitalist and communist countries come together for a major meeting. The goal of the meeting would be to "[exclude] war as a method of settling . . . problems, to stop the cold war and the [race for nuclear weapons] and to establish relations among states on the basis of coexistence." Conflict, Khrushchev went on, would be settled "by means of peaceful competition in the culture and in the best satisfaction of human requirements and needs."

Khrushchev's words gave many Americans hope that it still wasn't too late to realize Henry Wallace's vision for a century of the common man. Unfortunately, Eisenhower ignored him. In his November 1957 "Address to the American People on Science and National Security," the president chose to respond with bluster. Instead of agreeing to the meeting Khrushchev suggested, Eisenhower bragged about the vast military superiority of the United States and its intention to stay far ahead in the arms race:

> Our nation has . . . enough power . . . to bring near annihilation to the war-making capabilities of any other country. Atomic submarines have been developed. . . . A number of huge naval carriers are in operation, supplied with the most powerful nuclear weapons and bombers of great range to deliver them. Construction has started which will produce a carrier to be driven by atomic power. . . . In numbers, our stock of nuclear weapons is so large and so rapidly growing that . . . we are well ahead of the Soviets . . . both in quantity and quality. We intend to stay ahead.

Eisenhower made yet another decision that could very well have led to the end of life on the planet. By responding to Khrushchev as a bully would in a schoolyard, Eisenhower sent the Soviet Union a message that it would have to build more nuclear weapons, conduct more testing, and build better rockets. After all, if the United States intended to "stay ahead," the Soviet Union would need to at least keep pace.

The president backed up his words with action. Determined to make the race to space into a real contest, the United States tried to launch a satellite with a Vanguard rocket on December 6, 1957. The launch was a huge embarrassment. The rocket stayed in the air for only two seconds, reaching a height of four feet. Newspapers scornfully called the grapefruit-size sphere "Kaputnik," "Flopnik," and "Stayputnik." Eisenhower, undeterred, unleashed Wernher von Braun and his army rocket-development team—then working at Redstone Arsenal in Alabama—to put something, anything, up in the air. By January 31, 1958, they successfully orbited a thirty-one-pound Explorer satellite.

At one point, the United States even thought about exploding a Hiroshima-size atomic bomb on the moon to send a clear message to the Soviet Union that the United States intended to dominate the world. The resulting dust cloud would have been widely visible from the earth. A study was conducted from May 1958 to January 1959 by a ten-person staff that included the young astronomer Carl Sagan. Finally, the scientists joined with others in convincing authorities that "there was no point in ruining the pristine environment of the moon."

The air force devised even more cockamamie schemes. In February 1958, Lieutenant General Donald Putt disclosed secret plans for missile bases on the moon. Putt explained, "[Bombs] could be catapulted from shafts sunk deep into the moon's surface." Then, if the United States was destroyed in a major nuclear attack and all of its major missile bases were knocked out, it could still retaliate against the Soviet Union from the moon. So, if the Soviet Union really wanted to defend itself, it would have to figure out how to launch an attack on the moon.

Going even further, Putt added that if the Soviets ever figured out how to build their own bases on the moon, the United States could build bases on more-distant planets from which it could launch attacks against both the Soviet Union and its moon bases. When independent journalist I. F. Stone read about those plans, he smartly noted that the Latin word for "moon" is *luna* and suggested that the military establish a space warfare branch called the Department of Lunacy.

The Peaceful Atom

Indeed, lunatics were rampant inside the Eisenhower administration. In late April 1955, the president began a campaign at home and around the world to promote what he called "the peaceful atom." The Atomic Energy Commission marketed nuclear power not only as a protector against communism but as a magic potion that would power transportation vehicles, feed the hungry, light the cities, heal the sick, and excavate the planet.

The US Postal Service issued a stamp celebrating "Atoms for Peace: To Find the Way by Which the Inventiveness of Man Shall Be Consecrated to New Life." Eisenhower unveiled plans for an atomic-powered merchant ship that would visit ports all over the world to show the United States' commitment to a "just and lasting peace." In July, the United States generated its first commercial nuclear power and made agreements with Japan and thirty-six other nations to build atomic reactors. Meanwhile, the United States began building an atomic plane, but a proposed $60 million atomic-powered coast guard icebreaker proved too costly, and Eisenhower vetoed it.

On March 14, 1958, the *New York Times* reported on its front page that "atomic explosions up to ten times the power of the World War II Hiroshima bomb may be within a couple years an every-day occurrence almost anywhere in the country under a program being pressed by scientists of the Atomic Energy Commission (AEC)."

On July 28, 1955, the US Postal Service issued this "Atoms for Peace" stamp, designed by George Cox.

In June, the AEC released plans to create an entirely new harbor north of the Arctic Circle in Alaska by exploding four hydrogen bombs. Officials thought that the bombs might free hard-to-reach oil deposits trapped far beneath the ground. Other explosions could also create huge underground reservoirs, produce steam, desalinize water, crack copper and other impenetrably hard metals, and produce radioactive isotopes for use in medicine, biology, agriculture, and industry.

Some experts wanted to use nuclear weapons to blast a new, bigger, and better Panama Canal. Others wanted to use them to change weather patterns. Jack Reed of Sandia National Laboratories, headquartered in Albuquerque, suggested exploding a 20-megaton bomb alongside the eye of a hurricane to reverse its direction. He was sure that any radioactivity would fall harmlessly. A US Weather Bureau scientist, Harry Wexler, proposed a plan to speed up the melting of polar ice caps by exploding ten 10-megaton bombs near the Arctic Circle, which would warm the North Pole by about 10 degrees Fahrenheit.

In 1959, Eisenhower approved plans for a 10-kiloton explosion deep in a salt bed near Carlsbad, New Mexico. Project Gnome, as it was called, would explore the possibility of creating an underground reservoir of heat that would remain trapped in melted salt and could be used to produce electricity. A spokesperson for the National Park Service, which ran the nearby

Carlsbad Caverns National Park, reported that the department was "completely flabbergasted" by the announcement.

Popular Mechanics asked its readers the following questions: "Will we ever be driving cars powered by atomic energy? Will individual reactors ever heat and air condition homes? Will we fly cross-country in atomic-powered planes?" The magazine acknowledged that radiation might be a problem but went on to answer, "It's quite possible at this moment to design atomic-powered planes and cars, to build small reactors for heating and air-conditioning homes. But whether reactors ever will be built for these purposes is another question."

Despite Eisenhower's strong efforts to promote the peaceful atom, Americans were becoming ever more aware of the dangers of nuclear weapons. The *Lucky Dragon 5* incident and Sputnik's launch ignited more protests against civil defense and nuclear testing. In 1956, Democratic presidential candidate Adlai Stevenson had insisted that he could not "accept [Eisenhower's apparent] position that we are powerless to do anything to stop this headlong race for extinction." He, too, called Eisenhower's nuclear buildup "madness." British, US, and Soviet tests in 1957 angered many leaders around the world. Prime Minister Nehru of India demanded an end to all nuclear tests, fearing that they "might put an end to human life as we see it."

On the Beach

In November 1957, the National Committee for a Sane Nuclear Policy placed an ad, written by Norman Cousins, in the *New York Times*. Signed by forty-eight prominent citizens, it called for an end to nuclear testing as the first step toward arms control. People across the country responded with great enthusiasm. They cheered the committee's bold statement and overwhelmed its members with support. Committee members never imagined they would get such a response and set out to establish a new major national anti-nuclear organization called SANE.

SANE was only one of many efforts launched in 1957. The first Pugwash anti-nuclear conference was held in Nova Scotia in July. Scientists from all over the world, including five from the United States and three from the Soviet Union, called for abolishing war, ending the arms race, and halting nuclear testing.

That same year, Nobel Peace Prize winner Albert Schweitzer added his voice to the growing international anti-nuclear movement. Schweitzer broadcast his "Declaration of Conscience" to approximately fifty countries. The *New York Times* reported "world-wide concern that the continuation of tests poses a threat to the future existence of all living things on earth." A May Gallup poll showed that 63 percent of Americans wanted an international halt to bomb tests, more than double the 27 percent who opposed such a move. This was triple the number of Americans who wanted to halt tests the prior year.

In bookstores and movie theaters across the country, Americans came face-to-face with the potential horrors of nuclear war. British adventure novelist Nevil Shute wrote the riveting bestseller *On the Beach*, which described the aftermath of a thirty-seven-day nuclear war. The plot traced the final days of the last surviving pocket of humans in Melbourne, Australia, the earth's

Albert Schweitzer was a noted doctor, missionary, and philosopher and one of the world's most respected men. In 1957, his radio address warned people all over the world about the dangers of nuclear tests.

FOR A SANE NUCLEAR POLICY

A poster produced by the National Committee for a Sane Nuclear Policy, or SANE, in 1964.

southernmost major city, as a huge radioactive cloud descended upon them. Somewhere far away, way up north, a terrible misunderstanding between nations had resulted in nuclear war. Was it an accident? Was it on purpose? Did it matter? One character remarked, "No, it wasn't an accident. . . . It was carefully planned, down to the tiniest mechanical and emotional detail. But it was a mistake."

The *Washington Post* reviewed *On the Beach* in an article titled "The Facing of Certain Death." It read, "Nevil Shute has written the most important and dramatic novel of the atomic age, and if you read only one book a year this should be the one." The reviewer concluded, "I hope Nevil Shute's book will go into a few cornerstones or time capsules, so that if an atomic Armageddon ever comes, future civilizations may realize that this generation went down the road to destruction with its eyes wide open. It should be required reading on both sides of the curtain."

Filmmaker Stanley Kramer made the book into a movie. It premiered simultaneously in all the major capitals of the world in December 1959 to international fanfare. The film began with a chilling line: "This is how the world ends; not with a bang, but a whimper."

People across the world emerged from theaters asking themselves what they would do if they knew the end was near. Would they party like there was no tomorrow? Would they pretend it wasn't happening? Would they regret not having taken action sooner to prevent such a calamity?[1]

Nineteen-year-old Australian Helen Caldicott remembered how she felt after reading *On the Beach*: "Shute's story haunted me. Millions of words have since been written about nuclear war and its consequences, and much of the literature is more horrific and emotive than anything Nevil Shute wrote or perhaps imagined. But his novel was set in Melbourne, the city where I had grown up. It described places I knew, devastated by nuclear catastrophe. Nowhere was safe."

Helen had known that she wanted to be a doctor since she was eleven years old. She always loved biology and was passionate about helping sick people heal. Her parents told her all the time that if she worked hard enough, she could accomplish anything. But now, Helen realized that she had a higher calling. "After reading *On the Beach*, I knew I wouldn't just go through medical school and settle into a nice, cozy, well-paid niche somewhere, as doctors in Australia were apt to do."

Realizing her true calling, Helen spent the rest of her life teaching the public about how nuclear weapons impact the human body. In 1978, she revived an organization called Physicians for Social Responsibility, a group of doctors dedicated to the abolition of nuclear weapons. Over the years, she collected many awards for her work, received nineteen honorary degrees, and was nominated for the Nobel Peace Prize. Later in life, Helen reflected on the importance of preserving the earth for future generations: "The future of our children is a trust we have been given. To conserve and grow, not to squander wastefully on needless excesses. The earth is a trust, to protect and to honor. Our home, our livelihood, our future rests in the quality of our stewardship. Let us become better stewards."

Was Eisenhower an adequate steward of the earth? In September 1957, Winston Churchill declared that he planned to send a copy of *On the Beach* to Khrushchev. Someone asked him if he was also planning to send one to Eisenhower. Churchill replied, "It would be a waste of money. He is so muddle-headed now. . . . I think the earth will soon be destroyed. . . . And if I were the almighty I would not recreate it in case they destroyed him too the next time."

Some in Eisenhower's cabinet discussed ways to convince Americans who had read or seen *On the Beach* that nuclear weapons didn't have to be abolished to prevent nuclear war. Officials in the State Department and the Atomic Energy Commission tried to discredit the film by alleging that it contained serious errors. The US Information Agency created a file called "Possible Questions and Suggested Answers on the Film 'On the Beach.'"

However, despite the government's attempt to minimize the impact of Shute's work, throngs of moviegoers, many of whom left the theaters in tears, were probably more convinced by Julian, the scientist played by actor Fred Astaire, who was asked who he thought started the war. He responded:

> The war started when people accepted the idiotic principle that peace could be maintained by arranging to defend themselves with weapons they couldn't possibly use without committing suicide. Everybody had an atomic bomb. And counter bombs. And counter-counter bombs. The devices outgrew us. We couldn't control them. I know. I helped build them. God help me. Somewhere some poor bloke probably looked at a radar screen and thought he saw something. Knew that if he hesitated 1/1000th of a second his own country would be wiped off the map. . . . So he pushed a button and the world went crazy.

The logic of Julian's response did not escape Eisenhower. The president knew that, given how out of control things had gotten, something had to be done to prevent nuclear war. He resisted the Joint Chiefs' pressure to use nuclear weapons. He limited spending on civil defense and held back the growth of overall defense spending. He worked to enact a ban on nuclear testing. He resisted pressure for a massive nuclear weapons buildup after Sputnik. He confronted the powerful and sometimes hostile Soviet Union. And he was often a moderate voice among far more extreme advisers who often pushed for war.

Military Growth

Yet under Eisenhower, the United States went from having a little more than 1,000 nuclear weapons to having more than 22,000, aimed at 2,500 targets in the Soviet Union. Between 1959 and 1961, the United States added 19,500 nuclear weapons to its arsenal. The United States was producing new weapons at the rate of 75 per day. Total megatonnage increased sixty-five-fold in five years, reaching 20,491 megatons by 1960. That was the equivalent of 1,360,000 Hiroshima bombs.

What is little known is that Eisenhower had given military commanders below him the authority to launch nuclear weapons if they believed it was necessary. If they couldn't get in touch with the president, they could press the button without him. With Eisenhower's approval, some of those commanders in turn gave commanders below them the authority. All of a sudden, commanders of air forces, fleets, and navies—and in some cases, even pilots, squadron leaders, base commanders, and carrier commanders—had their fingers on the triggers. According to Research and Development (RAND) Corporation analyst Daniel Ellsberg, who had discovered all of this, "It was a doomsday machine on a hair trigger."

On some level, Eisenhower understood how dangerous the world had become under his leadership. He regretted the doomsday machine he was passing on to the next president. He was deeply disappointed that he was not able to conclude a test ban treaty before leaving office. But after eight years in office, there didn't seem like much he could do about it. The nuclear arms race had taken on a life of its own.

PART FOUR

Americanizing the World

The Cost of Oil: Iran

In the early 1950s, at a time of growing atomic anxiety and Cold War fears, cars reigned supreme. They were big and fast and bright. They were celebrated, idolized, and polished relentlessly by teenagers in their garages. Millions of Americans were moving away from cities and into newly built suburban neighborhoods. They needed a way to get to work and school. *Life* magazine reported that teenagers with the means were either receiving cars as gifts from their parents or buying them with their savings. By 1953, parking at Carlsbad High School in California had become so difficult that school administrators decided to open up a special parking area just for students. The same scene played out across the country. Parking lots were overflowing. They couldn't be built fast enough.

Automakers outfitted their latest products with heaters, air conditioners, radios, and other modern electronics. Special car washes sprang up along highways. Drive-through windows and drive-in theaters were built to accommodate them. There were drive-in religious services, liquor stores, diners, and banks.[1]

Unlike Ford's Model T, which was designed to be reliable and affordable, these new cars were designed as luxury items without luxury price tags. They were bright, highly visible, and aggressively styled. The average cost of a new car in 1953 was $1,650—low enough for most middle-class families to afford at least one.

Cars liberated teenagers from their parents, their communities, and their anxieties. To teens in particular, the car represented freedom. A generation growing up with the threat of nuclear annihilation lived for the present, and what better way to have fun than to cruise down the highway with the top down, listening to rock-'n'-roll with your sweetheart?

One key ingredient fueled the American car culture: gasoline. In the 1950s, gas in Europe and the United States was cheap and plentiful.

The West had become dependent upon oil to fuel cars, fight wars, and manufacture products. Landing massive boats at Normandy, for example, required a phenomenal amount of fuel, not just for the boats themselves, but also for the larger vessels that moved them across the Atlantic. Moving food from farms to grocery stores, transporting building materials to new suburban home lots, and heating homes and office buildings also depended on access to cheap gas.

In the early 1950s, the United States produced about half of the world's oil and was able to supply itself with the fuel necessary to fight Japan and Germany. The British, however, were in an entirely different position. An island nation, Great Britain had to secure many of its natural resources from abroad. It had a long tradition of capturing those resources by force. For its oil, Britain looked to Iran.

Shahs Get Rich While Workers Stay Poor[2]

Britain and Iran had a rocky history that began in the mid-nineteenth century when the British bought the rights to lay telegraph cable across Iranian soil. Since then, Britain struck deal after deal with corrupt Iranian royalty, known as "shahs." Those deals made the shahs richer and the Iranian people poorer.

For decades, the shahs betrayed the Iranian people to foreign countries. They sold Iran's natural resources to foreign companies. Those companies, in turn, forced many Iranians to work for very low wages in dangerous conditions. But perhaps the biggest sellout of all was when Iran gave the British Empire control over all of the country's oil. That deal gave British oil prospectors the right to extract oil from under huge expanses of Iranian land, setting off a chain of events that continues to threaten the security of the world today.

Most Iranians were absolutely furious that the shahs literally sold their riches out from under them. They were also desperate. Poverty and disease ravaged the country as Britain and other European nations took Iran's resources and sold them to the world. Iranians, whom the Europeans hired to work for them, earned barely enough to survive.

Still, decades passed, and the Iranian leaders granted Britain more power and control. In the Anglo-Persian oil fields at Abadan, conditions by the mid-1940s were the worst they had ever been. Royal-born, England-educated Manucher Farmanfarmaian, in his book *Blood and Oil: Memoirs of a Persian Prince*, remembered what it was like:

> Wages were fifty cents a day. There was no vacation pay, no sick leave, no disability compensation. The workers lived in a shantytown called Kaghazabad, or Paper City, without running water or electricity, let alone such luxuries as iceboxes or fans. In winter the earth flooded and became a flat, perspiring lake. The mud in town was knee-deep, and canoes ran alongside the roadways for transport. When the rains subsided, clouds of nipping, small-winged flies rose from the stagnant waters to fill the nostrils, collecting in black mounds along the rims of cooking

pots and jamming the fans at the refinery with an unctuous glue.

Summer was worse. It descended suddenly without a hint of spring. The heat was torrid, the worst I've ever known—sticky and unrelenting—while the wind and sandstorms whipped off the desert hot as a blower. . . .

To the management of [Anglo-Iranian Oil Company] in their pressed ecru shirts and air-conditioned offices, the workers were faceless drones. . . . In the British section of Abadan there were lawns, rose beds, tennis courts, swimming pools and clubs; in Kaghazabad there was nothing—not a tea shop, not a bath, not a single tree. . . . The unpaved alleyways were emporiums for rats. The man in the grocery store sold his wares while sitting in a barrel of water to avoid the heat.

Watching all of this unfold was thirty-seven-year-old Mohammad Mossadegh. Mossadegh, too, came from a wealthy Iranian family with royal lineage. Throughout his career in politics, he learned how much control the British had over Iran. He understood that British involvement came at the expense of the Iranian people.

Mossadegh realized that Britain was trying to strong-arm Iran into becoming just another one of its colonies. He couldn't accept that. Iran was too important to him to be further robbed of its resources and stripped of its dignity. He immediately called and wrote others to express his anger and frustration. He wrote a letter to the League of Nations denouncing the agreement and published flyers expressing his anger. What made his blood boil even more was that it seemed like the Iranian people were just going to go along with it, just as they had for over seventy years.

Mossadegh believed strongly in democracy, not monarchy and not imperial control. As a student in Europe, he had become enamored of the concepts of equality, fraternity, and liberty. Now, he would share those concepts with many people who had suffered at the hands of an unequal, tyrannical, and corrupt government. He was quickly becoming a popular leader, one whom Iranians so desperately needed given all they were up against.

Even though he came from a rich family, Mossadegh sympathized with the poor. He looked out at Iran through his sad, brooding eyes and dreamed of a future that provided economic prosperity for all, not just a select few. He declared before the Majlis (Iran's Parliament): "The Iranian himself is the best person to manage his house." With those words, Mossadegh pulled on the heartstrings of his countrymen. Independence was a cause worth fighting for! No longer should Iranians have to put up with the tyranny of their kings at the direction of foreign powers. If only they would stop accepting that reality and directly challenge British rule, perhaps they could realize true freedom for future generations.

Tudeh: Party of the People

How did workers deal with these incredible inequalities between themselves and their bosses? In Iran, as in other places throughout the world, they increasingly turned to communism. Groups of professors, intellectuals, and activists banded together to form a political party called Tudeh. The goal of the party was to fight for the workers, like those at Abadan, who were suffering so miserably. Tudeh pushed for better working conditions and sought to protect workers from their cutthroat bosses. Party members were young; they were optimistic; they were energized. Tudeh quickly caught on with Iranians who were, like Mossadegh, furious with the shahs and ready for change.

As the years went on, Tudeh got stronger and stronger. By 1944, it had aligned itself with the Soviet Union and committed itself to the philosophies of Karl Marx. The party caught on like wildfire between 1944 and 1946. On May Day 1946, Tudeh brought throngs of Iranians to the streets. They jammed the streets of Tehran and other cities, carrying banners and chanting in favor of workers' rights. If the shahs were going to continue to prioritize Great Britain and other Western countries over Iran, Iranians were not going to let them do so without a fight. Protesters cheered wildly in favor of a minimum wage, a forty-hour workweek, and maternity leave. They also pushed to regulate child labor, so that young children would not have to endure Abadan's backbreaking working conditions.

The Iranian people, determined to take back control of their lives and their land, had had enough. Sensing that a new day was on the horizon, Mossadegh ran for office in the Majlis. On October 13, 1949, he called all who were interested in democracy to the front steps of his house. Thousands showed up. Together, they marched through the capital city of Tehran to the entrance of Shah Mohammad Reza Pahlavi's Golestan Palace. They rushed

A pro-Mossadegh demonstration in Iran in February 1953. Enormously popular inside his country and well-respected internationally, Mossadegh was overthrown by the CIA in 1953.

the gate, chanting and waving. The crowd parted to reveal Mossadegh, who moved purposefully toward the front, from where he launched into an incendiary speech denouncing the shah. The crowd roared its approval. Mossadegh declared that he would stay exactly where he was until the shah agreed to hold fair elections. He would not budge. It was a remarkable act of civil disobedience. For seventy-two hours, Mossadegh and dozens of others camped out on the palace green. Remarkably, their efforts paid off. The shah, eager to embark on a trip to the United States, gave in and pledged to hold fair elections.

Though sympathetic to Tudeh, Mossadegh was uncomfortable with its alignment with the Soviet Union. His priority was Iran first. While gravely concerned about the plight of Iran's workers, Mossadegh was careful not to ally himself too closely with Tudeh's brand of communism. He didn't want to see Iran fall under the thumb of yet another imperial power, the Soviet Union. Nor did Tudeh support Mossadegh, who they believed was too weak to challenge Great Britain. Mossadegh and his allies decided to form a group called the National Front. They would forge a new era for Iran. They would take back control of its oil.

A New Day on the Horizon

Emboldened by Mossadegh and his fearless collaborators, the National Front and others decided that the only way to truly attain independence from Britain was to nationalize Iran's oil industry. Enough was enough. On April 28, 1951, the Majlis voted to appoint Mossadegh as prime minister. Immediately, Mossadegh submitted a bill to nationalize the Anglo-Iranian Oil Company, seizing control of the oil fields at Abadan. The bill became law on May 1. Mossadegh took office five days later.

The unthinkable had occurred. Mossadegh had done what generations before him had failed to do. He stood up to the British, looked them square in the eye, and, without flinching, revoked their power to do business in Iran. Gholam-Reza Sabri-Tabrizi recalled in his memoir:

> These days were a time of joy and grief, days of certainty and uncertainty—the days of gaining social consciousness. We were proud and full of joy to see and feel that—for the first time—a democratically elected government under Mossadegh's premiership had been established. There was a deep sense of pride and unity among the ordinary people of Iran. Mossadegh was the embodiment of a suppressed nation.[3]

Many in the United States, which had fought a war for independence from Great Britain 175 years earlier, initially sympathized with Mossadegh. The State Department declared in a public statement that Americans "fully recognize the sovereign rights of Iran and sympathize with Iran's desire that increased benefits accrue to that country from the development of its petroleum." At the time, many Iranians also viewed the United States positively. They thought of Americans as their friends. One observer reflected on how Americans in Iran had made incredibly positive contributions to the society: "Americans were regarded with nearly universal admiration and affection. . . . The American contribution to the improvement and . . . the dignity of our impoverished, strife-torn country had gone far beyond their small numbers."

Iranians drew inspiration from the State Department's words. They assumed that the United States would support their quest for democracy and independence from their colonial bondage. They had many reasons to believe that. After all, President Franklin Roosevelt had publicly rebuked Britain's rule over Gambia in 1944: "It's the most horrible thing I have ever seen in my life," he declared. "The natives are five thousand years back of us. . . . The British have been there for two hundred years—for every dollar that the

British have put into Gambia, they have taken out ten. It's just plain exploitation of these people." Later, Harry Truman called William Fraser, the head of the Anglo-Iranian Oil Company, a "typical nineteenth century colonial exploiter."

Man of the Year

Even though Truman was sympathetic to Mossadegh, he worried about the relationship between the United States and Great Britain, as Great Britain was America's closest ally. Staying on good terms with Great Britain was crucial, in Truman's mind, to keeping the Soviet Union in check. He decided to try to negotiate with the Iranians to come to some sort of compromise. In a letter penned at Blair House, Truman pleaded with Mossadegh to strike a deal:

> This matter is so full of dangers to the welfare of your own country, of Great Britain and of all the free world, that I have been giving the most earnest thought to the problems involved. . . . I have watched with concern the breakdown of your discussions and the drift toward a collapse of oil operations with all the attendant losses to Iran and the world. Surely this is a disaster which statesmanship can find a way to avoid.

He sent Averell Harriman, the longtime statesman and financier, to Tehran to try to broker a deal.

Mossadegh was in no mood to negotiate. He believed that Iran was experiencing a wave of freedom from the tyranny of British colonialism. He was willing to accept death rather than allow Great Britain to remain in his country. He told Harriman, "You do not know how crafty [the British] are. You do not know how evil they are. You do not know how they sully everything they touch." Finally, after days of meetings, Harriman was able to convince Mossadegh to negotiate with Britain. However, the hardheaded British simply wouldn't budge. They wouldn't recognize Iran's right to nationalize its oil, and Iran wouldn't recognize Britain's claim to it.

Mossadegh's resistance to Great Britain made him a global celebrity. On a trip to Egypt, he was greeted by throngs of frenzied supporters who craned their necks to get a mere glimpse of him. The Egyptian press feted him as a savior, a champion of the people who had "conquered history" and "won freedom and dignity for his country." King Farouk and Prime Minister Nahas Pasha pledged their devotion to him, declaring, "A united Iran and Egypt . . . will together demolish British imperialism."

On January 7, 1952, *Time* designated Mossadegh "Man of the Year." His face adorned the popular magazine's cover and was captioned with the phrase "He oiled the wheels of chaos." Though the article demeaned Mossadegh as "a willful little boy" and "a strange old wizard who lives in a mountainous land," it acknowledged that he was the only one strong enough to stand up to the British, who were "hated and distrusted almost everywhere."

For Great Britain, Mossadegh's newfound celebrity was the straw that broke the camel's back. As people around the world began to sympathize with him more and more, the British feared that the world might react similarly to other challenges to its imperial rule. This could not stand. Mossadegh was not just a threat to Great Britain's oil supply, he was a threat to the very survival of the empire. It became clear as day to Winston Churchill and other high-ranking British officials: Mossadegh had to be stopped. To make that happen, Britain turned to its closest ally, the United States, for help.

Operation Ajax

Britain understood that under Truman, the United States would continue to seek negotiations with Mossadegh. Time and time again, Truman scoffed at the idea of removing him from power. Eisenhower, however, was a different story. The British were ecstatic when he was elected in November 1952. No longer would they have to deal with an American leader who believed Mossadegh could be reasoned with.

Just two weeks after Eisenhower's election, British officials descended upon Washington. They came to convince the CIA to help them get rid of the democratically elected Mossadegh, who had the support of 95 to 98 percent of all Iranians. To do so, they argued that if Mossadegh was allowed to nationalize Anglo-Iranian, the communist Tudeh party would wrest control of the Abadan fields and send Iran's oil straight to the Soviet Union. This might cause Iran to fall behind the Iron Curtain. At the time, the United States was fighting ferociously in Korea to prevent the spread of communism across East Asia. The British figured that Americans would naturally want to prevent it from spreading in Iran as well. They used that argument to whip up support for Mossadegh's removal. The days of diplomacy were long gone. It was time to get serious.

The British received gleeful support form Eisenhower's secretary of state John Foster Dulles and his brother, CIA director Allen Dulles. The two brothers, both staunch anti-communists from a privileged family, understood the importance of keeping Iran's oil away from the Soviet Union. Given how dependent the entire world was becoming on cheap gasoline, they also knew how important it would be for Britain to maintain control. It was clear that the Eisenhower administration was much more inclined to take Britain's side against Iran.

The Dulles brothers summoned Kermit Roosevelt, son of Theodore Roosevelt and the CIA's top Middle East expert, to a late-night meeting deep in the bowels of a Washington office building. Together, they discussed ways to eliminate "that madman Mossadegh." How could they turn 95 percent of Iranians and the majority of the world against Iran's leader, then topple his government? If the British or the Americans sent in troops, it would look just like what it was: an invasion of a sovereign country. No, it had to be kept secret—secret from the Iranians, of course, but also secret from American and British citizens. Without congressional approval, Allen Dulles sent $1 million to the CIA outpost in Tehran to use "in any way that would bring about the fall of Mossadegh." The operation would come to be known as Operation Ajax and would set a dangerous precedent for the CIA to topple any government that it deemed a threat to American interests.

The plan was simple. The CIA and British spies would turn Iranians against Mossadegh. They would "create, extend and enhance public hostility and distrust and fear of Mossadegh and his government." To do so, the CIA paid Iranian journalists, preachers, army and police officers, and members of the Majlis to turn against Mossadegh. They also paid an Islamic fundamentalist group, Warriors of Islam, to threaten to kill supporters of the prime minister.

The objective was to depict Mossadegh as a communist tool of the Soviet Union, not an Iranian freedom fighter. If the CIA could convince Iranians that Mossadegh was going to nationalize their oil, then send it to the Soviet Union, they might turn against him. American spies designed booklets and posters, reading: MOSSADEGH FAVORS THE TUDEH PARTY AND THE USSR . . . MOSSADEGH IS AN ENEMY OF ISLAM . . . MOSSADEGH IS DELIBERATELY DESTROYING THE MORALE OF THE ARMY . . . MOSSADEGH IS DELIBERATELY LEADING THE COUNTRY INTO ECONOMIC COLLAPSE . . . MOSSADEGH HAS BEEN CORRUPTED BY POWER. They posted them throughout Tehran and other Iranian cities.

In August 1953, Kermit Roosevelt began setting mobs loose to create chaos across Tehran. He spread rumors among the largely Shiite Muslim population that Mossadegh was a Jew. His street thugs, pretending to be members of Tudeh, attacked Islamic clergy and destroyed a mosque. On August 19, in the midst of the anarchy, Roosevelt brought former Iranian army officer General Fazlollah Zahedi out of his CIA hiding place to assume the role of prime minister. After an armed battle, plotters arrested Mossadegh and thousands of his supporters. Some were executed. Mossadegh was convicted of treason and imprisoned. The CIA had successfully pulled off its first coup d'etat, or overthrow, of a country.

Death to America

After the coup, with Mossadegh in prison, Iran's relationship with Britain and the West got stronger and stronger. Mossadegh's dream of returning Iran's oil to its people was replaced with a nightmare. Between 1953 and 1979, Mohammad Reza Pahlavi, the shah of Iran, got rich as he sold more and more of Iran's natural resources to foreign companies and governments. The American CIA helped him establish SAVAK, a secret police force, which tortured and killed thousands of people who dared to stand up to Pahlavi. SAVAK officers whipped and beat prisoners, burned them with cigarettes, shocked them with electricity, pulled out their nails and teeth, pumped boiling water into their bodies, and, in some cases, raped them.

Meanwhile, flush with oil money, Pahlavi purchased $200 million worth of arms from the United States. At the same time, he destroyed Iran's judicial system and robbed citizens of their personal and civil liberties. According to one account, "[Pahlavi destroyed] the dignity of our people by treating them like backward savages to be pulled with an iron hand out of the middle ages into the light of the modern era. Nearly every source of creative, artistic and intellectual endeavor in our culture was suppressed."[4]

Outraged by what Britain and the United States had done to their country, the Iranian people rose up once again in 1979 and, chanting "Death to America," led a successful revolution fueled by a fundamental interpretation of Islam that appealed to many who had been at the butt end of capitalism for far too long. The shah fled to the United States. Iranian students stormed the grounds of the American embassy in Tehran, took fifty-two Americans hostages, and set the stage for another era of repression and instability.

Had democracy been allowed to flourish under Mossadegh, perhaps the United States and Iran would have a better relationship today. Perhaps generations of Iranians could have increased their wealth and provided better opportunities. Instead, the two countries are now enemies to the peril of the entire world.

Bananas for Bananas

The most popular fruit in the 1950s was the banana. As the US government fought a war against communism in Korea and toppled the Iranian government, Americans baked banana cream pies, banana chiffon cake, banana muffins, and banana cookies. They sliced bananas into their cereal when they woke up in the morning, wrapped bananas in ham for lunch, whipped up banana pudding with vanilla wafers for a snack, deep-fried SPAM and banana fritters for dinner, and paired bananas with ice cream for dessert. Banana peels were everywhere—on subway floors, trash-can lids, and park benches.

Even Elvis Presley, the so-called King of Rock-'n'-Roll, loved bananas in all forms. He was known to eat entire family-size bowls of banana pudding. His favorite food was the banana and peanut butter sandwich. He pasted one slice of toasted white bread with peanut butter, sliced a ripe banana atop that, placed another piece of toasted bread on top, and fried the whole thing, on each side, in a stick of butter.[1] He ate it for breakfast, lunch, and dinner—and always with a knife and fork. The sandwich caught on with groupies across the country who wanted to be just like Elvis.

Customers show off their banana milk shakes in front
of a Dairy Queen in Buzzards Bay, Massachusetts, 1950.

Bananas were a staple food for many Americans in the
1950s. In this photograph, a woman shops for bananas
and other items at a grocery store in 1948.

Americans consuming Bananas Foster at Brennan's Restaurant in New Orleans or scarfing down banana pancakes in their local diners had no idea that the CIA was about to engage in a secret war for the coveted fruit. That war sowed death and destruction across the Central American country of Guatemala. There, in 1954, the CIA backed American fruit company United Fruit as it put its boot firmly on the neck of the country's people. By convincing Guatemalans that their democratically elected leader was a communist, the CIA was able to overthrow him and install a leader friendly to United Fruit. While United Fruit made millions, Guatemalans would suffer the consequences for decades and decades. The Cold War had come to the Americas.

United Fruit

Bananas had not always been so popular or plentiful or affordable. In fact, seventy-five years before Elvis devoured his famous sandwiches, people thought of bananas as rare delicacies. At Philadelphia's Centennial Exhibition in 1876, seven-year-old Frederick Upham Adams paid ten cents for the exotic crescent-shaped fruit, wrapped in tinfoil and served with a fork and a knife. Years later, the famous author and inventor reflected on his experience: "To my young and impressionable mind, this was the most romantic of all the innumerable things I had seen at any of the [exhibition's] vast buildings. It was the tangible, living, and expressive symbol of the far-distant and mysterious tropics." Lorenzo Baker, a gruff, bearded sea captain with unruly sideburns, changed all that. Baker made money by transporting restless gold miners from New England to the shores of Venezuela. On one particular voyage, Baker was on his way home after dropping off ten miners when his ship sprang a terrible leak. He barely made it to the closest island, Jamaica, where he spent a few nights while islanders repaired his ship.

While on the island, Baker grew enamored of the sweet, yellow tropical

Captain Lorenzo Baker, the sea captain turned merchant who first brought bananas to the United States from Jamaica.

fruit that hung enticingly from the stalks of dark green-leaved trees. He picked 3,200 bunches and loaded them aboard the ship. Eleven days later, he returned to Jersey City, New Jersey, with the bananas and sold them immediately for two dollars a bunch.

Before the Jamaica voyage, his ship, the *Telegraph*, often returned from the tropics empty. Baker learned that by filling the ship with bananas, he could make more money bringing the fruit to the United States than he made bringing miners to Venezuela. So he bought land in Jamaica, built a huge house, and planted acres of banana trees. The fruit grew quickly. Baker hired plantation workers who picked the bananas while he made the long trips back and forth.

Whenever Baker landed at the Boston docks with a load of bananas, Andrew Preston, a local merchant, was always there to bargain for them. Once Baker and Preston agreed on a price, Preston loaded them onto wagons and transported them to the city's markets. Business was brisk. Bostonians wanted bananas and were willing to pay high prices for them. That meant people across the country would too. The only problem was that bananas were highly perishable and often spoiled on the long three-week journeys between tropical ports and northeastern American cities. For all of the fruit to survive the long voyage, it had to be kept cool.

Baker told Preston about his problem. Preston suggested that they figure out how to refrigerate the bananas so they wouldn't rot.

Men load bananas at a United Fruit Company farm in this 1926 photograph.

In 1938, ten cents bought eight bananas at this fruit car on Sixty-First Street in New York City.

Workers in a United Fruit banana warehouse prepare to ship ripe bananas out to stores, October 1948.

They decided to chill the fruit with ice on the ships and built refrigerated warehouses across the United States to enable them to send the bananas far and wide. The warehouses also depended upon ice to operate, so ice-making businesses sprang up at the ports and along railroad lines.

With refrigeration, the North American banana craze began. As bananas became more and more plentiful, they came down in price. Eventually, the fruit from 1,500 miles away cost half as much as apples, which farmers grew in orchards just outside major cities. Baker and Preston were a huge success. They got together to form a company called Boston Fruit. It later became United Fruit, one of the most powerful and ruthless companies in American history.[2]

Guatemala

As time went on, United Fruit ran into another problem. The company needed more land to harvest bananas. Baker and Preston looked to Central America, where the climate was ideal for banana growing.

United Fruit arrived in Guatemala in the early part of the twentieth century. Bordered by Mexico to the north and west, Guatemala had been one of the most vibrant hubs of Mayan civilization. When Spain conquered the region in the sixteenth century, the Mayan population was forced to endure brutal living conditions, horrible treatment, and mass death at the hands of both man and disease.

Guatemala declared independence from Spain in 1821. A series of weak governments ruled the region until 1898, when Manuel Estrada Cabrera took power after a rigged election. Cabrera told the Mayan descendants that the only way to become free and independent was to modernize. What the people did not know was that Cabrera was primarily concerned with two things: money and power. He welcomed United Fruit with open arms.

In order to build new banana plantations far into the country's interior, the company needed rail lines. To communicate between plantations, the company needed telegraph. To accommodate larger

Manuel Estrada Cabrera won a rigged election in 1898 to become president of Guatemala. He welcomed United Fruit with open arms.

and more modern ships, the company needed new ports. Cabrera allowed United Fruit to build everything it needed, regardless of the harm it caused to Mayan villages.

The Mayans were devastated. Fragile fishing villages disappeared almost overnight as United Fruit destroyed millions of acres of rain forest to grow banana trees. Villagers, who had already been exploited for 350 years by the Spanish, now faced another enemy: the American demand for bananas. They got poorer as United Fruit got richer.

Protesting United Fruit became incredibly dangerous. Cabrera eliminated freedom of the press. He sent death squads to kill his perceived enemies. He built monuments to himself in Guatemala's capital. Meanwhile, the

Three Mayan children in 1904. Mayan villages in Guatemala were devastated when United Fruit built massive banana plantations throughout Guatemala.

American company continued to expand into the country, take more land, and pay workers next to nothing to pick bananas in the blistering heat. The workers were basically indentured servants. They took loans from their bosses for room, board, and supplies. Often, they would be unable to pay them back. As a result, many were forced to live their entire lives on the plantation.

Eventually, in addition to controlling Guatemala's government, United Fruit controlled almost half of its economy. Guatemalans overthrew Cabrera in 1920, but working conditions continued to be deplorable. As Americans gleefully sang the famous song "Yes, We Have No Bananas" and ate banana fruit cocktail and fried bananas in butter during the Roaring Twenties, those who grew their fruit struggled under five more dictators until 1931, when General Jorge Ubico took power. Though the six dictators before him were shockingly cruel, Ubico would become perhaps the most bloodthirsty dictator in Central American history.

After his election, Ubico immediately changed Guatemala's laws to ensure he could remain in office as long as he wanted. Throughout the 1930s, with Ubico's approval, United Fruit bought even more land. Ubico told the Mayans that they had to spend at least 100 days per year working for United Fruit and other landowners. If they didn't follow that rule, Ubico's soldiers often shot them dead. Meanwhile, the US embassy gave Ubico an enthusiastic endorsement.

Ubico hated communism. He responded violently to any hint of worker protest. He told Guatemalans that they could not speak or write the words "strike," "petition," "trade union," and even "worker." People who worked for United Fruit were thereafter referred to as "employees."

Guatemala had become what American short story author O. Henry called a "banana republic." A foreign company, United Fruit, owned the majority of the country's land, employed the majority of its workers, and controlled its government. Two percent of the population owned 60 percent of the land, while 50 percent of the people eked out a living on only 3 percent of the land. The Mayan population barely survived on less than fifty cents per day.[3]

Guatemala's middle class had had enough. They couldn't understand why Guatemala had to be the world's largest banana plantation. How was an American company able to enter a foreign country, buy up most of the land, and control so much of the government? Why couldn't Guatemala have bananas *and* freedom, just like the United States? After decades of exploitation by United Fruit and the Guatemalan dictators who supported it, anger finally boiled over into action.

In 1944, Guatemalans took to the streets in protest. Teachers and their students walked out first. They demanded an end to Guatemalan misery. United Fruit paid no taxes. That meant that there was not enough money to build new schools or repair the old ones. Schools became so crowded that children had to attend in two shifts, one in the morning and one in the afternoon.[4]

In response to the protest, Ubico's soldiers marched down the streets of Guatemala City, firing on the demonstrators. More and more people poured into the streets to protest their brutality. One student protester recalled, "Everyone held their breath. . . . Beneath the anxiety, a new spirit was rising, nurtured by the bravery of the students and the wholehearted support of the teachers." Guatemalans rich and poor, agrarian and professional, demanded that Ubico resign.

On June 24, 1944, protesters brought Guatemala City to a standstill. Students and teachers led tens of thousands of people on a silent march through the capital. Suddenly, one of Ubico's soldiers fired a bullet into the crowd. It struck María Chinchilla, a thirty-one-year-old teacher. She died a short time later. The next day, all stores, businesses, gas stations, and newspaper offices closed in protest of the brutal murder. María had become a martyr for Guatemalan reform.

Amazingly, the protests worked. Ubico resigned on July 1, 1944. His departure paved the way for a new generation of Guatemalans to determine their own future. For a brief ten-year period, it looked like anything was possible. The long, hard winter of oppression seemed to be finally thawing into a spring of progress.[5]

Arbenz

In 1950, Guatemalans elected handsome, charismatic, young Colonel Jacobo Arbenz president. The election was the freest and fairest ever held in the country. At his inauguration, Arbenz vowed to improve working people's lives. He would ask the rich to spend more money on the country's welfare. He would tax United Fruit and use the money to modernize schools, provide cleaner drinking water, and build new homes for workers:

All the riches of Guatemala are not as important as the life, the freedom, the dignity, the health and the happiness of the most humble of its people . . . we must distribute these riches so that those who have less—and they are the immense majority—benefit more, while those who have more—and they are so few—also benefit, but to a lesser extent. How could it be otherwise, given the poverty, the poor health, and the lack of education of our people?

To feed his people, Arbenz needed more land for farming. He announced plans to buy 234,000 acres of United Fruit's land. Since the company wasn't using 90 percent of it, Arbenz decided that Guatemalan farmers could put it to better use. He offered the company $600,000, which was the amount the company declared it was worth. United Fruit refused. The company would not let go of any of its land, regardless of what it was going to be used for.

United Fruit's owners were alarmed. For decades, they were able to do what they pleased in Guatemala. Now, a new young leader was directly challenging them. The company would not allow its power to be threatened.

If the company could ruin Arbenz's reputation, it might be able to convince Guatemalans to turn against the popular leader. It might also convince American leaders to take action against him. United Fruit hired Edward Bernays, the "father of public relations," to tell riveting stories about how Arbenz was a dangerous threat to the United States and the world. Bernays, whose Austrian uncle Sigmund Freud had founded psychoanalysis, had friends at major newspapers, including the *New York Times*. Soon after the company hired Bernays, the *Times* began publishing articles about the communist threat in Guatemala. American congressmen, including Senator Henry Cabot Lodge, read the articles and attacked Arbenz for being a communist.

In June 1951, the *Times* warned of a "Guatemalan Cancer." The newspaper complained that "the Government's policy is either running parallel to, or is a front for, Russian imperialism in Central America." The *Washington*

Post printed an editorial a few months later called "Red Cell in Guatemala" that described Arbenz as a tool of the communists.

Many Americans read those articles and became concerned that communism was so close to American borders. Central American leaders who dared to stand up for the interests of their people were now threatening American companies. Was it only a matter of time before the entire system of American free-market capitalism was at risk?

Secret War

United Fruit had friends among the high and mighty in the Eisenhower administration. Apart from CIA head Allen Dulles and his brother, Secretary of State John Foster Dulles, who had written United Fruit's agreements with Guatemala when he was a lawyer in New York, Assistant Secretary of State for Inter-American Affairs John Moors Cabot owned many shares of United Fruit. His brother, Thomas Dudley Cabot, had actually been president of the company a few years earlier. White House National Security Council adviser General Robert Cutler had been chair of the company's board. John J. McCloy, who had been assistant secretary of war during World War II, was a former board member. President Eisenhower's private assistant was even married to Ed Whitman, United Fruit's public relations chief.

Eisenhower's State Department demanded that Guatemala pay United Fruit $16 million for the land it wanted, more than twenty-six times what the company said it was worth. Arbenz refused. The CIA and other branches of the Eisenhower administration then decided to take the matter into their own hands. The Guatemalan president posed too great a threat to American business in Central America. Arbenz had to go. The United States would involve itself again in removing a democratically elected leader from power.

In August 1953, the CIA began its secret war against Arbenz. Allen Dulles hired Tracy Barnes as chief of political warfare. Eisenhower appointed

John Peurifoy as his ambassador to Guatemala. Peurifoy was a fierce anti-communist and an admirer of Joe McCarthy. He had helped purge the State Department of liberals and leftists. Together, they launched Operation PBSUCCESS to turn Guatemalans against their president, force him from power, and install a government friendly to United Fruit.

The United States began working with Guatemalan Colonel Castillo Armas to train an army of Honduran and El Salvadorian soldiers. Arbenz found out about it. He asked Czechoslovakia, a communist nation in Eastern Europe, for a shipload of arms. Guatemala would have to defend itself against the invasion.

Guatemalan president Jacobo Arbenz speaking to supporters in 1954. After his reform efforts upset the United Fruit Company, he was branded a communist and overthrown by a military junta in a 1954 coup engineered by the CIA.

The Czechoslovakian arms made it onto a ship bound for Guatemala. The CIA knew about it but allowed it to land. When the news reached Americans that a communist ship had landed in Guatemala, it was all the proof they needed: Arbenz, they figured, was a communist and a tool of the Soviet Union.

Meanwhile, the CIA went to work convincing Guatemalans to turn against Arbenz. The agency found out about a student activist group in Guatemala City that opposed Arbenz's policies toward United Fruit. The CIA, along with American and Guatemalan businesspeople, gave money to the group so that they could make anti-communist flyers, banners, and stickers. On September 15, 1953, the students pasted 106,000 anti-communist stickers on road signs, telephone poles, and buildings all over the capital. They asked bus drivers and train conductors to hand out tens of thousands of flyers to riders. When riders got off of the buses and trains in other cities and towns, they took the flyers with them. This allowed the anti-communist and anti-Arbenz messages to quickly circulate around the country.[6]

The CIA took over a radio station in Miami and broadcast anti-communist messages through United Fruit's radio network. Radio programs played anti-communist music, broadcast comedy shows, and told stories about how bad Arbenz was for Guatemala and the rest of the hemisphere. Newspapers reported that Arbenz had killed himself. John Peurifoy even gave the American media photographs of dead civilians said to have been killed by Arbenz's forces. The photos were actually of earthquake victims.

In June 1954, a few hundred CIA-trained fighters and Colonel Armas attacked Guatemala from bases in Honduras and Nicaragua. US airplanes followed, some whizzing over Guatemala City. Armas's fighters encountered thousands of Guatemalan troops loyal to Arbenz and were forced to retreat back into Honduras.

Even though it had lost the battle, the CIA had won the propaganda war. The ground attack, the air raid, the stickers, the flyers, the radio broadcasts, and the newspaper stories convinced many Guatemalans, even Arbenz himself, that an American invasion was about to take place.

On June 27, Arbenz, assuming that it wasn't worth it to fight anymore, stepped down. That night, he delivered a final radio address. He told the Guatemalan people, "The United Fruit Company, in collaboration with the governing circles of the United States, is responsible for what is happening to us." He warned about "twenty years of fascist bloody tyranny." After his speech, he proceeded to the airport, where he boarded a plane bound for Mexico. Arbenz would never set foot in Guatemala again.

The Price of Cheap Bananas

After Arbenz left, the CIA bombed Guatemala's main military base and its government radio station. Colonel Castillo Armas returned to the country in a US embassy plane to head the new government. Secretary of State Dulles addressed the American public on June 30 and applauded the victory of "democracy" over "Soviet communism." He announced that the situation was "being cured by the Guatemalans themselves." Shortly thereafter, Armas visited Washington and told Vice President Richard Nixon that he was loyal to the United States—and to United Fruit.

The United States gave Armas $90 million in American aid over the next two years, 150 times as much as it had given the Guatemalan government in the entire ten-year spring of progress. Allen Dulles said that the country had been saved from "communist imperialism." Meanwhile, Armas set up a brutal dictatorship and was assassinated three years later. One retired Marine Corps colonel who participated in the overthrow wrote later that "[American] 'success' led to 31 years of repressive military rule." The actual price of cheap bananas was closer to 200,000 human lives.

17

Sweet Empire

In the winter of 1915, Catherine Hershey could barely stand up anymore. At just forty-two years of age, the avid writer could now hardly hold a book or a pencil. She was so weak that she rarely left home, and when she did, she limped along with great difficulty.

Late one afternoon after a particularly bad bout of illness, a doctor examined Catherine from head to foot. He diagnosed her with a mild case of pneumonia. It was certainly a serious illness, but one from which the doctor thought she would recover. Catherine knew better. She had been sick for a very long time, but she had done her best to minimize her condition.

The nurse called Catherine's husband, Milton, and told him what had happened. Within hours, he was at her bedside, tenderly stroking her thinning hair and desperately trying to make her more comfortable. He asked her if she would like anything to eat or drink. She replied, "Champagne." The anguished man stood up from the bedside, exited the room, and went to fulfill his wife's request. When he returned, it was too late. His beloved Kitty, the intelligent, witty, and strong woman he had traveled the world with for seventeen years was gone.[1]

For the first time in as long as he could remember, Milton felt truly alone. He knew that he had to channel his grief into something productive that would distract him from his loneliness. Determined to honor Kitty's memory, he directed his energies toward work. Over the next thirty years, he would expand his twelve-year-old Pennsylvania chocolate factory into one of the most famous food companies in the world.

Milton Hershey, the "Chocolate King," in 1903.

Seeking inspiration and needing an escape, Milton did what many other wealthy American businessmen did at the time: He packed his bags and headed south, to the beautiful Caribbean island of Cuba. Perhaps a trip to warmer climes would get his creative juices flowing again and distract him from his misery. But, as it turned out, this would not be the only reason for his trip to "America's playground."

An Exploding American Frontier[2]

Milton arrived in Cuba's capital, Havana, and checked into the Plaza, one of the most prominent hotels in town. He was greeted by a whirlwind of activity. In 1915, Cuba was fast becoming a haven for wealthy Americans who took advantage of the island nation's climate, lenient culture, and economic opportunities. Just seventeen years earlier, the United States had repelled the Spanish from Cuba, ending centuries of Spanish colonial rule.

In 1901, the United States had drafted the infamous Platt Amendment,

Havana's Paseo del Prado between 1900 and 1915. This scene is similar to what Milton Hershey would have encountered when he arrived in Havana after Kitty's death.

insisting it must be part of an "independent" Cuba's new constitution. The amendment cemented US influence over the country. It stipulated that Cuba could not make any treaties with foreign countries, or allow foreign military bases on its soil, without first asking the United States for permission. It allowed the United States to examine Cuba's public finances. It dictated to the Cubans that the United States had the right to buy or lease lands necessary for "coaling or naval stations," eventually resulting in the establishment of a military base at Guantanamo Bay. Perhaps most ominously to Cubans, who reluctantly included it in their constitution, the amendment gave the United States the ability to intervene in Cuba whenever it saw fit.[3]

The Platt Amendment dictated that the United States could intervene politically and militarily, but it was the influence of American culture that made perhaps the deepest impact on Cuba. In the late 1910s and 1920s, Cuba was an exploding American frontier.

As World War I receded into memory, the twenties began to roar. American hotels that had been built before the war were now filled with wealthy industrialists from the north eager to take advantage of everything the island had to offer. Havana seemed to have it all—beautiful weather, free-flowing booze, gorgeous modern hotels, gambling, dancing, and a sultry nightlife. A Cuban tourist brochure described the scene: "Beauty reigns, relaxation prevails, and by courtesy of license your personal liberty is unrestricted. Havana is one of the best-ordered capitals in the world and surely the liveliest."

In 1919, John McEntee Bowman, the American magnate who owned the storied Biltmore hotel line, bought Havana's stalwart Sevilla Hotel, renovated it, and renamed it the Sevilla-Biltmore. It opened to great fanfare in 1920. Just two years later, Bowman added a ten-floor addition, making it the most prestigious accommodation in Cuba. Impeccably adorned guests streamed in with their shopping bags from Havana's Paseo del Prado, a grand European boulevard that rivaled those of Barcelona, Paris, and Rome. After visiting their rooms to freshen up, they headed to the breathtaking rooftop garden to swill mojitos and take in incredible views of the rollicking scene below.

Bowman swallowed up properties in Havana like a shark. Between 1920 and 1930, the dapper American took over the city's Jockey Club, the Oriental Park Racetrack, and the Gran Casino Nacional. These were some of the most prestigious spots in town, where Cuban and American tycoons splashed out their money in the grandest style. Never satisfied with what he had, Bowman's appetite for money propelled him further into the real estate business. Together with wealthy American and Cuban benefactors, he started a real estate investment company, which set out to fully cement Cuba's status as "a playground of the rich."

During the day, tycoons like chemical giant Irénée du Pont and sugar magnate Julio Lobo munched on bite-size sandwiches, drank tea, and schmoozed with power brokers at elaborate country club banquets. When the sun went down, they emerged from their luxurious digs into the sultry Caribbean air, warm breezes blowing behind them as they prowled the Paseo in search of late-night debauchery. Casinos, bars, nightclubs, and brothels welcomed their well-heeled clientele with open arms.

Men and women waltzed in the moonlit garden of the Sans Souci cabaret and nightclub while world-renowned bands played the hottest music. Those with less cash beelined for the famous Dos Hermanos Bar, which was perfectly located directly across from the cruise ship terminal in Old Havana. There, they smoked cigars and sucked down Cuba libres (rum and Cokes with lime wedges) until dawn broke over the Florida Straits.

The most popular watering hole in Old Havana was unquestionably Sloppy Joe's, located just a block away from the Sevilla-Biltmore. In the early 1920s, it became a haven for drink-starved American tourists escaping the puritanical confines of Prohibition just ninety miles to the north.

Central Hershey

One of the biggest problems Milton Hershey faced in making chocolate bars was the ever-increasing price of sugar. World War I made sugar more expensive, as European nations cut production dramatically between 1914 and 1918. As a result, the cost of one pound of sugar doubled over the same period. In 1915, when Milton arrived in Cuba, there was no way of knowing how long the war would drag on. The "Chocolate King" realized that he would have to grow his own sugarcane, build his own sugar mill, and hire his own workforce in order to avoid the high cost of sugar. Cuba was the perfect place to do it.

Milton called his acquaintance Juan Batista Salo, a Cuban he had met back home some years earlier. Salo summoned Angel Ortiz, another Cuban who understood the rhythms of the island's sugar industry. They met Milton at his hotel, rented a car and driver, and headed out into the coastal countryside.

The trio drove along Cuba's northern coast, past wide expanses of sugarcane. Out in the fields, on the opposite side of long barbed-wire fences, workers with machetes thrashed canes more than twice their height, hoisted the bales onto wagons, then thrashed some more. The work, performed in the unforgiving tropical sun, was backbreaking. *Colonos*, or landlords, watched

Cuban plantation workers gather sugarcane and place it on a wagon.

Sugar plantation workers labor under the watchful eye of their boss on horseback.

over the workers like hawks to make sure they weren't falling behind on their quotas. As the men drove farther along past the workers' quarters, a dark storm cloud formed on the horizon.

Salo and Ortiz chose to take Milton to a sugar plantation and adjacent mill called Central San Juan Bautista. As they approached the fields, the now rain-slicked road became so laden with mud that the car could go no farther. While trying to figure out what to do about their predicament, they spotted a group of oxen way off in the distance. Driving the oxen was F. F. Aguirre, the owner of the San Juan Bautista mill. After pulling the car out of the mud, Aguirre took the men on a tour of the mill.

When the tour was over, Aguirre asked Milton what he thought of the property. Milton smiled at him with deep satisfaction—for less than $500,000, he could buy an entire modern mill and enough land to supply his burgeoning chocolate empire with sugar. Labor would also be cheap, as it was for many other industrialists in Cuba. He quickly snapped up the land. At Central San Juan Bautista, he would build his own private chocolate empire that he triumphantly named "Central Hershey."

Bateyes[4]

As he spent more and more time in Cuba, Milton shook the grief that had consumed him after Kitty's death and threw all of his energy into building an entire company town complete with modern housing for his employees. He built houses for them with electricity, indoor plumbing, and lush gardens surrounding the structures, along with soccer fields, parks, schools, a medical clinic, and an orphanage, just as he had 1,000 miles to the north in Hershey, Pennsylvania. He even built Cuba's first electric rail line, ranging 120 miles, to transport his goods from Central Hershey to port. For many workers, Milton's utopian sugar production community seemed too good to be true. By 1921, partly aided by Milton's decision to grow and process his own sugar, the Hershey Chocolate Company had become the largest candy company in the world, producing eight million pounds of chocolate annually.[5]

Between 1899 and 1920, many other American industrialists colonized Cuban sugar plantations and mills, filling the vacuum left behind by the Spanish. Some of the richest and most powerful American and Cuban industrialists raced to buy up Cuban land. They cashed in beyond their wildest dreams. In 1905, North American owners controlled 21 percent of Cuba's sugar production. By 1926, they controlled 63 percent.[6]

Like Hershey's enterprise, many owners built company towns called "bateyes" that ensured employees would rarely if ever have to leave. In addition to the factory itself, the batey typically contained neatly constructed tract housing, schools, churches, medical clinics, banks, hotels, stores, ball fields, tennis courts, theaters, and social halls. George Braga, a batey resident, recalled, "On

Before Milton Hershey's electric railway, sugar was transported by coal-driven train locomotives like the one above.

[the sugar plantations] lived some 40,000 people. The maintenance of the mill towns, the schools, the hospitals, the churches, all came under our supervision and were our responsibility."

Reporter Carlos Martí described the Cuban American Sugar Corporation's batey at Chaparra as a "flourishing and prosperous population" with "a manner of living according to the needs of modern civilized life," evidenced by "comfortable and modern [homes] equipped with electricity provided by the company." Spanish-Cuban author Eva Canel described Chaparra thusly: "It has very wide streets on which families gather; there are modest homes and elegant chalets. There is a very comfortable hotel where employees eat well at prices imposed by the company. There is bustle, there is movement: men of all kinds, races, and types, women well dressed, flirtatious, and as daring as in Havana."

To many, bateyes represented the ideal "American way of life." Healthy, clean, orderly, and prosperous, they afforded those in Cuba's middle class a higher standard of living than many had ever imagined. Adventurer and journalist Herbert Lanks observed of Central Hershey:

> The company has done much to help its employees toward a higher standard of living. Comfortable modern homes have been built for them, making the town a model for the whole countryside. Various clinics as well as education and social services have been established to go with the physical improvements. A clear attempt has been made to raise the children to a higher standard of living, and the result was particularly noticeable in the appearance of the children on the streets. Whereas in other towns and villages there are always a number of ill-kempt street urchins begging for money, here all are well dressed, playing together in an orderly manner, and with respectful answers to questions when spoken to.

New Spain

Unfortunately for the vast majority of Cuban workers, bateyes only benefited middle- and upper-class white-collar employees, most of them American. In fact, many company towns segregated themselves into two separate zones, one for Cubans and one for Americans. Cuban workers who actually operated the mills or harvested the cane lived in deplorable conditions. The sophisticated sewer systems, screen doors, and brightly painted fences of the American zone might as well have been worlds away from the reality they had to endure.

As American companies bought up more and more land, placing a greater stranglehold on Cuban life and work, working- and middle-class Cubans began to resent them more and more. To many of them, the United States had simply replaced Spain as a colonial power. Despite the independence Cubans had achieved on paper, the Platt Amendment, the flood of American tourism, and the power of the sugar industry made them feel like second-class citizens in their own country, working first to feed the American beast, and only then, afterward, to feed themselves and their families.

Meanwhile, Americans unwrapped Hershey bars, licked candy canes, baked Betty Crocker cakes, and ate lemon sticks at county fairs, blissfully unaware of the impact those activities had upon Cuban life and culture. By 1959, in addition to their control over the Cuban sugar industry, American corporations controlled more than 80 percent of the country's mines, cattle ranches, utilities, and oil refineries and 50 percent of the railroads. Cuba had essentially become a colony of the United States of America.

Big Sugar

Of course, American corporations could only profit if Cuba maintained a stable government. Between 1898 and 1959, the United States backed a series of Cuban leaders who were friendly to American business interests but hostile to the majority of the Cuban people.

During the Great Depression, the price of sugar crashed. This caused an almost complete collapse of the Cuban banking system. Much of the wealth that Cubans had acquired during better times evaporated. Many Cubans, especially those who had lost everything, seethed with anger as American bankers snapped up the property of those who had been bankrupted.[7]

Angry Cubans directed their ire toward Cuba's leader, Gerardo Machado y Morales, who ruled the island from 1924 until 1933. In order to hold on to power during the Depression, Machado brutally suppressed dissent. His personal army tortured and, in some cases, shot to death those who disagreed with him. As student opposition groups formed to protest Machado's unconstitutional actions, Machado continued to place his boot on the neck of the Cuban people.

Despite the violence, and against the will of the vast majority of Cubans, the United States steadfastly supported Machado. US companies had made a tremendous amount of money during his reign, and the United States believed that Machado would ultimately be able to maintain control over the country. Democracy would have to take a backseat to profits.

It soon became clear that Machado would not be able to hold on to power. The US ambassador to Cuba told the dictator that it would be best for him to resign. But before he could put pen to paper, the Cuban army revolted in August 1933, forcing Machado to flee. The dictator's departure resulted in an explosion of revolutionary energy, as Cubans took to the streets in excitement. Citizens young and old, white and black, poor and middle-class celebrated the departure of Machado and hoped for better days to come.

Unfortunately for many Cubans who reeled from crushing repression for years at the hands of Machado and other dictators, big sugar would not go quietly. As brutal as Machado had been, nothing could prepare the Cuban

Cuban dictator Gerardo Machado y Morales meets with US president Calvin Coolidge and other American officials at the Cuban embassy in Washington, DC, on April 22, 1927. The United States supported Machado until 1933, when the Cuban army revolted against him.

people for the bloodshed, the violence, and the sheer terror of what would come next: the reign of Fulgencio Batista y Zalvídar.

After Machado left, Batista emerged as the best hope for stability in Cuba. In fact, to the United States, he appeared to be the only hope. According to US ambassador Sumner Welles, he was the "only individual in Cuba who represented authority."[8] In January 1934, Batista took control over the ineffective President Ramón Grau San Martin. The United States supported Batista's efforts and immediately recognized the new government, abolishing the Platt Amendment to make it look like Batista would stand up to its northern neighbor. Eventually, Batista was elected president in 1940.

Sumner Welles, US undersecretary of
state and former US ambassador to Cuba,
greets Fulgencio Batista when he arrives
in Washington on November 10, 1938.

American officials breathed a massive sigh of relief. Batista seemed to be just the man to right Cuba's course. Possessing African, Spanish, Indian, and Chinese blood, he seemed to be a literal man of the people. For a time under Batista, things seemed to go in the right direction. The onset of World War II increased the worldwide demand for Cuban sugar. Output rose from 2.7 million tons in 1940 to 4.2 million tons by 1944. This injected desperately needed cash into the country's coffers. Batista governed as a social democrat, spending some of that money on social programs designed to help Cubans rebuild their lives after the Depression. He even welcomed communists into his government at a time when the entire world was grappling with the rise of Hitler.[9] But, as always seemed to be the case with Cuba's economy, the relatively stable times were not to last.

Batista's Rule

After World War II and into the early 1950s, Cuba's economy began to sputter once again as European nations increased their sugar production. Batista had left office in 1944 and moved to the United States but could not stay away for long. In 1952, he returned to Cuba and ran for president a second time. When he realized that he did not have the support of the voters, he turned to Cuba's military for help. Together, they denied the will of the Cuban people, canceled the election, and led a successful coup against President Carlos Prio Socarrás. Now Batista was the absolute dictator. And despite its commitment to democracy and free elections, the United States again supported his regime.

In order to maintain power, Batista ruled with an iron fist. Almost immediately after he seized power, he denied Cubans their civil liberties and cracked down on those who dared to protest against big sugar and his corrupt government. Paid off by wealthy

US Army Chief of Staff Malin Craig chats informally with Batista at Arlington Cemetery. Together, they await President Franklin Roosevelt's arrival on Armistice Day, November 11, 1938.

American and Cuban industrialists, Batista acted in their interests, torturing and imprisoning anyone who spoke out against them. While the dictator lounged in his palace, dined on luxurious meals, and viewed American horror films, his secret police rounded up and imprisoned tens of thousands of people.[10]

The dictator used torture, public executions, and other extreme forms of violence to scare Cubans into silence. He censored the media and intimidated reporters. With money and weapons from Washington, Batista murdered from 10,000 to 20,000 people between 1952 and 1959. Meanwhile, the gap between rich and poor continued to grow as Batista helped American mobsters expand their gambling, drug, and prostitution empires.

Major General Craig shows off American weapons to Batista at a war museum in Arlington, Virginia. Batista was fascinated with the many different types of bullets and their capabilities.

Though browbeaten into silence, many Cubans could hardly contain their outrage. Batista had become so brutal, so dangerous, and so unpredictable that the world recoiled with horror. By 1958, such extreme violence prompted the United States to finally withdraw support for the dictator, but the damage had already been done. Arthur M. Schlesinger Jr., who would advise President John Kennedy on foreign policy in the coming years, remarked of the situation, "The corruption of the government, the brutality of the police, the regime's indifference to the needs of the people for education, medical care, housing, for social justice and economic justice is an open invitation to revolution."

That is exactly what happened. Five years earlier, on July 26, 1953, rebels led by twenty-eight-year-old lawyer Fidel Castro mounted a brazen and incredibly dangerous assault on the Moncada Barracks, guarded by Batista's army. The army defeated the rebels, and those who were not imprisoned or killed fled the country. Batista's forces captured Castro and imprisoned him, but he was released two years later. He then fled to Mexico, where he and a band of eighty revolutionaries hatched their plan to take Cuba back from the arms of a madman.

On November 25, 1956, the men, led by Castro and Argentinean freedom fighter Che Guevara, boarded a wooden ship called the *Granma* and cast off from the Mexican coastline. While in Mexico, they had developed detailed plans for the overthrow of Batista. Now it was time to put their plan into action. The men pointed the *Granma* east toward Cuba.

After they traversed the Gulf of Mexico, the *Granma* ran aground in a remote region of the island. The revolutionaries got off the damaged ship one by one and waded through chest-deep water until they reached a marsh,

A hand-painted mural of Che Guevara in Havana, Cuba.

where sharp, unforgiving bushes cut into them like hundreds of needles. They were not alone. All of a sudden, Batista's army ambushed them. Bullets rained down as Castro's men fled in all directions. A bullet ripped through Guevara's neck. He fell to the ground in agony. Later, he recalled, "I immediately began to wonder what would be the best way to die, now that all seemed lost."[11]

The ambush killed all but a dozen of the revolutionaries. Castro, Guevara, and Castro's brother Raúl—wounded, parched, and utterly exhausted—barely made it into the dense jungles of the Sierra Maestra mountain range. There, they regrouped and recuperated. They had made it this far. They couldn't let their comrades die in vain. They decided to go ahead with the plan they had hatched in Mexico. In a matter of time, their actions would reverberate across the globe and set the stage for one of the most dire conflicts in world history.

Rebel with a Cause[1]

On a balmy evening in December 1957, an overweight twenty-nine-year-old American named William Alexander Morgan disembarked from a ship in Havana's harbor. Suitcase in hand, he emerged into the bustling streets of the capital city, illuminated by the bright lights of the nightclubs, hotels, and casinos. Dressed in a $250 white suit and a brand-new pair of shoes, Morgan later recalled, "I looked like a real fat-cat tourist."

Though dressed like a wealthy American businessman, William didn't travel to Cuba to dance the night away at the Sans Souci or get sauced on Cuba Libres at Sloppy Joe's. He had grander ideas in mind. William walked furtively along the Paseo, past the Plaza Hotel, where Milton Hershey had stayed many years before, along a deserted wharf, and into the back streets of Old Havana, toward the secret meeting place. He could hardly contain his excitement.

William stopped next to a phone booth. There, he waited in silence for his Cuban contact, Roger Rodríguez. The two had met in Miami years before. Rodríguez was a revolutionary who had encountered Batista's wrath. He had been shot by police during a political protest, further inflaming his opposition to the dictatorship.

Out of the darkness, the mustached Cuban approached William. Both men smiled and embraced. It had been too long! Together, the two strolled through the darkened streets, speaking in low voices about the dangerous adventure William was about to embark upon.

William told Roger that he had read about Batista's ambush of Castro and the revolutionaries in the *New York Times*. The article described Castro as a man with "strong ideas of liberty, democracy, social justice, [and] the need to restore the Constitution." William admired Castro's devotion to his country. He wanted to join him and the others in the effort to wrest Cuba from Batista's paws. But why would an American want to fight and risk his life in a Cuban revolution?

William told Roger that he had a very good reason. To convince Roger that he should help him, William made up a story that one of his good friends had traveled to Cuba years earlier. After he was caught smuggling guns to rebels, Batista's men hunted him down, captured him, "tortured [him] and tossed [him] to the sharks." William told Roger that he was in Cuba to avenge his friend's death. He then told Roger of his plan: He would leave Havana, travel hundreds of miles across Cuba, then steal away into the Sierra Maestra to rendezvous with Castro and his men. He told Roger that he had already made contact with another rebel who would lead him into the rugged mountains.

Roger's face turned white with fear. He knew the rebel William was talking about. He was an agent for one of Batista's death squads. William would almost certainly be arrested and killed. No, Roger could not let that happen to his comrade. He told William that he would lead him as far as the Escambray Mountains to a group of anti-Batista radicals who would hopefully take him the rest of the way.

The two men hired a driver and made their way southeast out of

Havana toward Cienfuegos. They agreed that if anyone asked, William was an American coffee magnate on his way to look at plantations. Sure enough, not long after they began driving, they came upon an army roadblock. An armed soldier approached the car. The men's hearts began to race. What if this guy didn't believe their story? The soldier came close to the window. He slipped his sunglasses down his nose so he could get a better view of the inside of the car. His steely eyes stopped on William. Where was this nattily dressed American headed? The soldier asked his question out loud. Roger recited William's cover story. Warily, the soldier backed away from the car. He bought it! Whew. The men breathed a sigh of relief, then put the car in gear and zoomed away into the Cuban backcountry.

The men continued to the village of Banao, where they met up with a campesino, a local farmer, who led them into the Escambray forests. The campesino thrashed at thick vegetation with his machete as they plunged farther and farther into the remote wilderness. It was a grinding hike. Finally, they reached an open area. The campesino cupped his hands to his mouth, then let out a distinct birdcall. It echoed across the steep ravines. The men heard another similar call in return. Suddenly, a guard slipped out of the unforgiving jungle and led William and Roger to a clearing. Guns and water jugs littered the ground. About thirty men, parched and almost malnourished, were strewn about on hammocks that had been strung between the shady banana trees. They had arrived in a rebel camp.

The rebels eyed William with uncertainty. Who was this American who had descended upon their secret hideout? Was he an agent of the CIA, there to infiltrate their movement? The CIA had been known to send spies disguised as journalists into rebel territory. Was William one of them?

William came before the group's leader, twenty-three-year-old Eloy Gutiérrez Menoyo. He told Menoyo how much he hated Batista and how much he desired to get back at the dictator for killing his friend. He imparted that he had served in the US Army, knew martial arts, and could disarm opponents with his bare hands. In fact, William was such a good warrior that he would be able to train Menoyo's rebels, many of whom had never participated in guerrilla warfare before.

Menoyo was still skeptical. William sensed his hesitation. He would have to prove himself. The American rebel, still dressed in his business suit, asked for a knife. He grabbed it by its handle, then flung it toward a tree some sixty feet away. Bull's-eye! It hit the tree square and embedded itself in the textured bark. The men were taken aback by William's feat. Still, they did not fully trust him, and the American outsider would have to prove himself over and over again as the rebels did everything in their power to get rid of him.

Every day, the rebels led William up, down, and across the unforgiving mountainous terrain. They pushed him until he fell to the ground in hunger and utter exhaustion. They marched him through poisonous bushes that stung like swarms of bees, causing his face and chest to swell up in red, painful blotches. It was so painful that William lay awake all night long, squirming in agony.

William soldiered on. He kept a good spirit regardless of the trials the men put him through. He lost thirty-five pounds in very short order and grew a thick, mangy beard. One rebel later remarked, "The gringo was tough, and the armed men of the Escambray came to admire his persistence."

One day, as the rebels marched along a ridgeline, one of them eyed 200 soldiers loyal to Batista. This could become the catastrophe that they had feared since the beginning of their campaign. They were grossly outnumbered and at risk of being massacred.

The rebels began to panic. William, who had gained Menoyo's admiration for his fighting skills and his perseverance, devised a plan. He told the rebels to arrange themselves in a semicircle behind a set of massive rocks. Hearts pounding, they crouched down and clutched their rifles with white-knuckled anticipation.

The troops came closer and closer. The rebels waited in determined silence. Finally, when it seemed like Batista's men were about to literally stumble on the rocks the rebels were hiding behind, Menoyo gave the command to open fire. The forest exploded into gunfire. William lunged out from his hiding place, trained like a laser on his enemies. While others retreated, the American stayed put, determined to beat back the invaders and save the lives of his newfound comrades.

It worked. The soldiers, facing a barrage of gunfire from all sides, began to run away. One rebel, Armando Fleites, recalled, "They folded. . . . It was a complete victory."

From that point on, the rebels regarded William with great esteem. He finally earned the trust of the group, which called itself the Second National Front of the Escambray. He eventually learned Spanish, then took an oath to "fight and defend with my life this little piece of free territory," to "guard all the war secrets," and to "denounce traitors." The American boy, who had grown up in the Midwest, who had gone to Catholic school, and who had been a top Boy Scout, had succeeded in becoming part of Fidel Castro's revolution.

William had always been a misfit and a dreamer. He was also deeply insecure about himself. Though he received high grades, he did not like school. The *New Yorker* described his childhood:

> [He] often slipped away to read stories of adventure, especially tales about King Arthur and the Knights of the Round Table, filling his mind with places far more exotic than the neighborhood of cropped lawns and boxy houses outside his bedroom window. His mother once said that [William] had a "very, very vivid imagination," and that he had brought his fancies to life, constructing, among other things, a "diving helmet" worthy of Jules Verne. He rarely showed "fear of anything," and once had to be stopped from jumping off the roof with a homemade parachute.

By age fifteen, William had grown tired of life in the suburbs. A fire burned within him to escape the confines of his boring neighborhood and his insular high school, to strike out into the world in search of meaning and adventure. One night, while his parents slept, William tiptoed downstairs and stole his dad's car keys. He opened the door, careful to turn the handle slowly in order not to make noise. Soon he was in the driver's seat, zooming through the streets of Toledo, Ohio. When the police caught him, he ended up at a juvenile detention center, but he escaped from there as well. After a feverish search, his dad found him in Chicago, caring for elephants and eating fire in the Ringling Brothers circus.

He went home with his dad, but he didn't stay there for long. He dropped out of school in ninth grade and traveled across the country, seeking adventure and freedom. To move around, he freeloaded on buses and boats. To keep himself alive, he took odd jobs bagging groceries, herding cattle, shoveling coal, and ushering movie patrons to their seats. He ran errands for the Mafia, joined the army, and got stationed in Japan in 1946. He deserted his post in 1947 and received a five-year jail sentence for it in 1948. He got out two years later in 1950, then worked on and off again for the Mafia until 1955. His parents were upset about William's decisions, but his dad came around to understanding. He wrote William, "Get as much adventure as you can and we will be glad to see you whenever you decide you want to come home."

By the summer of 1958, William had seen more adventure, and more horror, than his parents could have possibly imagined. Deep in the Cuban jungles, he and the Escambray rebels had fought off Batista's troops many times. The battles were intense. William remembered, "We were always outnumbered at least thirty to one. . . . We were a small outfit, but we were mobile and hard-hitting. We became known as the phantoms of the mountains." Sometimes, they looked on in disbelief as Batista's army destroyed and torched villages, executed people at point-blank range, and, in one case, cut an old man's tongue out. These horrors further reinforced William's resolve to fight. He couldn't sit idly by while human beings did such horrific things to other human beings.

Though fighting against a regime backed by the American government, William was proud that he was born in the United States and admired many of the ideals that his country supposedly stood for. The rebels of Escambray wanted to replace Batista's dictatorship with American-style democracy. They were also fiercely anti-communist. In fact, at the time, Fidel Castro himself declared, "I have never been, nor am I now, a Communist. If I were, I would have sufficient courage to proclaim it." Of his purpose, William declared:

> I am here because I believe that the most important thing for free men to do is to protect the freedom of others. I am here so that my son when he is grown will not have to fight or die in a land not his own, because one man or group of men try to take his liberty from him [sic] I am here because I believe that free men should take up arms and stand together and fight and destroy the groups and force that want to take the rights of people away [sic]

¡Cuba Libre!

As the Escambray rebels fought, the revolution in other parts of the country was taking shape in earnest. In October, Che Guevara and a band of 100 soldiers arrived on the mountainside. Together with William and his comrades, they prepared to descend from the mountains into the foothills and cities. Che and William were at each other's throats the whole time. The very serious, intellectual, and morose Che, steeped in the teachings of Karl Marx, butted heads with the affable, anti-communist American. Nevertheless, for the time being, they had a common enemy and recognized that they would have to work together to take Batista down.

In December, the Escambray rebels and Che's forces decided it was time to take their fight toward the capital. By then, they had become a tight unit, a well-oiled, battle-tested machine. More than 1,000 men strong, they marched out of the Sierra Maestra into the Santa Clara province and beat back Batista's troops. The battle was a turning point. Shortly thereafter, the rebels occupied the village of Manicaragua. Next came El Hoyo. Then La Moza. Then San Juan de los Years. While Che, William, and the rest of their army drew closer to Havana from the southeast, Fidel Castro launched a major offensive from the west. His brother Raúl and his soldiers approached from the north. They had Batista and his army surrounded. Finally, as Che and William reached Topes de Collantes, a mere 160 miles from the capital, one of Batista's officers declared urgently, "Headquarters can't resist anymore. The Army doesn't want to fight."

It was January 1, 1959. In Havana, CIA agent David Atlee Phillips swigged champagne in celebration of the New Year. He heard a sound and looked up into the dark, star-studded sky. One of those stars seemed to be blinking and moving. It was moving away from the city, out over the open ocean toward the Dominican Republic. Phillips put down his champagne glass and picked up the phone. He called his superior, who gave him the astounding news: "Batista just flew into exile."

The next day, Cubans found out that Batista, the man who had wreaked havoc on their country for so long, had been literally forced out of the country. They flooded the streets in joyous pandemonium. They torched the office of the government newspaper, raided casinos, ransacked the ticket offices of international airlines, and looted American banks. Then they lowered the flag of Batista's army and set it aflame.[2] Rebels occupied Havana. So used to fighting, they commandeered cars and trucks and drove toward the center of town, ready at a moment's notice to be fired upon. But no fire came. Instead, throngs of jubilant Cubans jammed the streets. Smoking cigars and swilling dark rum, the Castro brothers, the rebels, and their admirers reveled in their victory. The revolution had been successful. Cuba basked in the dawn of a new day.

Eleven days later, in a field overlooking Cuba's beautiful San Juan valley, Raúl Castro and a battalion of rebel forces lined up hundreds of Batista's former soldiers shoulder to shoulder. The rebels tied their hands behind their backs and told them to step down into a predug trench. Then they opened fire with machine guns. The men, many of whom were still teenagers, had joined Batista's army simply because they were dirt poor and needed to survive. To Raúl, it didn't matter. They were the enemy. Raúl gunned them down as a warning to others who might choose to speak out against the new government.[3] The executions proved that the Castro brothers, though they sought a more equal society for all Cubans, would use violence and intimidation when necessary to achieve their goals.

Secret Army

The revolution took the Eisenhower administration by surprise. Almost immediately, the CIA began spying on Fidel and Raúl Castro. It even came up with a code name for Fidel: AMTHUG. The Americans knew that Raúl had been a communist for a long time. When he was eighteen years old, he joined the Communist Youth Movement, traveling behind the Iron Curtain to Romania and Czechoslovakia. He was also friendly with certain influential Soviets. While in Eastern Europe, he met Nikolai Leonov, a Soviet diplomat. The two got along famously. Their relationship would endure for many years.

The CIA was paranoid and on edge. Would Fidel follow in the footsteps of his brother and embrace communism as the official form of government? That would mean a communist country, hostile to the United States, only ninety miles from Florida. As close as Guatemala was, this was closer. Over time, the CIA became more and more convinced that Fidel, who had

Soviet premier Nikita Khrushchev and Cuban president Fidel Castro elbow their way through a crowd, 1960.

assumed the Cuban presidency, was a threat. Even though Fidel kept saying that he was opposed to communism and that he would hold free and fair elections within a year and a half, the United States did not believe him.

The CIA, fresh off victorious secret wars in Iran and Guatemala, believed that if it became necessary, it could easily get rid of Castro, as it had Arbenz and Mossadegh, and replace him with another leader friendly to the United States. After all, the United States had been able to control Cuba so easily for sixty years. This should be a piece of cake. But how would the United States be able to turn the Cuban people, who were so enthusiastic about their victory over Batista, against Che and the Castro brothers?

Strange Things

The evening of August 26, 1960, was hot and humid in south Florida. In Homestead, sixteen-year-old John Keogh ran around his family's chicken farm, hopelessly trying to corral a flock of rogue chickens that had broken through a fence. The chickens ran in all directions, and John, desperately trying to capture them, called on a bunch of his friends to help. They chased down the free-range birds, but they couldn't hold them long enough to round them up. After giving it a valiant try, the kids got bored and abandoned their efforts. They hopped in John's pickup truck and headed to a local general store to buy sodas and talk about girls. On the way, one of the boys told a spectacular story about strange things he had seen at a nearby camp of migrant farmworkers. John remembered that his friend told them that at the camp, late into the night, the workers "danced around [campfires] and acted weird." The boys decided that they wanted to see for themselves. They downed their sodas, paid the shopkeeper, then sped off into the fields.

The boys arrived at the camp. They peered over the fence. Their friend was right. Something strange was up on the other side. They decided to get the workers' attention. One of the boys had brought with him a stash of firecrackers. He lit them one by one and hurled them over the fence as the others smiled in mischievous delight. The farmworkers turned toward them. John immediately thought to himself, *These are not your average immigrant farmworkers.* Everything after that was a blur. The workers opened fire with machine guns, spraying bullets in every direction. John and his friends turned around and darted back toward the pickup. They jumped in and attempted to drive away, but not before one of the bullets pierced the back window of the truck, striking John in the head and permanently blinding him.

When the cops arrived, they asked the workers exactly what they were doing there. Given how well they were armed, it was clear they weren't just thrashing sugarcane. They were certainly up to something else. To the surprise of the police, the men explained to them that they were Cubans who had been forced to flee from their homeland after the revolution. In Homestead, they were being trained to invade Cuba and overthrow Castro. As outlandish as the story was, the cops didn't care. The men had shot at a sixteen-year-old kid, taking away his eyesight. The cops arrested fifteen of them and charged two with attempted murder.

Cuban exiles gather to demonstrate against Fidel Castro in Washington, DC.

Even though the men had been charged with such serious crimes, their trials did not begin on time. In fact, they did not begin at all. After a brief period in captivity, the police quietly released all of the men. Curious about why accused criminals would suddenly go free without trials, a reporter for the *Miami Herald* named David Kraslow began asking questions. He found out that the US State Department had asked for the men to be released and the cases against them thrown out.

Why in the world would the State Department let these Cuban exiles off the hook for such serious crimes? Kraslow dug deeper, determined to get to the bottom of the story. He found out that the men were being trained by the CIA as part of a larger plot to invade Cuba and overthrow Castro. Ever since the revolution, the CIA had secretly recruited Cuban soldiers, students, and workers who were furious at Castro for disrupting their lives, ruining their careers, killing their friends, or forcing them out of their homeland. Before the revolution, some of them had been employed as middle-class workers for American companies in Cuba. Now they found themselves in a foreign country with little more than the shirts on their backs. They had lost their homes, their livelihoods, and many of their possessions. Castro had forced the companies they worked for to either stop operating in the country or come under the control of the Cuban government. If owners did not obey Castro's order, they faced persecution or even death.

Kraslow couldn't believe what he was learning. The CIA was trying to wage a secret war against Cuba! The agency was training Cubans to fight so it would look to the world like a civil war, not a war the United States was instigating. It would have looked horrible in the world's newspapers if it became known that the United States, a huge superpower, was drawing up plans to invade its tiny neighbor. The CIA knew better. Kraslow furiously wrote up the article and submitted it to his editors for approval.

His editors read the article and reacted with caution. They were very skeptical about publishing a story that was so critical of the federal government. In those days, newspapers most often reported exactly what the government wanted them to report, especially as it pertained to military matters. Now they were reading a story that described a secret military mission to illegally invade a foreign country. This was explosive. Finally, after many discussions, they decided that Kraslow should contact the Eisenhower administration for more information.

Stranger Than Fiction

Kraslow traveled to the capital. He went from office to office. Everyone he spoke with denied knowing anything about the Cubans. Nobody would acknowledge that there was anything out of the ordinary going on. Finally, Kraslow got ahold of Allen Dulles, the director of the CIA, whom many magazines referred to admiringly as "America's Master Spy."

Kraslow was determined to get a straight answer from the master spy. He rode the elevator up to Dulles's office, then sat impatiently in the waiting room. Finally, Dulles called him in. Kraslow breathlessly shared his story. He asked the director if he would confirm that it was true. Dulles's bright blue eyes focused on him expressionless through circular, thin-framed glasses. He took a few puffs from his pipe. He stroked his mustache methodically with his thumb and forefinger, perhaps mildly amused by Kraslow's request.

If this reporter only knew that training Cuban exiles was just the tip of the iceberg. In addition to plans for invasion, the CIA had dreamed up other outlandish schemes to mess with Castro. Just five months earlier, Dulles had recommended to Vice President Nixon that the United States poison Castro's food with a drug to make Cubans think he was crazy. The agency also thought about sprinkling powder into his shoes, causing all of the hair on his body to fall out, including his iconic beard.

The plans read like the plot of a James Bond novel. That was no coincidence, given how much Dulles loved the spy series. The CIA director spoke publicly about how fascinated he was with James Bond spy tools, including "one device . . . a special kind of homing radio outfit which Bond installed in cars his opponents were using and which permitted him, with the appropriate radar type of gadget, to follow the hostile car and home in on it from his own car even at many miles' distance."[4] Dulles actually tried to persuade CIA employees to make such a gadget, but it never really caught on.

When Kraslow pressed him further, Dulles finally sat up in his chair. He tapped his pipe against the side of a glass ashtray. His eyes opened wide as he looked the earnest reporter square in the eye. He warned Kraslow ominously, "If you publish that kind of information, you'll seriously damage national security."

Flabbergasted, Kraslow left Washington and flew home to Miami. When he got there, his editors told him that they intended to obey Dulles. The *Herald* buried the story.[5] Americans would be left in the dark about their government's secret war plan. Kraslow knew that it was unconstitutional for the CIA to wage war without Americans' consent. Still, he had no choice but to comply if he wanted to keep his job. Little did he know that six months later, the truth would come out in ways literally explosive.

PART FIVE

Dangerous Moments

19

Jack Kennedy

On September 26, 1960, exactly one month after John Keogh lost his eyesight in Homestead, the young, charismatic, and handsome John F. Kennedy splayed out on a chaise lounge on the roof of a Chicago hotel. The senator from Massachusetts gazed eastward over Lake Michigan as warm winds gently pushed a set of giant sun umbrellas to and fro. He momentarily lost focus, but he was jolted back to reality by his friend and speechwriter Ted Sorenson, who was lounging next to him. It was time to get back to work. Tonight would be a huge night.

Between the two men, on a small glass table, sat a tall pile of note cards. Kennedy, who most people referred to as Jack, sat up slowly, slathered on another layer of suntan lotion, then focused his gaze on his friend, who stared back at him intensely through a pair of horn-rimmed glasses. The two had been at it for hours, and the routine was familiar. Ted read questions off of the cards. Jack answered them. As they went back and forth, Jack's answers got better and better. If Ted didn't like them, he suggested ways that Jack could improve. Ted challenged Jack with unexpected curveball

Newlyweds John F. Kennedy and his bride, Jackie Bouvier Kennedy, beam as they cut their wedding cake, September 12, 1953.

questions, and Jack responded deftly. Finally, the two men decided that Jack was ready. Or at least as ready as he would ever be. Jack went downstairs to his room to take a nap. When Ted came in later to wake him up, his friend was fast asleep with the note cards strewn across the bed.[1]

Before September 26, not many Americans knew much about John F. Kennedy. Some knew that at forty-three years old, he was quite young to be running for president. Others knew that if he won, he would be the first Catholic in the White House. A handful knew that he was married to the very attractive and worldly Jacqueline, who was pregnant with their second child.

When the Going Gets Tough, the Tough Get Going

Though Jack appeared youthful and strong, many different illnesses plagued him throughout his life. As a very young child, he suffered from measles, chicken pox, and whooping cough. Just before he turned three years old, he came down with a terrible case of scarlet fever, which had been known to kill many young children in the early 1920s. He recovered, but he was always suffering from one malady or another from birth until death.[2]

Growing up, Jack went with his family each summer to Hyannis Port on Cape Cod. His father, Joseph Kennedy Sr., was an investor on Wall Street and had become very rich by buying stock and real estate. Jack, therefore,

The Kennedy family poses for a photograph on the beach in Hyannis Port, Massachusetts. From left to right: Robert Kennedy, John F. Kennedy, Eunice Kennedy, Jean Kennedy (on lap of) Joseph P. Kennedy Sr., Rose Fitzgerald Kennedy (behind) Patricia Kennedy, Kathleen Kennedy, Joseph P. Kennedy Jr. (behind) Rosemary Kennedy. The dog in front is Buddy.

lived the life of privilege, and nowhere was that more visible than on the compound of their summer home. There, he and his siblings swam, sailed, played football, and sunned themselves on the back lawn. Their father wanted his children to be tough and encouraged them to compete with one another. He wanted the boys in particular to win the sports they played, always telling them, "When the going gets tough, the tough get going." Jack took those words to heart.

At the boarding school he attended in Connecticut, Jack was very popular and well liked by his peers. He was a voracious reader, devouring book after book. He was always interested in world affairs. Unlike any of his friends, Jack maintained a subscription to the *New York Times*, which he read every day. His headmaster recalled that Jack had a "clever, individualist mind" but that he was not the greatest student. Jack worked hard only in the subjects he found to be the most interesting: history and English.

When he graduated high school, he went to Harvard University, where he played football. He wasn't the best player, but he could hold his own against opponents. Like Paul Robeson, he was incredibly determined and gave it his all on the football field. One afternoon, Jack thundered downfield. With all of his might, he tackled one of his opponents with the force of an ox, knocking him to the ground. As Jack hit the ground himself, he felt a snap in his back, followed by unbearable pain. He had blown a disk in his spine. Even after extensive medical treatment, he never really healed from the injury. He faced back problems for the rest of his life.

PT-109

After college, Jack enlisted in the US Navy. He was stationed in the South Pacific during World War II, where he commanded *PT-109*, a patrol torpedo boat. On August 1, 1943, while scanning the sea for Japanese ships, one of his crew members called frantically to the deck. A destroyer was headed right for them, coming fast. Jack was at the wheel. He turned hard to try to avoid the attack, but the maneuver came too late. The huge Japanese ship slammed into *PT-109*, slicing it in two. Two men were killed instantly.

The remaining crew members, including Jack, jumped from the deck as the entire boat exploded into flame. Jack flew against the front of the ship, his back slamming into the steering column. He tried to find his way to the door of the ship, or at least to an opening from which he could escape. Suddenly, he heard a cry for help coming from the direction of a piece of the wreckage. One of the crew, Patrick McMahon, had been terribly burned by the fire and was struggling to keep his head above water. Jack, himself writhing in pain, grabbed his shipmate from behind with both arms and towed him across the water to another piece of the boat. Shipwrecked and bobbing up and down in the cold Pacific Ocean, the remaining crew members waited all night in the pitch black until sunrise.

The next morning, Jack, who had also been a member of Harvard's swim team, tied McMahon to a belt, bit down on the loose end of it, and towed him by mouth toward a distant island. Behind them swam the other crew members, who themselves were towing others who couldn't swim. Exhausted beyond imagination, the men finally reached the beach, where Jack collapsed in a heap. There they stayed for two days with very little food and water.

Jack, fearing that he and his men would die on the island, convinced them to get back in the water later that day in search of another island where they might find food. He again tied McMahon to the belt. They swam and swam until an island appeared in the distance. Filled with hope but taxed with exhaustion, they swam feverishly toward it. When they felt sand beneath them, they straggled out of the water. They had somehow done it again.

After resting up for a little while, the men went off in search of something, anything to eat. The search was desperate, but all of a sudden, one of the men

Lieutenant John F. Kennedy (shirtless, at right) stands with the crew members of PT-109, 1943.

cried out in joy. Behind a tree and amid thick brush, he had miraculously found a box of Japanese candies, along with a container of freshwater and a small canoe. Relieved, the men tucked into the candy and shared the water among them. They remained there for three more days, rationing their supplies and hoping for rescue.

Each day, Jack went out in search of anyone who might be able to relay a distress signal. He knew how dangerous his explorations could be. What if he crossed paths with Japanese patrols? What if hostile islanders spotted him? He knew that he had to take the risk. On August 6, Jack and George Ross stumbled upon two islanders willing to help. Amazingly, the islanders had been patrolling the entire chain of islands by canoe and knew the location of the rest of their American crew! Jack's heart pounded with excitement. He carved a message into a coconut shell, then asked the islanders to take it to the other Americans. Late on the evening of August 7, boats came to the rescue of the *PT-109* crew. Jack and his crew members reached safety very early the next morning.[3]

For his bravery and his leadership, Jack received the Navy and Marine Corps Medal, along with a Purple Heart. After the war, he went on to run for Congress in Massachusetts in 1946 and won. Jack served for three consecutive two-year terms in the House of Representatives before winning election to the Senate in 1952.[4]

Missile Gap

Though an undisputed war hero, Jack did not display the same courage in Congress that he did in the Pacific. He supported politicians, including Richard Nixon, who launched attacks against people they said were communists. He avoided criticizing Joseph McCarthy for his attacks on the Hollywood Ten and missed the December 1954 Senate vote to rebuke the Wisconsin senator. His brother Robert actually served on McCarthy's staff.

In 1957, Jack wrote a Pulitzer Prize–winning book called *Profiles in Courage*, which told the stories of eight courageous senators throughout history who did what they felt was right in the face of great pressure. After it was published, Eleanor Roosevelt said of Jack that she wished he had "a little less profile and a little more courage." He tried to win Eleanor's support, along with the support of other liberals in the Democratic Party, but never fully gained their trust.

As a senator, Kennedy scared Americans into thinking that the Soviets had many more missiles than the United States. He warned that very soon, the Soviet advantage would create "a peril more deadly than any wartime danger we have ever known." Some of his advisers had warned him hysterically that the Soviet Union would have 2,000 ICBMs by 1963. Those advisers recommended that the United States build and station 600 ICBMs in 1959 and place 240 IRBMs (intermediate range ballistic missiles) in Europe. The idea that the United States lagged far behind the Soviet Union in the number of missiles the countries possessed became known as the "missile gap."

Even Eisenhower thought that Kennedy's comments were ridiculous and inappropriate. He knew that the United States had far more missiles than the Soviet Union. His administration had been spying on the Soviet Union for years with U-2 surveillance planes. None of those missions proved that the Soviet Union possessed even one missile. Regardless, Kennedy regularly used the missile gap to his advantage in his political campaigns, betting that people would vote for him if he appeared tougher than his opponents. His run for the Oval Office was no exception.

Cold Warrior

After he awoke from his nap in his Chicago hotel room that beautiful September day in 1960, Jack took one more trip up to the hotel roof to breathe in the fresh evening air. Then he went back downstairs, piled up his note cards,

"Kennedy for President"
campaign pamphlet, 1960.

dressed himself in a black suit and dark tie, and descended to the lobby. After waiting for a few minutes, he got into a car and headed over to the television studio to meet his opponent, Vice President Richard Nixon. Anticipation filled the air. Pressure on both candidates was intense. This would be the first presidential debate ever to air on television. Seventy-four million Americans would tune in to watch the vice president duke it out with the young, idealistic senator from Massachusetts.[5]

The two candidates shook hands, then took their seats on the darkened stage. CBS journalist Howard K. Smith, the debate's moderator, sat at a wood-paneled desk between them. The room was hushed. Cameramen positioned themselves. Smith leafed through his questions once more and cleared his throat. The candidates steeled themselves.

Lights flooded the studio as televisions flickered on across the nation. Nixon, pasty and underweight from a recent hospital stay, couldn't shake his sick appearance. He sat awkwardly on the left side of the stage, his back rigid in an uncomfortable pose. His light-colored suit further washed out his already-pale face. Sweat beaded on his chin.

On the other side of the stage, Kennedy sat poised, confident, and self-assured. He bounded to the podium and launched into his introductory statement, cameras focused on his youthful, handsome, distinguished face and his perfectly combed hair. Unlike his opponent, he displayed vim and vigor, beckoning Americans to look forward into the future, not backward into the past. He was the candidate of change, representing the hopes and dreams of all who had come of age during a very frightening time.

This debate, the first in a set of four, was supposed to deal with issues at home, like health care, education, taxation, and debt. However, both candidates were clearly focused on communism and the Soviet Union. Tensions were higher than they had ever been before. Earlier in the year, the Soviet

Kennedy and Nixon debate on the CBS set of WBBM-TV in Chicago, September 26, 1960.

Candidates Richard M. Nixon and John F. Kennedy pause for a photo after one of their presidential debates in 1960.

Union had shot down an American spy plane and took prisoner its pilot, Francis Gary Powers. The Soviets had known that the United States was spying on them for years.

First, Eisenhower had ignored Khrushchev's appeal for peace after Sputnik. Then, the Soviet Union found out that the United States had plans to increase military spending by billions of dollars. Now, it became clear to the entire world that the United States was actually invading Soviet airspace to take photos of their power plants, their cities, and their military bases. It looked to many in the Soviet Union like the United States was making plans to invade.

Onstage in Chicago, Kennedy framed the conflict as one of freedom versus slavery. He blasted the Eisenhower administration for not doing enough about the Soviet threat. He promised Americans that he would be tougher on communism than even the fire-breathing Nixon had been. In his opening statement, Kennedy went beyond the missile gap. He warned Americans that the Soviet Union was graduating "twice as many scientists and engineers" as the United States, and he ominously predicted that the Soviets would be able to produce more energy than the United States by 1975.

Kennedy also blasted the Eisenhower administration for not doing enough to grow the economy and warned that economic weakness would cause the United States to fall behind the Soviets.[6] Privately, Kennedy didn't think the Soviet Union would actually attack the United States, but he wouldn't take any chances. He promised that, when elected, he would spend much more money on defense than Eisenhower had.

To Americans watching at home, this was the first time they had heard a Democrat speak so forcefully against the Soviet Union. They were used to Adlai Stevenson, Henry Wallace, and others from the New Deal era urging cooperation and peaceful competition. Now, Kennedy represented a new generation of Cold War Democrats who seemed to be out-toughing the Republicans. After fifteen years of rising tension with the Soviet Union, both parties were now parties of war.

Richard Nixon was perplexed. How was it possible that Kennedy could convince Americans that he was tougher on communism? After all, Nixon had built his career on attacking suspected communists at home. He strongly supported Eisenhower's decision not to respond to Khrushchev's appeal for peace, and he was vice president during the secret wars in Guatemala and Iran. Now this young son of a rich Wall Street banker dared to call him weak?

Kennedy Wins

During the debate series, Kennedy brought up Cuba again and again. He called on the United States and the rest of the world to support "freedom fighters" in their effort to beat back Castro's strengthening government.

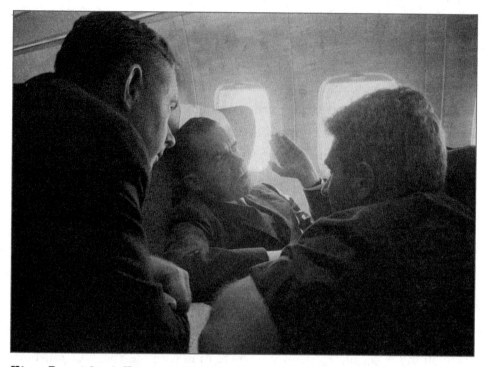

Vice President Nixon talks to the press on the way to the Soviet Union, August 5, 1959.

In the final debate, Kennedy pledged that, if elected, he would support Cuba's liberation and intervene to crush Castro if necessary. He warned that Cuba was just the tip of the iceberg—that Castro's success would cause communists in Mexico, Panama, Bolivia, and Colombia to become more powerful.[7] He attacked Nixon and the Eisenhower administration for doing nothing while a communist country rose up just ninety miles from American shores.[8]

Nixon recoiled in shock. Nothing?! If that guy across the stage only knew! At that very moment, the Eisenhower administration was, in fact, planning to secretly invade Cuba! As David Kraslow had found out one month earlier, the CIA under Eisenhower and Nixon was training Cuban exiles in Florida and parts of Central America to wage war against Castro. The vice president was tongue-tied. He couldn't say anything about the secret plan. How would he handle Kennedy's attack without mentioning it? He decided that he would denounce Kennedy's ideas for intervention in Cuba as "dangerously irresponsible."[9] This made Nixon seem weaker on Cuba than his younger opponent. Nixon later reflected, "Kennedy conveyed the image—to 60 million people—that he was tougher on Castro and Communism than I was."[10]

On Election Day, Kennedy squeaked by Nixon by one of the thinnest popular-vote margins in American history, beating the vice president by just over 100,000 votes. His strategy of hammering Nixon for being weak on communism worked. Shortly thereafter, Kennedy was inaugurated to great fanfare as the thirty-fifth president of the United States. At his inauguration, eighty-six-year-old Robert Frost became the first poet ever to participate in a presidential inauguration. Marian Anderson, the talented African-American singer whom the Daughters of the American Revolution had once barred from Constitution Hall because of her race, sang the national anthem. Then Kennedy delivered a ringing inaugural address. Though he ran his campaign as a strong cold warrior, he extended an olive branch to the Soviets in hopes of rebuilding trust and friendship. He welcomed the fact that his generation had been granted the opportunity to "defend freedom in its hour of maximum danger" and would "pay any price, bear any burden, [and] meet any hardship" in order to do so.

Kennedy and his beautiful young family moved into the White House amid a blanket of fresh snow in January 1961. The new president surrounded himself with intelligent, high-achieving, hopeful advisers who became known as "the best and the brightest." Though they were smart, most of them were also arrogant and ignorant about the complicated world. Products of the Cold War, they saw the world only in black-and-white—communist versus anti-communist. Their minds were churning about how to handle the Cuba situation. By the time Kennedy took office, Castro had taken control over the property of American oil companies like Esso and Texaco. The United States

Surrounded by a huge crowd, John F. Kennedy is inaugurated as the thirty-fifth president of the United States on January 20, 1961. He is the first Catholic to take the oath of office.

responded by reducing the amount of sugar it bought from Cuba. Castro, in turn, began to sell more sugar to the Soviet Union. The Soviet Union and China began sending arms to Cuba. Cold War storm clouds were forming rapidly just ninety miles south of Florida's coast.

One thing was very clear to the young president: After convincing Americans how tough he would be on communism, Kennedy would have to live up to his new reputation as a cold warrior. He talked the talk in his campaign. Now he would need to walk the walk.

20

Bay of Pigs[1]

What would President Kennedy do about Cuba? Would he carry out the invasion plans that were hatched under Eisenhower? Or would he back down? By the time Kennedy took office, it was clear that Cuba's relationship with the United States was getting worse. Fidel Castro was becoming closer and closer with the Soviet Union.

Seventeen days into his term, the president asked his national security adviser, McGeorge Bundy, for advice. Bundy told him that the CIA was enthusiastic about invading Cuba and that the agency was training troops in Guatemala to storm Cuban beaches. If the invasion did not go according to plan, the United States might risk its reputation in the world. If it got out that the United States had trained Cuban exiles to start a civil war, the Soviet Union might throw more support to Cuba. The Soviets might even send Castro nuclear weapons.

Bundy was smart and rational. He warned the president that an "invasion adventure" could be disastrous. Others, including Secretary of State Dean Rusk, Chester Bowles, Arthur Schlesinger

Jr., and Richard Goodwin, also had major problems with the plan. Senate Foreign Relations Committee chair J. William Fulbright urged Kennedy to forget about it. Schlesinger warned that even if the invasion went well, the rest of the world would find out that the United States was behind it. This could cause huge protests and a major backlash against the United States throughout the rest of Latin America. It might also make Kennedy look like the monstrous leader of a large nation invading its much smaller neighbor that was fighting for its independence. In other words, it would have the exact opposite result they were looking for.

Kennedy listened to his advisers. He valued their opinions and trusted their judgments. Perhaps they were right. Maybe the invasion wasn't worth the risk to his reputation and the reputation of the United States.

The CIA had other ideas. By 1961, the agency had spent many months planning the invasion. The agency was convinced that the United States needed to take Castro out immediately. Otherwise, it was almost certain that Cuba would become a strong communist nation, allied with the Soviet Union. That could inspire countries throughout Latin America to become communist too. Like dominoes, they might fall one after another. The Cold War would move closer and closer to US soil until, finally, the United States might itself fall to the Soviet Union.

The CIA strongly warned Kennedy that if he didn't act soon, Castro would quickly become too strong to remove. The exiles were in place, ready to fight. They had devoted their lives to the cause. If the new president decided not to invade, he might look like a spineless hypocrite. Even worse, if Kennedy didn't invade and Castro became more and more powerful, the American people would never forgive their president for not invading when he had the chance. Robert Kennedy later remarked, "If he hadn't gone ahead with it, everybody would have said it showed that he had no courage."

Finally, over strong protests from Schlesinger, Kennedy agreed to go ahead with the invasion—on three conditions. The first was that the invasion needed to take place in an isolated part of Cuba, so as not to arouse Castro's suspicion. The second was that the CIA needed to promise that Cubans on the island would definitely join the exiles in a revolt against Castro. The third was that the United States could never appear to be involved at any stage of the operation.

The CIA replied that the invasion would indeed take place in an isolated spot, Bahía de Cochinos, or Bay of Pigs. They reassured Kennedy that Cubans across the country would join the revolt against Castro. It would be a slam dunk. They also agreed that if something went wrong, the United States would not send in planes and helicopters to rescue the exiles. To do so would confirm to the world that the invasion was, in fact, an American invasion.

What Kennedy didn't understand, and what the CIA didn't tell him, was that by moving the invasion to an isolated part of the island, the revolt would have trouble spreading to the rest of the population. After all, if the rest of the population didn't know what was going on, how could they possibly join the exiles in revolt? Still, the CIA was so convinced that the invasion would be successful, it pushed ahead with its flawed plan.

Steeling for Battle

On April 15, 1961, fourteen hundred men sailed across the Caribbean Sea on six ships. A strong sun glinted off the starboard side and off the faces of the Cuban exiles on deck, eager to get their revenge on Castro and other rebels who had turned their homeland upside down. The CIA had leased four of the ships from the García Line, a freight company owned by Cubans who also hated Castro. Two other ships belonged to the CIA.

The men played cards, joked, and talked with anticipation about the mission they were about to embark upon. Most of the men chain-smoked anxiously, unsure about what was going to happen to them when they arrived at Bahía de Cochinos. The majority of them had never fought before. Some were doctors, lawyers, and students who couldn't have imagined going to war against their own country just two years before. Now they found themselves on the front lines of the Cold War. They believed that if something went wrong when they hit the beaches, American planes would be there to take out Castro's troops and save them.

When the sun went down that night, the men tried to sleep, but to no avail. Conditions aboard ship didn't help much. There was very little food besides crackers, stale bread, and cold sausage. No cooking could be done for fear that flame might ignite the thousands of pounds of fuel sloshing around just below the deck. To make matters worse, there were no bathrooms or even buckets. To relieve themselves, men had to walk out on a plank over the open ocean, take down their pants, and hope that they didn't lose balance, lest they fall straight down into shark-infested waters.

At 6:00 p.m. on April 16, the exiles emerged from their quarters and gathered somberly on deck. Pepe San Román, the group's military commander, and Manuel Artime, the man who would become Cuba's leader once Castro was removed from power, gave an emotional speech about how important their mission would be. They were about to free Cuba from Castro's grasp! The men ran the Cuban flag up the flagpole and saluted their leaders, more determined than ever to prevail. They sang the Cuban national anthem and prayed with all their might. They double-checked to make sure all their gear was packed in their backpacks. Hunting knives? Check. Ponchos? Check. Sun visors? Check. They brandished their M1 Garand semiautomatic rifles and secured .45-caliber pistols on their hips. They put on their green-and-brown camouflage uniforms and steeled themselves for battle.

The Invasion Begins

The Bay of Pigs was calm and quiet just after midnight on April 17. Gentle waves lapped up against the rock-studded sandy beaches. Had there been a moon that night, it would have glinted off the waves, ever so slightly illuminating the six ships quickly approaching the mouth of the bay. However, with no moon to light the water, very few could have detected the boats from shore. With engines at low throttle, four of the boats turned toward Playa Giron. The others turned into the bay and headed due north toward the tiny village of Playa Larga.

Three of the boats halted about a mile from Giron. If they went any farther, they risked tearing holes in their hulls. Five men, dressed in wet suits and swim fins, descended from one of the ships and eased themselves onto a small powerboat. They were outfitted with machine guns, ammunition, and other survival equipment, and their faces were blackened with grease. The powerboat shuttled them closer to shore, where they transferred to a small raft that would take them the rest of the way.

The men could finally see the shore. Strangely, bright floodlights illuminated the sand, and the sound of tropical music echoed out over the bay. Beneath a grove of palm trees sat a group of construction workers who, after a long day working to build a new resort hotel, sat drinking and socializing. The workers did not yet see the invaders.

The exiles held their breath. This wasn't supposed to happen. The CIA had promised them that the beach would be deserted. Now they were in a position they hadn't anticipated. What would happen once they landed? Would the workers alert the Cuban militia? As they contemplated the danger they were sailing into, their raft ground to an abrupt halt against deposits of hard coral. This would be terrible news for the many hundreds of men who would follow them onto the beach later that night.

The men tried to navigate their raft around the coral but kept getting caught up on it. Suddenly, out of the corner of his eye, one of the men noticed a military jeep speeding over the sand. It turned toward the bay, illuminating the men with its blinding headlights. Inside the jeep were two Cuban soldiers. They figured that the invaders were fishermen who had gotten caught up on the coral and decided to head toward them to warn them about the danger. The invaders froze. This was what they had feared the most. Here they were, face-to-face with Cuban soldiers before they'd even landed on the beach. Petrified, they reached for their guns.

Pop! Pop! Pop! Pop! Pop! The exiles opened fire, raining bullets on the jeep like a hailstorm. Almost immediately, the lights on land went out, plunging the entire beach into darkness. Under fire, the soldiers turned the jeep around and gunned it away from the bay, back along the beach toward the village to alert others about the invasion. The exiles frantically radioed their comrades offshore, telling them to sail in close. They were going to need backup, *now!*

As they waited for help to arrive, dozens of Cubans emerged from the village of Giron, leaped aboard trucks, and thundered toward the bay. Trapped between the coral and the beach, the exiles opened fire once again. This time, the Cubans returned fire in earnest, and the entire beunach lit up with their shots. Finally, one of the ships maneuvered close enough to fire its huge guns toward Giron. The ferocity of the attack forced the Cubans to jump back into their trucks and retreat. But the word was out. Cuba was under attack.

21

Disaster at Playa Giron

Little did the exiles know, but Castro had been tipped off that an attack was going to take place. He had found out that Americans were training Cuban exiles in Guatemala and that they were being recruited in Miami. A couple of months earlier, the Cuban leader ordered tens of thousands of men to stand at the ready. He stationed guards all along the southern coast and prepared them for an invasion from the sea. The CIA had lost the element of surprise.

At Giron, exile commanders sailed the rest of the ships close to shore, but the coral hampered their progress and ripped holes in their boats. Everything that could go wrong did go wrong. The men were forced to jump into the water and wade through the spiny coral with all of their heavy equipment. Boats sank left and right. Those that remained afloat had engine problems because they had been fueled with the wrong ratio of oil to gas. On one boat, the engine hadn't been properly fastened, causing it to fall off. Finally, the invaders were down to only eight landing boats. Each boat could hold only ten people. With 400 men still waiting to land, the operation dragged on for hours.

As the exiles struggled through the coral-laced water toward Playa Giron, chaos reigned 1,000 miles away in Washington. CIA deputy director Charles Cabell heard about the failing invasion. He jumped out of bed, threw on whatever clothes he could find, grabbed his keys, and ran out the door. He needed to talk to President Kennedy immediately. If the United States just left the exiles on the beach to die, the invasion would fail and it would make everyone look terrible. The exiles who survived would blame the United States for promising to protect them, only to withdraw support when they needed it the most. Many of them would be captured, tortured, or killed. The only way to save the invasion would be for American planes to swoop in and provide air cover so the exiles could make it back to their ships. Otherwise, Castro's planes would bomb the ships and overwhelm the beaches, making it impossible for them to escape. Time was of the essence. Tens of thousands of Cuban militiamen were now scrambling toward the southern coast.

Cabell gripped his steering wheel tightly as he raced toward the Sheraton-Park Hotel, where Secretary of State Dean Rusk was monitoring the operation. It was 4:15 in the morning.

Cabell screeched to a halt outside the hotel, went up to Rusk's room, and pounded on the door, probably louder than he should have. Rusk answered in his bathrobe. Cabell laid it on the line for the secretary of state. Barely able to contain the emotion in his voice, he pleaded with Rusk to protect the ships. The two men went back and forth until, finally, at 5:00, Rusk agreed to call Kennedy so Cabell could share his concerns with the president. Cabell implored Kennedy to send in planes. He told the president that the invasion could fail without them.

Kennedy couldn't believe what he was hearing. The CIA had promised him that American planes and ships were not going to be involved. The United States could never appear to be behind the invasion. That was the deal. Now, under an intense amount of pressure, Kennedy had to make a decision. Would he send in planes to save the exiles and risk the world finding out that the United States was invading the tiny country to its south? Or would he stick to his guns and let the exiles fight it out so the United States could deny being involved? If he sent in planes, what would happen if the Soviet Union found out? Would the Soviets respond by attacking West Berlin . . . or even the United States?

For all of his tough talk about the Soviet Union, Kennedy did not want to risk a wider war. After listening to Cabell's impassioned plea, the president asked him to put Rusk back on the phone. Kennedy had made his decision. American planes and ships would not rescue the exiles. Cabell recoiled in stunned silence. He knew that from that moment on, the entire invasion was doomed.

Sea Fury

Four hours after Cabell left Rusk's hotel room, Cuban airman Enrique Carreras angled his jet, the *Sea Fury*, over the Bay of Pigs. Fully fueled and armed with heavy ammunition, he flew toward the *Río Escondido*, one of the ships belonging to the exiles. The ship was crucial to the success of the mission. It contained fuel, ammunition, explosives, food, and radios necessary to communicate with the CIA. The men on the deck started shouting, "*Sea Fury! Sea Fury!*"

Out of the glare of the sun thundered Carreras's gleaming jet, descending rapidly toward them. Carreras opened fire. Bullets pelted down on the ship as men jumped overboard from the bow and stern. All of a sudden, one of the bullets penetrated the ship's hull and ignited the thousands of pounds of fuel in the hold. The ship exploded into a massive fireball, propelling scattered fragments skyward. An incredible boom echoed across the bay as dust and smoke rose high into the air, bellowing out in a massive cloud.

Precisely as Cabell had warned, the exiles did not stand a chance without American planes. Fearing that they were about to get blown up, the crew on board two of the other ships turned their vessels around and began steaming out to sea, leaving their men to fend for themselves on the beaches. The men, sleep-deprived and hungry, fought valiantly all day, clinging to the hope that American planes would come to their rescue.

At 12:30 a.m. on April 18, Máximo Cruz, one of the exile commanders, spotted Cuban tanks coming toward his battalion. He immediately instructed his men to fire. They bombarded the tanks with everything they had, including bazookas, mortars, and smaller weapons. Fire darted across the dark beach. The tanks kept on coming. The exiles kept fighting, knowing that they were outgunned and probably going to die. The tanks pressed forward, crushing the bodies of those already injured and dead. The battle waged for hours and hours.

One of the exiles, Gilberto Hernández, stormed out from behind the brush and bounded toward one of the tanks. In his hands he held a single rifle. He began firing at the hulking machine. Though the bullets did not actually break through the tank's fortified shell, the Cubans inside surrendered out of fear.

Gilberto's feat was so courageous that his comrades started calling him El Barberito, "The Cruel One." After forcing the crew of the tank to surrender, El Barberito charged another one. This time, he wasn't so lucky. The tank's gunner trained his sights on the brave exile and shot him dead. Shortly thereafter, Máximo Cruz died too after his arm was shredded with shrapnel. This episode became known as the Battle of the Rotunda. Though the exiles were able to force the Cubans to retreat, it would be their last victory. As ships exploded in the bay and others turned out to sea, hopes quickly faded that the exiles would ever make it back to safety.

As the Battle of the Rotunda raged, Kennedy, Vice President Lyndon Johnson, Secretary of Defense Robert McNamara, and Dean Rusk huddled together in the White House with General Lyman Lemnitzer, the chair of the Joint Chiefs; Navy Chief Admiral Arleigh Burke; and the CIA's chief of clandestine services, Richard Bissell. Burke and Bissell spent three hours trying to persuade Kennedy yet again to send in air support and ground troops. They fully expected that the young, inexperienced Kennedy would cave in to their pressure. Kennedy said, "They were sure I'd give in to them and send the go-ahead order." Lemnitzer bullied the president, saying that his failure to rescue the exiles was like "pulling out the rug" from underneath them, that it was "absolutely reprehensible, almost criminal." But Kennedy stood strong. As he explained to an old friend, "We're not going to plunge into an irresponsible action just because a fanatical fringe in this country puts so-called national pride above national reason."

A Kick in the Teeth

The invasion was an utter failure. When all was said and done, victorious Cubans captured 1,189 exiles and killed 114. Even though Kennedy had not sent in American ships and planes, it became clear to the entire world that the CIA was behind the invasion. After thoroughly defeating the exiles, Castro declared triumphantly that his forces had beaten back the United States and defeated the "imperialists." In a rousing speech in Havana, he blasted Kennedy and declared independence from American companies, along with all other foreign powers. He had shown the world that his little island nation could stand toe-to-toe with a superpower, stare it right in the eye, and defeat it.

Castro became a hero across the communist world. Among his own people, he was seen as almost godlike for defeating the United States. He announced that Cuba was now a "socialist regime," one that was not a threat to Americans, but rather a beacon of hope and equality for all Cubans. Castro addressed Americans directly: "What threatens [your] security is the aggressive policy of the warmongers of the United States. What threatens the security of the North American family and people is the violence, that aggressive policy, that policy that ignores the sovereignty and the rights of other peoples."[1] If Americans hadn't fully realized it before, they knew it now: The botched invasion had pushed Cuba further down the road toward communist dictatorship.

On April 20, Americans woke up to the news that the American-backed invasion had failed. The front page of the *Detroit News* screamed, INVASION CRUSHED. The *San Francisco Chronicle* declared, CASTRO REPORTS EXILES WIPED OUT. The *Chicago Tribune* reported starkly, "The main results of the supposed Cuban 'invasion' are that the Castro dictatorship is more firmly installed than ever, the communists have made hay all over the world, and the United States has taken a dreadful kick in the teeth." The *Wall Street Journal* lamented that "the U.S. finds itself in a sorry mess. . . . This country is reviled around the world. . . . But we suspect that the deeper feeling, especially in [communist countries], is one of astonishment at U.S. weakness."

Cuban exiles after their capture in the Bay of Pigs. These were some of the lucky ones. In the botched invasion, 114 men were killed and 1,189 were captured.

The world was shocked. Other countries simply couldn't believe that the United States had made such a terrible mistake. Kennedy was shocked too. He couldn't believe that the CIA had broken its promises. The agency had told him that the Cuban invasion would go just as easily as Guatemala and Iran before it. Instead, Kennedy faced a new, terrible reality. Castro was becoming more and more powerful every day. The Soviet Union was buying Cuba's sugar and providing the small country with enormously powerful weapons.

So upset at the CIA for lying to him, Kennedy vowed to destroy the agency. He threatened to "shatter the CIA into a thousand pieces, and scatter it to the winds." The young president was beginning to understand what Eisenhower had warned the country about in his farewell address. If he let the military and the CIA get away with everything they wanted, the results could be disastrous. He fired Allen Dulles. He fired Richard Bissell. He forced other important CIA and military officers to resign. Then he made plans to cut the CIA budget by 20 percent by 1966. The CIA had burned him once. Kennedy would not allow the agency to do it again.

Killing Castro

Even though the Bay of Pigs invasion failed, Kennedy still wanted to get rid of Castro. In fact, the invasion made the president more determined than ever. His brother Robert explained in January 1962 that overthrowing Castro was "the top priority of the United States government." The Kennedys approved Operation Mongoose, a CIA terror campaign designed to turn Cubans against their government. The objective was to wreck the Cuban economy and assassinate Castro. Kennedy put Edward Lansdale in charge. Lansdale was an expert in sabotage. He recruited 600 CIA officers in south Florida and nearly 5,000 CIA contractors to help.

Castro was one of the most protected people on the planet. How would the CIA be able to get rid of him? The team considered blowing up Cuban factories and burning sugar plantations to the ground to make it impossible for Cubans to make a living. This could, in turn, cause Castro's own people to rise up against him and kill him. If that didn't work, perhaps they could plant explosives in the cigars Castro liked to smoke or taint them with fatal poison?[2] Castro enjoyed scuba diving. Maybe they could replace the air in his tank with some sort of chemical or biological agent? Or perhaps they could embed a bomb in a seashell on the ocean floor that would explode when Castro swam near it?[3] They would have to choose a brightly colored one to pique the dictator's interest while underwater. Or how about infecting Castro's wet suit with a fungus that would cause him to contract a nasty skin disease?

The CIA even recruited one of Castro's girlfriends to poison him with pills. She hid them in a jar of facial cream. When Castro fell asleep, she tried to take the pills out of the jar but discovered that they had melted.

The CIA also tried to blow Castro up while he was giving a speech in Panama. They placed 200 pounds of explosive beneath the lectern that he was about to speak from. Castro's men discovered the explosives just before they were timed to detonate.[4] All in all, the CIA developed hundreds of plans to assassinate the Cuban dictator. None of them were ever successful.

If assassination proved too difficult, perhaps another invasion would work better. The trick would be to convince Americans to support military action. That would not be such an easy feat after the Bay of Pigs disaster. The CIA would have to persuade them that a war was really necessary. But how?

New Ideas

Brigadier General William Craig, Operation Mongoose's program officer, had an idea. The United States was about to launch a rocket to orbit the planet Mercury. If that flight failed, maybe they could blame Cuba for interfering with it. This could convince Americans to rally their support for another invasion of Cuba.

What else could they try? They might have to take more drastic steps. Another idea, code-named Operation Northwoods, was to blow up an American ship and make it look like Castro had done it. After all, the explosion of the USS *Maine* sixty-four years earlier had outraged Americans and convinced them to declare war on Spain in Cuba then. Why couldn't the same thing work again? Perhaps the CIA could stage the fake hijacking of an American commercial jet and blame it on Castro. Maybe it could even stage the shoot-down of an American plane full of vacationing college students and make it look like the Cuban air force was responsible. That would be certain to outrage Americans. How about exploding bombs around Guantanamo Bay to make it look like Castro was attacking an American military base? CIA contractors or Cuban exiles could blow up aircraft on the base, lob bombs, incite riots, and sabotage ships, then blame it all on the Cubans.

While the CIA was dreaming up ways to convince Americans to support another invasion, the US military was already rehearsing it. In April 1962, 40,000 US troops engaged in a two-week exercise that simulated an invasion of Cuba. Two smaller exercises followed in May. In October, the United States announced Operation Ortsac, a large exercise including a mock invasion by 7,500 marines of another Caribbean island. Once the mock invasion took place, the objective was to overthrow the island's government. The message was clear: "Ortsac" was "Castro" spelled backward.

Berlin

After the Bay of Pigs invasion, the mood darkened around the world. Castro understood that the United States would stop at nothing to crush the revolution in his country. Khrushchev couldn't believe that Kennedy would allow himself to be so fooled by the CIA and the military. The Soviet premier sensed weakness and saw an opening. He blasted the young president for trying to deny the will of the Cuban people. Then he doubled down on his demand that the United States, Great Britain, and France withdraw from West Berlin.

Since the end of World War II, Berlin had been a divided city inside Soviet-controlled East Germany. Though entirely within East Germany, Berlin's western part was still controlled by the United States, Great Britain, and France. The Soviets controlled the city's eastern part. The problem for the Soviet Union was that as the Western powers rebuilt after World War II, West Germany became a hub for new jobs and technology while East Germany lagged behind. This caused 2.8 million refugees from the east to flee west between the late 1940s and 1961.

Most of the refugees exited East Germany through Berlin. Though communist guards tried to prevent them from crossing the border into West Berlin, they couldn't stem the tide. Many East Berliners had passes to cross over to the west for school and work. About 60,000 people did so each day. Many of them never returned. By 1961, the population of West Berlin was more than twice that of East Berlin. Meanwhile, East Berlin languished in poverty and joblessness.

Khrushchev was certainly worried about the flight of refugees from East Berlin to West Berlin. What worried him more, though, was that East Germany seemed to be getting weaker and weaker. Doctors, engineers, lawyers, teachers, and artists were leaving every day for the west. What would happen if East Germany became so weak that it dissolved into the hands of the Western powers? Would Germany eventually be able to get its own nuclear weapons, then point them at the Soviet Union?

Khrushchev had good reason to worry. Germany had invaded Russia twice already in the twentieth century. The Soviet premier was determined not to have it happen again. He explained to an American journalist, "We have seen how quickly governments in Germany can change and how easy it is for Germany to become an instrument of mass murder. . . . We have a saying here: 'Give a German a gun; sooner or later he will point it at the Russians.' . . . We fear the ability of Germany to start a world atomic war. . . . How many times do you have to be burned before you respect fire?"

A Very Cold Winter

In June 1961, Kennedy met with Khrushchev in Vienna. The Soviet premier was in a sour mood. After the Bay of Pigs, he had very little respect or patience for the American president. He demanded that all of Berlin fall under the control of East Germany. Kennedy said no, responding, "I see it's going to be a very cold winter." He simply couldn't allow the Soviet Union to control West Berlin.

The two men butted heads. Kennedy knew that in order to defend Berlin, he would have to consider using nuclear weapons. The scenario went like this: If the Soviet Union attacked West Berlin, the United States and its allies would retaliate. The Soviet Union might respond by launching nuclear weapons on European or American cities. If the Soviets launched first, would the United States be able to respond before possibly millions of Americans were killed? This was too big a risk.

The military decided that in such a situation, the United States should have the upper hand. They drew up a plan. Within twenty-four hours of the beginning of any war, the United States would launch nuclear weapons first to destroy Soviet missile bases, government offices, and industrial cities. The goal was maximum destruction.

The Joint Chiefs of Staff estimated that if such a war were to occur, 325 million people might be killed in the Soviet Union and Asia, another 100 million in Eastern Europe, a similar number in Western Europe from fallout, and up to another 100 million from fallout in bordering countries including Finland, Sweden, Austria, Afghanistan, Pakistan, and Japan. Those figures did not include deaths that would be caused by Soviet nuclear weapons. Nor did they consider that a war of this scale would almost certainly trigger nuclear winter, raising the possibility of extinction.

Kennedy knew that he couldn't risk nuclear war with the Soviet Union. He also knew that he couldn't just allow the Soviets to invade West Berlin. So what could he do?

The two leaders left Vienna without an agreement. Kennedy called the meeting the "roughest thing in [his] life." The stage was now set for one of the tensest summers of the Cold War. Dean Acheson, former secretary of state who was now one of Kennedy's advisers and who had helped prepare him for the Vienna meeting, told the president that he should not compromise

Woman in fallout shelter.

with Khrushchev at all. He felt that nuclear war was worth risking. If the Soviet Union or its allies confronted US troops in Berlin, the United States was ready to launch an all-out nuclear attack. In September, General Lyman Lemnitzer shared with Kennedy the military's plans for a full-scale attack against the Soviet Union.

Nuclear war? Is that what this conflict could really come to? Millions of people killed across the world over the one city of Berlin? Couldn't human beings solve complicated problems without resorting to mass death and destruction? These thoughts all coursed through President Kennedy's head. The thought of pushing the button, of making the decision to kill thousands or hundreds of thousands of people deeply disturbed him. After such an attack, those Americans who survived would have to remain in fallout shelters for at least two weeks. Probably much longer. The weight of the Cold War now sat firmly on his shoulders. He turned to Secretary of State Rusk and, in utter disgust, remarked, "And we call ourselves the human race."

Even though Kennedy balked at the idea of nuclear war over Berlin, he actually made the crisis worse by antagonizing the Soviet Union. On July 25, he addressed the nation:

> The immediate threat to free men is in West Berlin. But that isolated outpost is not an isolated problem. The threat is world-wide. . . . We do not want to fight—but we have fought before. And others in earlier times have made the same dangerous mistake of assuming that the West was too selfish and too soft to be divided. . . . The source of world trouble and tension is Moscow, not Berlin. And if war begins, it will have begun in Moscow, not Berlin.

A Wall Is a Hell of a Lot Better Than a War

Kennedy's speech pushed the Soviet Union and the United States closer to confrontation. Even though the idea of nuclear war nauseated him, he didn't want to seem weak to the Soviets. The Bay of Pigs incident had sent Khrushchev a message that Kennedy would cower in the face of strength. No, he would have to be strong. The president announced that the United States would spend an additional $3.45 billion on weapons. He also told Americans that he might have to draft them into service if it became necessary to fight the Soviets. The army would have to expand by 25 percent, and fallout shelters would need to be built across the country to prepare for nuclear war. He warned Americans that nuclear war with the Soviets "could rain more devastation in several hours than has been wrought in all the wars of human history." He sent strong signals to the Soviet Union that the United States was willing to risk war over Berlin.

On August 13, 1961, East German troops began building barbed-wire fences and roadblocks to stop East Germans from escaping to the west. Construction workers soon replaced the barbed wire with concrete. The barrier became known as the Berlin Wall. Kennedy sent 1,500 troops by road from West Germany to West Berlin, where they were met by Vice President Lyndon Johnson. The world teetered nervously on the brink of nuclear war. Would the United States, Britain, and France retaliate? If they did, could the world survive? The world waited breathlessly.

That night, at the Pentagon, eighteen-year-old James Carroll waited to pick up his father, Joseph Carroll, the director of the newly created Defense Intelligence Agency. His dad emerged from the hulking structure, spotted his son, and walked slowly toward the idling car. In an unsettled, somber mood, he opened the door and got in. He lit up a cigarette, then looked his son in the eye. In his powerful memoir *An American Requiem: God, My Father, and the War That Came Between Us*, James recalled one of the scariest conversations of his life:

> [Dad] is smoking, flicking ashes out the window. He has said nothing. Finally crushes the cigarette in the dashboard ashtray and turns to me. "Son, I want to say something to you. I'm only going to say it once, and I don't want you asking me any questions. Okay? You read the papers. You know what's going on. Berlin . . . I may not come home one of these nights. I might have to go somewhere else. The whole Air Staff would go. If that happens, I'm going to depend on you to take my place with Mom and the boys." "What do you mean?" "Mom will know. But you should know too. I'll want you to get everybody in the car. I'll want you to drive south. Get on Route One. Head to Richmond. Go past it. Go as far as you can before you stop." He didn't say anything else . . . neither did I. We must have driven the rest of the way

home in silence. I do remember very distinctly . . . what I felt . . .
fear. . . . Despite all the talk of war, I had believed that my father
and the others like him . . . would protect us from it. Now I saw
that Dad himself no longer thought they could. I felt my father's
fear, which until then I'd thought impossible. I began to be afraid
that night and I stayed afraid for many years, first of what our
enemy would do, later of what we would do.

Luckily for James and the rest of the world, the construction of the Berlin
Wall defused the immediate danger. Kennedy could have responded with
force, but he chose not to retaliate for the wall's construction. West Berlin
would remain out of Soviet hands, but the wall now prevented people from
leaving East Germany. The city was literally divided, and it stayed that way
until 1989. Sighing with relief, the president told his aides, "It's not a very
nice solution, but a wall is a hell of a lot better than a war." He continued,
"This is the end of the Berlin crisis. The other side panicked—not we. . . . It's
all over, they're not going to overrun Berlin."[1]

Kennedy had learned a lot in a very short period of time. It was important to be firm in these conflicts. However, it was also important to stay cool
and not to react impulsively. He was realizing quickly that in the nuclear age,
one false move could lead to a war more horrific than anyone could imagine.

Gun Thy Neighbor

Like Joseph Carroll and his son, a lot of people were scared by the Berlin crisis. The world was now closer than ever to nuclear war. What would happen
if Soviet bombs actually rained down upon American cities? By 1961, most
Americans realized that the government would not be able to save them.
Some of them decided that they would have to save themselves.

At the time, few people could afford to spend the several thousand dollars it cost to build fallout shelters in their homes. Nobel Prize–winning UCLA nuclear expert Willard Libby came up with a solution. To much fanfare, he built a shelter at his Bel Air, California, home for $30. He lectured, "If your life is worth $30, then you can afford a fallout shelter such as this." Libby dug a five-foot-wide, five-foot-deep, seven-foot-long hole in the side of a hill. He lined the sides, top, and entrance with 100 dirt-filled burlap bags. He made the roof from sixteen eight-foot-long railroad ties. Unfortunately for Libby, a fire swept through the Santa Monica Mountains in February 1961, destroying his home. His wife had time to save only two items: Libby's Nobel Prize and her mink coat.

But what about the fallout shelter? Did it survive the fire? Sadly, the *Washington Post* reported that it had been utterly destroyed. After all of Libby's speeches about how fallout shelters could save lives in a nuclear attack, his own couldn't even survive a forest fire! Physicist Leo Szilard commented that this "proves not only that there is a God but that he has a sense of humor."

Americans began talking more and more about what life would actually be like after Soviet bombers attacked. What would happen in major American cities like New York, Chicago, and Los Angeles? Everyone knew that there were no large public fallout shelters. This made Americans wonder if they really should have their own. Despite Libby's contention that shelters cost only $30 to build, the reality was that they cost much more than that. Not everyone would be able to afford one.

If the bombs fell, would people who had shelters allow others to share them? In August 1961, *Time* magazine published an article titled "Gun Thy Neighbor," which quoted one Chicago suburbanite as saying, "When I get my shelter finished, I'm going to mount a machine gun at the hatch to keep the neighbors out if the bomb falls. I'm deadly serious about this. If the stupid American public will not do what they have to do to save themselves, I'm not going to run the risk of not being able to use the shelter I've taken the trouble to provide to save my own family."

A model home fallout shelter designed by the US Office of
Civil and Defense Mobilization. The 1961 Berlin crisis infused
the fallout shelter debate with a new sense of urgency.

At public meetings, neighbors with shelters told next-door neighbors
and best friends that they would shoot them if necessary. Clergy weighed in
on both sides of the issue. Reverend L. C. McHugh wrote in the Jesuit magazine *America*: "Think twice before you rashly give your family shelter space to
friends and neighbors or to the passing stranger . . . others try[ing] to break
in . . . may be . . . repelled with whatever means will effectively deter their
assault. . . . Does prudence also dictate that you have some 'protective devices'
in your survival kit, e.g. a revolver for breaking up traffic jams at your shelter
door? That's for you to decide, in the light of your personal circumstances."

The Right Reverend Angus Dun, the Episcopal bishop of Washington, DC, thought that the every-family-for-itself approach was "immoral, unjust and contrary to the national interest." He observed that the kind of person who would be "most desperately needed in a post-attack world is least likely to dig himself a private molehole that has no room for his neighbor."

Many people couldn't believe how the Cold War and the threat of nuclear attack made Americans turn against one another so quickly. *Bulletin of the Atomic Scientists* editor Eugene Rabinowitch called home fallout shelters "pathetic." He couldn't believe Americans were actually talking about killing their friends and neighbors if an attack occurred. One cabaret skit asked why people shouldn't just shoot their neighbors now rather than wait until they tried to break into their shelters. Bob Dylan recorded a song titled "Let Me Die in My Footsteps." The song began, "I will not go down under the ground / 'Cause somebody tells me that death's coming 'round." In perhaps the most creative response, one protester carried an umbrella labeled PORTABLE FALLOUT SHELTER. An arrow pointing to the end opposite the handle read, *For stabbing shelterless neighbors.*

Americans contemplated what steps they would take to move underground and keep their neighbors at bay. Little did they know that their preparations were about to be put to the test once more. The Berlin crisis had brought the world perilously close to nuclear war. But that paled in comparison to what was about to happen.

The Most Dangerous Moment
in Human History

On Saturday, October 13, 1962, an American U-2 spy plane rocketed skyward from Edwards Air Force Base. Moonlight glinted off of the jet's long, slender wings as it turned eastward over the Southern California desert. It was 11:30 p.m. By early the next morning, the plane was sailing fourteen miles over western Cuba, between the capital city of Havana and the municipality of San Cristobal. From that height, the plane's pilot, Richard Heyser, could see the curvature of the earth. But the plane's crew was concerned with another view, that of the lush green countryside directly below them. Suspicious military movements had been reported in the area. Their mission was to observe and take photographs of anything that looked out of the ordinary. Sophisticated cameras snapped away.

A short time later, Heyser and his crew landed at Florida's McCoy Air Force Base. After unstrapping themselves and descending the stairs from the flight deck, the men gave the film to another crew, who flew it on to Washington. When it arrived in the capital, the Naval Photographic Intelligence Center developed the film and examined the photographs. Experts meticulously pored over the images, searching for anything that looked suspicious.

All of a sudden, one of the men gasped. He was looking at a set of medium-range SS-4 Soviet missiles, capable of reaching targets 1,000 miles away. From western Cuba, they could hit targets all across the southern United States, including major cities like Atlanta, Dallas, and New Orleans. They could even make it as far as Washington, DC.

Slightly panicked, the director of the center picked up the phone and began calling offices throughout Washington. He knew that the SS-4 missiles were each capable of carrying one-megaton nuclear warheads. Once they were assembled, they would present a clear danger to the survival of the United States and the entire world. By late afternoon on October 15, phones were ringing off the hooks in government offices across the country. Everyone was trying to figure out if the Soviet Union had just placed missiles in Cuba, a mere ninety miles away from American shores.[1]

Photo taken over Cuba by a US U-2 surveillance plane on October 14, 1962. The photo revealed that the Soviets had placed medium-range ballistic missiles (MRBMs) on the island that were capable of delivering one-megaton warheads to the continental United States. This revelation sparked the Cuban Missile Crisis.

Early the next morning, national security adviser McGeorge Bundy arrived at the White House. He walked briskly toward the front door, his mind burning with the bad news that he had to share with the president. He entered the East Wing and ascended a flight of stairs, where he encountered Kennedy. Bundy spoke first. "Mr. President, there is now hard photographic evidence . . . that the Russians have offensive missiles in Cuba."

Kennedy nodded with grim understanding. He had been worrying about this for a while. The CIA and leading Republicans had warned him that the Soviets would one day put nuclear missiles in Cuba. If they did, Kennedy replied, he would respond swiftly and forcefully. Now, the situation was staring him in the face. It was no longer hypothetical. It was real.

A Bit of Their Own Medicine

Why would the Soviets put missiles in Cuba? The last thing they wanted was war with the United States. They knew that they had only ten ICBMs that could actually reach US soil and only between 300 and 500 nuclear warheads. They stood no chance against the 5,000 nuclear bombs and nearly 2,000 ICBMs and bombers of the United States.

The Soviets feared that if war should break out, the United States would strike them first. They gambled that by placing missiles in Cuba, they could force Americans to think twice about that. At the same time, they could protect Cuba against an American invasion. Hard-liners in Moscow had been pushing Khrushchev to confront the United States with force all along. Khrushchev saw this as an inexpensive way to show them that he was doing something about the American threat to both Cuba and the Soviet Union.

In recent years, the United States had placed its own nuclear missiles in Western Europe and Turkey, which bordered the Soviet Union. Khrushchev explained that by placing missiles in Cuba, he was giving Americans "a little bit of their own medicine." If the United States could threaten the Soviet

Union with missiles so close to its borders, the Soviet Union could too. Khrushchev remarked defiantly, "It's been a long time since you could spank us like a little boy—now we can swat *your* ass."

At the time, Kennedy could not figure out why the Soviet Union would make such a dangerous move. He did not know that American missiles had been placed in Turkey. Incredulously, the president turned to his advisers and remarked, "It's just as if we suddenly began to put a major number of [missiles] in Turkey. Now that'd be goddamn dangerous, I would think." The room fell silent. Nobody said a word. Finally, Bundy replied sheepishly, "Well, we did [that], Mr. President."

General Curtis LeMay.

Kennedy was stunned. He knew that he would have to stop the Soviets before the missiles could be fully assembled. For three days, he huddled with his advisers to figure out what to do. They had to tread carefully. As was the case with the Berlin crisis, one false move could mean catastrophe.

On October 19, Kennedy met with the Joint Chiefs of Staff. The majority of them wanted to bomb Cuba and destroy the missiles. Some even wanted to go to war with the Soviet Union and wipe it out for good. General Curtis LeMay announced to the room, "The Russian bear has always been eager to stick his paw in Latin American waters. Now we've got him in a trap, let's take his leg off right to his testicles. On second thought, let's take off his testicles, too." LeMay told Kennedy that the Soviets would not respond to an attack on the missiles. Kennedy, wary of listening to military command-ers after the Bay of Pigs, replied that he believed the Soviets would have to respond—if not in Cuba, then in Berlin. LeMay would have been fine with that. He believed that it was long past time to get rid of Castro and the Soviet Union in one fell swoop.

Kennedy was shaken by LeMay's comments. Did LeMay know what would happen if the Soviets responded to an attack on Cuba with nuclear weapons? LeMay was famously responsible for burning 150,000 people to death in one night during the firebombing of Tokyo in 1945. It was clear that he didn't have any qualms about killing massive numbers of civilians in order to win a war. After the meeting, Kennedy turned to his aide Kenneth

President Kennedy meets with General Curtis LeMay (fourth from the left) and the pilots who flew reconnaissance missions over Cuba.

O'Donnell. "Can you imagine LeMay saying a thing like that? These brass hats have one advantage in their favor. If we listen to them, and do what they want us to do, none of us will be alive later to tell them that they were wrong."

Quarantined

Many of the chiefs wanted to send in planes to bomb the missile sites, then invade. Some of them who were more cautious knew better. They recommended that Kennedy blockade the seas surrounding Cuba to prevent any more missiles from being delivered to the island. Kennedy agreed with that idea, but he also knew that he had to figure out a way to rid Cuba of the missiles already there. If he didn't, other leaders in Latin America might strike deals with the Soviet Union to place missiles in their countries. And those at home who already saw Kennedy as weak after the Bay of Pigs would never let him hear the end of it. He might even be impeached.

Kennedy made a decision. He would blockade the island with warships. Any boat bound for Cuba would have to turn around and return to its port of call. If any boat tried to break the blockade, it would be fired upon. LeMay and others were furious. They accused Kennedy of being weak for not invading. However, the president knew that invading Cuba would almost certainly result in nuclear war.

Tensions rose for six days. Kennedy knew that he needed to tell the American people about what was going on. On the evening of October 22, he entered the Oval Office to deliver one of the most chilling speeches ever given by an American president. Millions across the country tuned in to watch. The camera trained on Kennedy's sturdy but clearly troubled face. After all the turmoil of the previous year and a half, what could possibly be happening now? Americans waited with uneasy anticipation. Kennedy began: "Good evening, my fellow citizens. This Government, as promised, has maintained the closest surveillance of the Soviet military build-up on the island of Cuba. Within the past week unmistakable evidence has established the fact that a series of offensive missile sites is now in preparation on that imprisoned island. The purposes of these bases can be none other than to provide a nuclear strike capability against the Western Hemisphere."[2]

Kennedy explained that the missiles represented "an explicit threat to the peace and security of all the Americas" and that the United States and the rest of the world could not "tolerate deliberate deception and offensive threats on the part of any nation, large or small." He told Americans about the blockade, which he called a "quarantine." He explained that the military was prepared for war and that war would be justified if the Soviets continued to assemble the missiles. Then he declared ominously, "It shall be the policy of this nation to regard any nuclear missile launched from Cuba against any nation in the Western Hemisphere as an attack by the Soviet Union on the United States, requiring a full retaliatory response upon the Soviet Union."

An attack by the Soviet Union on the United States? Full retaliatory response? This scared many people to death. After years of thinking about nuclear war, reading about nuclear war, and preparing for nuclear war, the president was now telling them that it might really happen. Could this be the end? What might happen if Soviet ships ran the blockade? Would the United States retaliate with nuclear weapons? If the Soviets didn't withdraw the missiles from Cuba, would the United States invade?

Generalized Anxiety

Americans across the country gasped as they contemplated the unthinkable. Panic began to set in. Seven-year-old Marta Maria Darby watched Kennedy's speech with her family. She remembered thinking, "The world is going to end. . . . Where would they strike first? . . . And then the adults . . . started wondering, well, maybe they'll hit New York first. And so I didn't sleep for days.

It was quite frightening." Marta went to school with a group of Cuban students. She recalled talking with them about the crisis: "I think at the time we were afraid that maybe something would happen to us much like the Japanese internment camps during World War II. And there were whispers of that. Maybe they'll take us away and hide us somewhere. And that was a little bit scary."[3]

A young John Tierney remembered going to school the following day, scared that missiles might rain down upon his Denver neighborhood at any moment. "Out on the playground at lunchtime, the macho fifth-grade boys joked about kissing our asses good-

As the Cuban Missile Crisis unfolded, hundreds of women took to the streets near UN headquarters in New York City to demand a peaceful resolution.

bye, but there was genuine anxiety lurking behind our usual bluster." Barbara Barnett, nine years old at the time, reflected, "The thing I remember most was being scared because I kept thinking there was going to be a war and the second thing was we will be blown up." Her teacher told her "that there probably was going to be a war and that the Russians were going to attack us and that we were probably going to be hit because we were near a military base."

Fifth graders at Wadsworth Elementary School outside Atlanta and students across the country passed notes to one another about the crisis. One girl wrote to the boy sitting next to her, *Are you scared?* He wrote back, *No.* The girl responded, *I am.* Another girl in Massachusetts wrote to a friend, *Can you imagine not seeing another Christmas, Thanksgiving, Easter, birthday, dance, or even Halloween? . . . We're just too young to die.* A boy attending boarding school in New England called his father in a panic. "Dad, should I come home?" His dad responded, "Peter, you try hard to do your job well, and I'll try to do my job well. And I think we'll be all right." A seventh-grade teacher in South Dakota made light of the situation: "If the Russians attack during my history test, I'm going to be really upset."

Lou Oschmann, a young naval officer from New Jersey, decided to cut loose during the crisis: "I took the bus to New York City, which probably would have been a major target, too. I just didn't care: I wanted to escape. I went to museums and spent my days in New York City. I went to a couple of bars. I figured that if I'm going to die in a few days, I might as well be doing something I enjoy—and it made me feel better."

Clois Williams, an African-American woman who cleaned the homes of white families in North Carolina, went to work the day after Kennedy's speech. The woman she worked for "had me take her vacuum cleaner downstairs and look in all the cracks and get rid of the spider webs so the basement could be their fallout shelter. And to tell you the truth, that dark basement scared me more than Khrushchev. I thought cleaning out the basement was silly, because if you're scared, what difference does it make if it's clean?"

Shoppers in Los Angeles, Miami, and other cities rushed supermarkets after civil defense directors announced that stores would be closed in the event of war. One woman purchased twenty cases of bottled water. Another bought forty containers of instant coffee, but no water. An employee at Vons grocery store in Los Angeles told reporters, "Calls have been received from all stores, particularly for staples and canned goods, which are going by the case."

Everywhere Sowing Death and Destruction

Across the country, people dumped sugar, chocolate, coffee, water, canned goods, powdered drinks, rifles, handguns, shotguns, and ammunition into their shopping carts. Guns flew off the shelves in Dallas, St. Petersburg, and Richmond. A gun shop owner in Richmond explained that his customers weren't protecting themselves against the Soviets as much as they were protecting themselves against "American city dwellers who might seek shelter in rural areas."

A store in New Orleans sold out of transistor radios. Americans grabbed as many batteries as they could in Houston. Auto parts dealers in South Carolina sold out of tires, and people rushed hardware stores for camping stoves, fans, and portable toilets. New cars disappeared from showroom floors throughout Texas. Depositors across the country withdrew their cash from banks. Patients rushed to pharmacies to fill months' worth of prescriptions.[4] Concerned citizens flooded their local police departments with calls, wondering what they should do when the bombs started falling.

Tensions rose every day. The crisis dragged on for almost two weeks. Students ducked under desks. Civil defense officers drilled and practiced. Cities braced. People prayed. By October 25, Soviet leaders finally decided they would have to remove the missiles. But first, they wanted something from the United States. The Soviets hoped to trade their missiles in Cuba for US missiles in Turkey. Khrushchev appeared ready to strike a deal with Kennedy.

But before Khrushchev could act on that decision, he received word from his advisers that the United States was about to invade Cuba. Determined to avoid nuclear war, he frantically fired off a cable to Kennedy. Secretary of Defense McNamara described it as "the most extraordinary diplomatic message I have ever seen." Khrushchev warned that the United States and the Soviet Union were headed unstoppably toward war; "if war should indeed break out, then it would not be in our power to stop it . . .

war ends when it has rolled through cities and villages, everywhere sowing death and destruction."

In the letter, Khrushchev asked simply for the United States to promise not to invade Cuba. The Soviet leader was frightened. A series of "incidents" had already occurred, any one of which could have triggered the nuclear holocaust that he and Kennedy desperately sought to avoid. A test missile was launched from Vandenburg Air Force Base toward the Marshall Islands. Not having all the information about it, US officials mistakenly reported that Tampa and Minnesota were under attack.

DEFCON 2

On October 24, for the first time in history, the US Air Force's Strategic Air Command declared Defense Condition 2 (DEFCON 2), the highest level of alert before all-out war, and prepared to strike targets in the Soviet Union. General Thomas Power made the decision to go to the brink of nuclear war on his own authority without asking the president. To make matters worse, instead of sending out his order as code, he sent it out in the clear to make sure that the Soviets would read it. Now at DEFCON 2, American bombers flying over 3,000 nuclear weapons around the world prepared to launch. The weapons that the planes carried had the ability to kill hundreds of millions of people.

Three days later, on October 27, the world came to the literal brink of nuclear war. Arthur Schlesinger Jr. described it as "not only the most danger-ous moment of the Cold War. It was the most dangerous moment in human history." A Soviet B-59 submarine breached the American blockade around Cuba. The sub was carrying nuclear weapons. The crew aboard the American ship the USS *Randolph* didn't know that. They began dropping depth charges. Aboard the sub, Soviet signals officer Vadim Orlov described the scene: "The [depth charges] exploded right next to the hull. It felt like you were sitting in a metal barrel, which somebody is constantly blasting with a sledgehammer. The situation was quite unusual, if not to say shocking, for the crew."

The temperature rose sharply, especially in the sub's engine room. The ship went dark. Only emergency lights continued to function. Carbon dioxide filled the air. It became almost impossible to breathe. "One of the duty officers fainted and fell down. Then another one followed, then the third one. . . . They were falling like dominoes. But we were still holding on, trying to escape. We were suffering like this for four hours." Then "the Americans hit us with something stronger. . . . We thought—that's it—the end."

The rest of the crew panicked. Commander Valentin Savitsky tried to reach his comrades at the surface to no avail. They had no way of knowing what was going on above. Savitsky ordered the officer in charge of the nuclear torpedo to prepare it for battle, shouting, "Maybe the war has already started up there, while we are doing somersaults here. We're going to blast them now! We will die, but we will sink them all—we will not disgrace our Navy."

Savitsky turned to the two other officers aboard. One of them, Vasili Arkhipov, did not agree. What if Savitsky was wrong? If he was, and if they launched a nuclear torpedo, they could be responsible for lighting the world on fire.

After an intense argument, Arkhipov managed to calm Savitsky down and persuade him to bring the sub to the surface. By doing so, Commander Arkhipov single-handedly prevented nuclear war. People around the world had no idea just how close they had come to the end.

The Brink of Armageddon

While Arkhipov fought with Savitsky under the sea, the United States received word that a U-2 spy plane had been shot down over Cuba. Another American U-2 plane accidentally entered Soviet airspace protected by Soviet jets with nuclear missiles. Then the Soviets prepared to launch nuclear weapons at the US base at Guantanamo. The crisis had reached a fever pitch.

American military commanders demanded that Kennedy authorize an air strike and invade Cuba. The Soviets began readying the Cuban missiles for launch. Kennedy acknowledged that "time was running out." He could not allow those missiles to become operational. The United States prepared to invade; 250,000 troops were mobilized and ready to go in. The invasion seemed imminent.

In Cuba, Castro urged Khrushchev to launch a nuclear attack against the United States before the United States attacked Cuba. Then Kennedy received another cable from Khrushchev. Unlike the first one, this one was strange, impersonal, aggressive. It demanded that the United States not invade Cuba and that the United States remove all of the missiles from Turkey. Kennedy was stunned. Why had Khrushchev sounded so willing to compromise in his first letter, yet so demanding in his second? Was the second letter written by someone else? Maybe the Soviet military had staged a coup and toppled Khrushchev from power?

Under unimaginable pressure, Kennedy decided to respond to the first letter and ignore the second one. He offered not to invade Cuba. He promised to take the missiles out of Turkey within four to five months, but only if Khrushchev kept the agreement secret. Robert Kennedy met with Soviet ambassador Anatoly Dobrynin and told him the United States was about to attack unless the Soviet Union removed the missiles immediately.

Kennedy waited on pins and needles for a response. He told a friend, "I'd rather my children be red than dead." McNamara went to bed that night thinking that he may not live to see another Saturday night.

They all waited through the night. The hours dragged on. How would Khrushchev respond? Early the next morning, the Soviet premier cabled back. He decided that it was not worth killing hundreds of millions of people or more just to prove he was tough. He announced that the Soviet Union would withdraw the missiles from Cuba.

The United States had come within a hairsbreadth of invading Cuba. Had it done so, Americans would have found out that in addition to the missiles the United States knew about, the Soviet Union had also shipped in 100 battlefield nuclear weapons. Secretary of Defense McNamara didn't find out about that until 1992. When he did, he couldn't believe what he was hearing. He admitted that if the United States had invaded, 100,000 Americans would have died and the United States would have responded by wiping out Cuba. An ensuing nuclear war might have caused hundreds of millions of people to die. Such a war could have very well ended all life on the planet.

Conclusion and Reflections

The world had come to the brink of nuclear annihilation. In the mere seventeen-year span of 1945 to 1962, human beings had developed the capability of destroying the earth many times over. Though people around the world breathed a massive sigh of relief after the Cuban Missile Crisis, their minds raced with deep fear and uncertainty. Just how much longer could anyone survive in such a world?

Shaken by how close the world had come to nuclear holocaust, Khrushchev wrote Kennedy a long letter on October 30, 1962. "Evil has brought some good," he reflected. "The good is that now people have felt more tangibly the breathing of the burning flames of thermonuclear war and have a more clear realization of the threat looming over them if the arms race is not stopped." The Soviet premier invited the United States to join the Soviets in getting rid of "everything in our relations capable of generating a new crisis."

The world could finally reflect on the monstrous nature of the Cold War. In just seventeen years, Henry Wallace's vision of peace and prosperity—his Century of the Common Man—had been replaced by dread of a nuclear World War III. People across the world heaved with anxiety as a culture of war swept over the United States.

That culture was fueled by fear of enemies both at home and abroad. At home, people like Paul Robeson, the Hollywood Ten, and thousands more had their careers and lives destroyed by such hysteria. Abroad, ordinary people in Guatemala, Iran, and other countries suffered because of the actions the US government took to contain communism and counter the Soviet Union. And though this book concentrates specifically on the actions of the United States, the Cold War policies of the Soviet Union caused incalculable suffering and death across Eastern Europe.

Meanwhile, as Americans and the rest of the world contemplated worst-case scenarios, dug fallout shelters, and protested civil defense drills, corporations like Dow Chemical, Lockheed, and Boeing profited handsomely by making weapons of war and selling them to the US government and foreign allies.

Even presidents and other world leaders seemed powerless to stop the madness. The "military-industrial complex" that Eisenhower had warned the nation about in his farewell address had only expanded by 1962. It had gotten so out of control that national "defense" accounted for over 50 percent of all government spending that year. Kennedy, a cold warrior early on, had come to understand that if war was the country's first priority, people worldwide would forever live under its cloud. His attempts to untie the knots of war would put him at odds with those who benefited from its spoils.

Would future generations be able to solve the problems their parents had created, so that their children might live peacefully and prosper in a world free from fear? Many of the children who ducked under their desks in the 1950s became antiwar activists in the 1960s. They protested the military as it got larger, nuclear weapons as they got more destructive, and wars as they continued to spread. They also crafted a blueprint for an alternative future, one that didn't prioritize war over other human needs and pursuits. Their efforts to combat an increasingly belligerent American foreign policy will be the focus of volume 3.

Chapter Notes

Chapter One

1. Paul Boyer, *By the Bomb's Early Light: American Thought and Culture at the Dawn of the Atomic Age* (Chapel Hill: University of North Carolina Press, 1985), 11.

2. Vincze Miklós, "The Terrifying Age of Radioactive Toys for Kids," *Gizmodo*, accessed June 8, 2017, io9.gizmodo .com/the-terrifying-age-of-radioactive-toys-for-kids-1501777693.

3. Allison Meier, "Objects of Intrigue: The Atomic Bomb Toy," *Atlas Obscura*, accessed June 8, 2017, atlasobscura.com/articles/objects-of-intrigue-the-atomic-bomb-toy.

4. Boyer, *By the Bomb's Early Light*, 16.

5. Cover image accessed June 8, 2017, at herseyhiroshima.com/nyk12.jpg.

6. Robert J. Lifton and Greg Mitchell, *Hiroshima in America: A Half Century of Denial* (New York: Avon Books, 1995), 86–87.

7. John Hersey, *Hiroshima* (New York: Alfred A. Knopf, 1946), 3–4.

8. Hersey, *Hiroshima*, 18.

9. Lifton and Mitchell, *Hiroshima in America*, 88.

10. Sadako's story in this section is based on Eleanor Coerr, *Sadako and the Thousand Paper Cranes* (New York: Penguin, 2004).

Chapter Two

1. Material about the Maidens in this chapter is largely based on Norman Cousins, "Hiroshima Maidens," Hibakusha Stories, accessed May 22, 2017, hibakushastories.org/wp-content/uploads/2013/10/Hiroshima-Maidens.pdf.

2. "History of Plastic Surgery," American Society of Plastic Surgeons, accessed May 22, 2017, plasticsurgery.org/news/history-of-plastic-surgery.html.

3. "25 Hiroshima Victims Land in US," *New York Times*, May 9, 1955, p. 10.

4. Norman Cousins, "Hiroshima Maidens," Hibakusha Stories.

5. Mike Meginnis, "The Atomic Bombing of Hiroshima: The Stuff of Reality TV," Electric Lit, accessed May 22, 2017, electricliterature.com/the-atomic-bombing-of-hiroshima-the-stuff-of-reality-tv.

6. "Kiyoshi Tanimoto, This is Your Life," YouTube video, accessed May 22, 2017, youtube.com/watch?v=KPFXa2vTErc.

7. Hersey, *Hiroshima*, 40.

8. Evelin Lindner, "Hiroshima and What We Can Learn Today: The Story of Koko Kondo," Human Dignity and Humiliation Studies, accessed May 22, 2017, humiliationstudies.org/documents/evelin/KokoKondo.pdf.

Chapter Three

1. Material in this chapter on Bikini is generally based on Jack Niedenthal, *For the Good of Mankind: A History of the People of Bikini and Their Islands* (Majuro: Bravo, 2001), 43–47.

2. David Vine, *Island of Shame: The Secret History of the U.S. Military Base on Diego Garcia* (Princeton, NJ: Princeton University Press, 2009), 64.

Chapter Four

1. Patrik Alac, *Bikini Story* (New York: Parkstone Press, 2015), unnumbered digital version.

2. Elaine T. May, *Homeward Bound: American Families in the Cold War Era* (New York: Basic Books, 1990), 110–113.

3. "A. Powell Davies: A Brief Biography," Davies Memorial Unitarian Universalist Church, accessed May 22, 2017, dmuuc.org/aboutworship/dr-a-powell-davies-bio-sermons.

4. "The Atomic Cake Controversy of 1946," *Conelrad Adjacent* (blog), accessed May 22, 2017, conelrad.blogspot.com/2010/09/atomic-cake-controversy-of-1946.html.

5. "The Atomic Cake Sermon," *Conelrad Adjacent* (blog), accessed May 22, 2017, conelrad.blogspot.com/2010/09/atomic-cake-sermon-1946.html.

6. "The Atomic Cake Controversy of 1946," *Conelrad Adjacent*.

Chapter Five

1. Material based on Joseph Dorinson and William Pencak, eds., *Paul Robeson: Essays on His Life and Legacy* (Jefferson, NC: McFarland, 2002), 32–55.

2. "A History of the Provincetown Playhouse," Provincetown Playhouse, accessed May 22, 2017, provincetownplayhouse.com/history.html.

3. Lindsey R. Swindall, *Paul Robeson: A Life of Activism and Art* (Lanham, MD: Rowman & Littlefield, 2013), 46.

4. Dorinson and Pencak, eds., *Paul Robeson*, 81–83.

5. Dorinson and Pencak, eds., *Paul Robeson*, 81.

6. Martha Biondi, *To Stand and Fight: The Struggle for Civil Rights in Postwar New York City* (Cambridge, MA: Harvard University Press, 2006), 69.

7. "VIDEO: Pete Seeger Recalls the 1949 Peekskill Riot Where He and Paul Robeson Were Attacked," Democracy Now!, accessed May 22, 2017, democracynow.org/2014/1/31/video_pete_seeger_recalls_the_1949.

8. Dorinson and Pencak, eds., *Paul Robeson*, 131.

9. Dorinson and Pencak, eds., *Paul Robeson*, 89.

10. "VIDEO: Pete Seeger Recalls the 1949 Peekskill Riot."

11. Dorinson and Pencak, eds., *Paul Robeson*, 91–92.

Chapter Six

1. Susan E. Reed, "Atomic Lake," *New Republic* 205, no. 18 (1991): 12.

2. Farangis Najibullah and Ukulyay Bestayeva, "Slow Death in Kazakhstan's Land of Nuclear Tests," RadioFreeEurope/RadioLiberty, accessed May 22, 2017, rferl.org/content/soviet_nuclear_testing_semipalatinsk_20th_anniversary/24311518.html.

3. Jacob Baynham, "From Russia, with Radiation," *Slate*, September 2, 2013, accessed May 22, 2017, slate.com/articles/news_and_politics/foreigners/2013/09/kazakhstan_was_site_of_the_soviet_union_s_first_atomic_bomb_the_kazak_people.html.

4. Stephen F. Cohen, *The Victims Return: Survivors of the Gulag After Stalin* (London: I. B. Tauris, 2012), 4.

5. Helen Rappaport, *Joseph Stalin: A Biographical Companion* (Santa Barbara, CA: ABC-CLIO, 1999), 123.

Chapter Seven

1. Boyer, *By the Bomb's Early Light*, 239.

2. Eric S. Singer, "Saving City X: Planners, Citizens, and the Culture of Civil Defense in Baltimore, 1950–1964," PhD diss., American University, 2012.

3. Bo Jacobs, "Atomic Kids: *Duck and Cover* and *Atomic Alert* Teach American Children How to Survive Atomic Attack," *Film & History* 40, no. 1 (2010).

4. Kenneth D. Rose, *One Nation Underground: The Fallout Shelter in American Culture* (New York: NYU Press, 2004), 133.

5. Rose, *One Nation Underground*.

6. Singer, "Saving City X," 75–78.

Chapter Eight

1. Guy Oakes, *The Imaginary War: Civil Defense and American Cold War Culture* (New York: Oxford University Press, 1994), 95.

2. "Operation Alert 1955 Protests," *Conelrad Adjacent* (blog), accessed June 7, 2017, conelrad.blogspot.com/2010/12/operation-alert-1955-protests.html.

3. Joanne Meyerowitz, ed., *Not June Cleaver: Women and Gender in Postwar America, 1945–1960* (Philadelphia: Temple University Press, 1994), 207.

4. "Mary Sharmat's Statement Regarding Her Civil Defense Protest," PBS *American Experience*, accessed March 1, 2007.

5. Dee Garrison, "Our Skirts Gave Them Courage," in *Not June Cleaver: Women and Gender in Postwar America, 1945–1960*, ed. Joanne Jay Meyerowitz (Philadelphia: Temple University Press, 1994), 216.

6. Meyerowitz, ed., *Not June Cleaver*, 215–217.

Chapter Nine

1. Julius W. Becton, *Becton: Autobiography of a Soldier and Public Servant* (Annapolis, MD: Naval Institute Press, 2017).

Chapter Ten

1. Bruce Cumings, "Why Did Truman Really Fire MacArthur? . . . The Obscure History of Nuclear Weapons and the Korean War Provides the Answer," History News Network, accessed June 7, 2017, hnn.us/articles/9245.html.

2. Mark Selden and Alvin Y. So, *War and State Terrorism: The United States, Japan, and the Asia-Pacific in the Long Twentieth Century* (New York: Rowman & Littlefield, 2003), 73.

3. John S. D. Eisenhower, *Soldiers and Statesmen: Reflections on Leadership* (Columbia: University of Missouri Press, 2012), 112–113.

4. "The President Is Very Acutely Ill," *Prologue Magazine*, National Archives, accessed June 7, 2017, archives.gov/publications/prologue/2012/fall/truman-ill.html.

Chapter Eleven

1. Choe Sang-Hun, "Korean War Survivors Tell of Carnage Inflicted by U.S.," *New York Times*, July 21, 2008, accessed June 7, 2017, nytimes.com/2008/07/21/world/asia/21iht-incheon.1.14657938.html?_r=0.

2. Linda Granfield, *I Remember Korea: Veterans Tell Their Stories of the Korean War* (New York: Clarion Books, 2003), 9–12.

3. James Wright, "What We Learned from the Korean War," *The Atlantic*, July 23, 2013, accessed June 7, 2017, theatlantic.com/international/archive/2013/07/what-we-learned-from-the-korean-war/278016.

4. "Ideal Countdown Toy Commercial (1962)," YouTube video, accessed June 7, 2017, https://www.youtube.com/watch?v=4AWnEs0PRrc.

5. Ann Marie Kordas, *The Politics of Childhood in Cold War America* (London: Pickering & Chatto, 2013), chap. 3.

6. JT Dykman, "Fifty Years Ago: Winter of Discontent: Winter 1951–52," Eisenhower Institute, accessed June 7, 2017, eisenhowerinstitute.org/about/living_history/winter_1952.dot.

7. "Irving Berlin," Songwriters Hall of Fame, accessed June 7, 2017, songwritershalloffame.org/exhibits/bio/C3.

8. Lawrence Bergreen, *As Thousands Cheer: The Life of Irving Berlin* (New York: Da Capo Press, 1996), 507–509.

9. Dykman, "Fifty Years Ago."

Chapter Twelve

1. "Eisenhower Answers America: A Political Announcement Paid for by Citizens for Eisenhower," 1956 (dated incorrectly) Eisenhower campaign ad, YouTube video, accessed June 7, 2017, youtube.com/watch?v=lEINBjHHvHE; and Linda Lee Kaid and Christina Holtz-Bacha, *Encyclopedia of Political Communication*, vol. 1 (Thousand Oaks, CA: Sage Publications, 2008), 204.

2. "Eisenhower Answers America: A Political Announcement Paid for by Citizens for Eisenhower," Eisenhower campaign ad, YouTube video, accessed June 7, 2017, youtube.com/watch?v=OJ3BngTJJS4.

3. Kaid and Holtz-Bacha, *Encyclopedia of Political Communication*, 204

4. "Election of 1952," American Presidency Project, University of California Santa Barbara, accessed June 7, 2017, presidency.ucsb.edu/showelection.php?year=1952.

5. Herbert York, *The Advisors: Oppenheimer, Teller, and the Superbomb* (Stanford, CA: Stanford University Press, 1989), 91.

6. "The Effects of a 300 Kiloton Nuclear Warhead Detonated Above Washington, D.C.," Nuclear Age Peace Foundation, accessed June 7, 2017, wagingpeace.org /the-effects-of-a-300-kiloton-nuclear-warhead-detonated-above-washington-d-c.

7. Tommy Swenson, "*Lucky Dragon 5* and the Terrifying Truth That Inspired *Godzilla*," Birth. Movies. Death. July 28, 2013, accessed June 7, 2017, birthmoviesdeath.com/2013/07/28/ lucky-dragon-5-and-the-terrifying-truth-that-inspired-godzilla.

Chapter Thirteen

1. This section on Sputnik is based on Paul Dickson, *Sputnik: The Shock of the Century* (New York: Walker Books, 2001), 12–34.

2. David E. Newton, *Latinos in Science, Math, and Professions* (New York: Facts on File, 2007), 57–58.

3. Franklin Chang-Díaz and Janet Vondra, *Dream's Journey* (self-published, 2014), 2–4.

4. Lily Rothman, "Meet the First Hispanic American in Space," *Time*, January 12, 2016, accessed June 7, 2017, time.com/4168255/franklin-chang-diaz.

Chapter Fourteen

1. Beverly Gray, "The Continuing Calamity of 'On the Beach,'" *Bulletin of the Atomic Scientists*, August 3, 2015, accessed June 7, 2017, thebulletin.org/continuing-relevance-beach8589.

Chapter Fifteen

1. Jerry Carrier, *Tapestry: The History and Consequences of America's Complex Culture* (New York: Algora Publishing, 2014), 192.

2. Unless otherwise indicated, the material on Iran is based on Stephen Kinzer, *All the Shah's Men: An American Coup and the Roots of Middle East Terror* (Hoboken, NJ: John Wiley & Sons, 2008), 58–133.

3. Gholam-Reza Sabri-Tabrizi, *Iran: A Child's Story, A Man's Experience* (New York: International Publishers, 1989), 108.

4. "Life Under the Shah," *Harvard Crimson*, December 6, 1979, accessed June 8, 2017, thecrimson.com/article/1979/12/6/life-under-the-shah-pit-was.

Chapter Sixteen

1. Maria Godoy and April Fulton, "Elvis Left the Building Long Ago, but His Food (and Music) Lives On," from "All Things Considered" radio show, NPR, January 8, 2013, text and audio accessed June 8, 2017, npr.org/sections /thesalt/2013/01/08/168871751/elvis-left-the-building-long-ago-but -his-food-and-music-lives-on.

2. Material in this section based on Peter Chapman, *Bananas: How the United Fruit Company Shaped the World* (Edinburgh, Scotland: Canongate, 2014).

3. David A. Graham, "Is the U.S. on the Verge of Becoming a Banana Republic?" *The Atlantic*, January 10, 2013, accessed June 8, 2017, theatlantic.com/politics /archive/2013/01/is-the-us-on-the-verge-of-becoming-a-banana -republic/267048.

4. Leo A. Suslow, *Aspects of Social Reform in Guatemala, 1944–1949* (Hamilton, NY: Colgate University, 1949), 21.

5. Material in this section based on Piero Gleijeses, *Shattered Hope: The Guatemalan Revolution and the United States, 1944–1954* (Princeton, NJ: Princeton University Press, 1992), 11–25.

6. CIA document (title illegible), est. date December 1, 1953, accessed June 8, 2017, foia.cia.gov/sites/default/files/document_conversions/89801 /DOC_0000923963.pdf.

Chapter Seventeen

1. Michael D'Antonio, *Hershey: Milton S. Hershey's Extraordinary Life of Wealth, Empire, and Utopian Dreams* (New York: Simon & Schuster, 2007), 166–167.

2. This section is based on Peter Moruzzi, *Havana Before Castro: When Cuba Was a Tropical Playground* (Layton, UT: Gibbs Smith, 2008), 26–36.

3. Richard Gott, *Cuba: A New History* (New Haven, CT: Yale University Press, 2005), 111.

4. Unless otherwise indicated, this section on bateyes is based on Bartow J. Elmore,

Citizen Coke: The Making of Coca-Cola Capitalism (New York: W. W. Norton, 2016).

5. Kathleen Morgan Drowne and Patrick Huber, *The 1920s* (Westport, CT: Greenwood, 2004), 136.

6. The rest of this section is based on Louis A. Perez, *On Becoming Cuban: Identity, Nationality, and Culture* (Chapel Hill: University of North Carolina Press, 1999), 242–245.

7. Gott, *Cuba*, 129.

8. David F. Schmitz, *Thank God They're on Our Side: The United States and Right-Wing Dictatorships, 1921–1965* (Chapel Hill: University of North Carolina Press, 1999), 88–92.

9. Gott, *Cuba*, 142–144.

10. David Grann, "The Yankee Comandante," *New Yorker*, May 28, 2012, accessed June 8, 2017, newyorker.com/magazine/2012/05/28/the-yankee-comandante.

11. Grann, "The Yankee Comandante."

Chapter Eighteen

1. Material on William Alexander Morgan is based on Grann, "The Yankee Comandante."

2. Alistair Cooke, "Cuban Dictator Flees," *The Guardian*, January 2, 1959, accessed June 8, 2017, theguardian.com/world/1959/jan/02/cuba1.

3. Armando Valladares, *Against All Hope: A Memoir of Life in Castro's Gulag* (New York: Alfred A. Knopf, 1986), 5.

4. Jim Rasenberger, *The Brilliant Disaster: JFK, Castro, and America's Doomed Invasion of Cuba's Bay of Pigs* (New York: Simon & Schuster, 2011), 63, 74–75.

5. Glenn Garvin, "The *Miami Herald*, the CIA, and the Bay of Pigs Scoop That Didn't Run," *Miami Herald*, April 17, 2015, accessed June 8, 2017, miamiherald.com/news/local/community/miami-dade/article18792675.html.

Chapter Nineteen

1. Kayla Webley, "How the Nixon-Kennedy Debate Changed the World," *Time*,

September 23, 2010, accessed June 8, 2017, content.time.com/time/nation /article/0,8599,2021078,00.html.

2. "Life of John F. Kennedy," John F. Kennedy Presidential Library and Museum, accessed June 8, 2017, jfklibrary.org/JFK/Life-of-John-F-Kennedy.aspx.

3. "John F. Kennedy and PT 109," John F. Kennedy Presidential Library and Museum, accessed June 8, 2017, jfklibrary.org/JFK/JFK-in-History/John -F-Kennedy-and-PT109.aspx.

4. "Life of John F. Kennedy," John F. Kennedy Presidential Library and Museum.

5. Webley, "How the Nixon-Kennedy Debate Changed the World."

6. "September 26, 1960 Debate Transcript: The First Kennedy-Nixon Presidential Debate," Commission on Presidential Debates, accessed June 8, 2017, debates .org/index.php?page=september-26-1960-debate-transcript.

7. "October 21, 1960 Debate Transcript: The Fourth Kennedy-Nixon Presidential Debate," Commission on Presidential Debates, accessed June 8, 2017, debates .org/index.php?page=october-21-1960-debate-transcript.

8. David Talbot, *Brothers: The Hidden History of the Kennedy Years* (London: Simon & Schuster, 2007), 37.

9. "October 21, 1960 Debate Transcript: The Fourth Kennedy-Nixon Presidential Debate."

10. Talbot, *Brothers*, 37.

Chapter Twenty

1. This chapter on the Bay of Pigs is based on Rasenberger, *The Brilliant Disaster*, 98–344.

Chapter Twenty-One

1. "Excerpt from Fidel Castro's Speech at Havana's May Day Celebrations on May 2, 1961—Less Than Two Weeks After the Bay of Pigs Invasion," HistoryofCuba.com, accessed June 8, 2017, historyofcuba.com/history/speech1 .htm.

2. Rasenberger, *The Brilliant Disaster*, 418.

3. Darren Boyle, "From Poisoned Cigars to Exploding Seashells: How Half a Century of Crackpot CIA Plans to Overthrow Fidel Castro Were Born When JFK Invited James Bond Author Ian Fleming to Dinner," *Daily Mail*, December 18, 2014, accessed June 8, 2017, dailymail.co.uk/news/article-2878730/The-ill -fated-schemes-upend-Castro.html.

4. Duncan Campbell, "638 Ways to Kill Castro," *The Guardian*, August 6, 2006, accessed June 8, 2017, theguardian.com/world/2006/aug/03/cuba .duncancampbell2.

Chapter Twenty-Two

1. Berlin material in this chapter is based on Greg Mitchell, *The Tunnels: Escapes Under the Berlin Wall and the Historic Films the JFK White House Tried to Kill* (New York: Penguin, 2016).

Chapter Twenty-Three

1. David E. Schmidt, *The Folly of War: American Foreign Policy, 1898–2005* (New York: Algora Publishing, 2005), 211.

2. "John F. Kennedy: Address on the Cuban Crisis, October 22, 1962," *Modern History Sourcebook*, accessed June 8, 2017, http://sourcebooks.fordham.edu/ halsall/mod/1962kennedy-cuba.html.

3. "Childhood Memories of the Cuban Missile Crisis," from "Tell Me More" radio show, NPR, October 22, 2012, accessed June 8, 2017, npr .org/2012/10/22/163395079/childhood-memories-of-the-cuban-missile-crisis.

4. Alice L. George, *Awaiting Armageddon: How Americans Faced the Cuban Missile Crisis* (Chapel Hill: University of North Carolina Press, 2003), 80–85.

A Time Line of Events

1821 Guatemala declares independence from Spain.

1898 Manuel Estrada Cabrera takes power over Guatemala in a rigged election.

1901 The United States drafts the Platt Amendment, which stated that Cuba could not make treaties with foreign countries, or allow foreign military bases on its soil, without first asking the United States for permission.

1920 Guatemalans overthrow President Cabrera.

1931 General Jorge Ubico takes power in Guatemala.

1940 Fulgencio Batista y Zalvídar is elected president of Cuba.

July 1, 1944 Guatemalan dictator Ubico resigns amid protests.

April 12, 1945 President Franklin Roosevelt dies.

August 6, 1945 The United States drops an atomic bomb on Hiroshima, Japan.

August 9, 1945 The United States drops an atomic bomb on Nagasaki, Japan.

September 1945 Japan surrenders, officially ending World War II.

March 1946 Residents of the Bikini Atoll island chain are evacuated onto a US Navy tank landing ship to Rongerik.

July 1, 1946 An American B-29 plane drops an atomic bomb over the Bikini lagoon.

August 31, 1946 *New Yorker* magazine publishes John Hersey's "Hiroshima," an article that describes the bombing of Hiroshima through the eyes of its victims.

May 1, 1946 The Iranian communist party Tudeh organizes a protest on the streets of Tehran to fight for workers' rights.

1947 The House Un-American Activities Committee (HUAC) accused many Hollywood actors and artist of being members of the Communist Party, including the ten writers and directors who were called in as witnesses and became known as the "Hollywood Ten."

August 1949 Paul Robeson is asked to sing at a benefit concert hosted by the Harlem chapter of the Civil Rights Congress near Peekskill, New York, but the concert is disrupted by violent protestors.

August 29, 1949 The Soviet Union successfully explodes its first atomic bomb at the Semipalatinsk Test Site.

September 3, 1949 An American RB-29 flying from Japan to Alaska detects dust from the Semipalatinsk explosion, alerting the federal government to the USSR's new nuclear capabilities.

September 4, 1949 Paul Robeson's benefit concert, rescheduled by the Civil Rights Congress, takes place. It is again disrupted by violent protestors, ultimately resulting in a riot that left 150 people injured.

June 25, 1950 North Korea invades South Korea, marking the start of the Korean War. President Truman would soon commit US troops to assist South Korea on behalf of the UN.

October 13, 1949 Mohammad Mossadegh leads a march to the entrance of Shah Mohammad Reza Pahlavi's Golestan Palace in Iran, and camps out on the palace green for seventy-two hours until the shah pledges to hold fair elections.

October 25, 1950 China becomes involved in the Korean War by attacking UN positions at Unsan.

November 12, 1950 Colonel Jacobo Arbenz is elected president of Guatemala.

November 24, 1950 US General Douglas MacArthur launches an offensive toward the Chinese border.

December 9, 1950 General MacArthur asks for permission to use atomic bombs whenever he felt necessary.

March 1951 President Truman begins to actively seek a cease-fire in the Korean War.

April 11, 1951 President Truman fires belligerent General MacArthur, destroying his own approval ratings in the process.

April 28, 1951 Mohammad Mossadegh is voted as prime minister of Iran by the Majlis, or Iranian parliament.

May 1, 1951 A bill—submitted by Mossadegh—to nationalize the Anglo-Iranian Oil Company, seizing control of the oil fields at Abadan, becomes law.

March 1952 President Truman announces that he will not run for a second full term.

January 6, 1952 Senator Henry Cabot Lodge Jr. enters Dwight D. Eisenhower's name in the New Hampshire presidential primary.

February 1952 Thousands come to Madison Square Garden in New York in support of Eisenhower, popularizing the chant "I Like Ike."

November 1, 1952 The United States destroys the island of Elugelab with its first ever hydrogen bomb test. The island disappears after burning for six hours following the explosion.

January 20, 1953 Dwight D. Eisenhower is sworn in as the thirty-fourth president of the United States.

February 1953 The United States begins to roll out "duck and cover" civil defense films in schools to provide a plan for the possibility of a nuclear attack.

July 26, 1953 Fidel Castro leads rebels on a dangerous assault on the Moncada Barracks, guarded by the army of Cuban dictator Batista, and is subsequently arrested.

July 27, 1953 Representatives from the United Nations meet with North Korean leaders in Panmunjom, Korea, to sign a truce that would end the Korean War at a stalemate. They divided North and South Korea along the 38th parallel and promised a peace treaty within three months, which was ultimately never written.

August 12, 1953 The Soviet Union successfully tests its first prototype hydrogen bomb over Semipalatinsk Test Site.

August 1953 The CIA launches Operation PBSUCCESS to turn Guatemalans against President Arbenz and put in power a government friendly to United Fruit.

March 1, 1954 The detonation of an American hydrogen bomb devastates the Japanese fishing industry as fear of radiation poisoning by contaminated fish spreads across Japan.

June 27, 1954 Jacobo Arbenz announces that he is stepping down as president of Guatemala.

June 15, 1955 The Operation Alert 1955 drill occurs in New York City, met with peaceful protest led by pacifist Dorothy Day.

November 25, 1956 Fidel Castro and Che Guevara lead a band of eighty revolutionaries from Mexico to Cuba in an attempt to overthrow Batista but are ambushed and barely escape.

August 1957 The Soviet Union successfully tests the world's first intercontinental ballistic missile, or ICBM, making it possible to launch nuclear weapons without planes, and to send satellites into space.

November 1957 The National Committee for a Sane Nuclear Policy calls for an end to nuclear testing and receives overwhelming support, leading them to establish a national antinuclear organization called SANE.

October 4, 1957 The Soviet Union launches Sputnik Zemlya, the first earth satellite.

Late 1958 The United States withdraws support for Cuban dictator Batista.

January 1, 1959 Batista is forced into exile.

May 3, 1960 The Civil Defense Protest Committee stages a protest of young mothers during a civil defense drill in New York City.

September 26, 1960 John F. Kennedy spars with Vice President Richard Nixon in the first nationally televised presidential debate.

January 20, 1961 John F. Kennedy is inaugurated as the thirty-fifth president of the United States.

April 17, 1961 Cuban exiles trained by the US government invade the Bay of Pigs along the coast of Cuba, but are met by Cuban soldiers and, without the assistance of US troops, ultimately fail in their mission to overthrow Castro.

August 13, 1961 East German troops begin building barbed-wire fences to stop East Germans from escaping to the west. The barrier would eventually be replaced by a concrete wall known as the Berlin Wall.

October 13, 1962 An American spy plane notices a set of medium-range SS-4 Soviet missiles in western Cuba.

October 22, 1962 President Kennedy announces his plan to have a blockade formed around Cuba.

October 24, 1962 The US Air Force declares DEFCON 2, the highest level of alert before all-out war, and prepares to strike targets in the Soviet Union.

October 25, 1962 Soviet leaders prepare to remove their missiles from Cuba, but hear of US intention to invade Cuba.

October 27, 1962 The Cuban Missile Crisis reaches its peak. A Soviet submarine carrying nuclear weapons breaches the American blockade around Cuba and is attacked by an American ship. Vasily Arkhipov convinces Soviet Commander Valentin Savitsky not to launch a nuclear torpedo on the United States. Meanwhile, a US spy plane is shot down over Cuba, and the Soviets prepare to launch nuclear weapons at Guantanamo while Kennedy authorizes for an air strike and mobilizes 250,000 troops.

October 28, 1962 Soviet leader Nikita Khrushchev agrees to withdraw missiles from Cuba in exchange for the United States removing its own missiles from Turkey.

Photo Credits

Part One: Atomic Fallout

Chapter 1: Hiroshima: Imagination and Reality

p. 11: *John Hersey, Pulitzer . . . author of* Hiroshima. *Library of Congress*

p. 13: *This map shows . . . in every direction. Public domain*

p. 16: *Sadako. Public domain*

p. 18: *In 1958, a . . . and her bravery. Public domain*

Chapter 2: Maiden Voyage

p. 20: *This girl sits . . . as she lives. Hiroshima Peace Culture Foundation.*

p. 25: *The Hiroshima Maidens . . . arrive in Hawaii. Peace Resource Center, Wilmington College.*

p. 26: *Hiroshima Maiden Shigeko . . . and newfound friend. Peace Resource Center, Wilmington College.*

p. 28: *After their surgeries . . . a newspaper photograph. Peace Resource Center, Wilmington College.*

Chapter 14: On the Beach

p. 143 (left): *Albert Schweitzer was . . . of nuclear tests. Library of Congress*

p. 143 (right): *A poster produced . . . SANE, in 1964. Library of Congress*

Part Four: Americanizing the World

Chapter 15: The Cost of Oil: Iran

p. 156: *A pro-Mossadegh . . . CIA in 1953. Nasser Sadeghi via Wikimedia Commons, public domain*

Chapter 16: Bananas for Bananas

p. 166 (top): *Customers show off . . . Bay, Massachusetts, 1950. Library of Congress*

p. 166 (bottom): *Bananas were a . . . store in 1948. Library of Congress*

p. 168: *Captain Lorenzo Baker . . . States from Jamaica. Library of Congress*

p. 169 (top): *Men load bananas . . . this 1926 photograph. Library of Congress*

p. 169 (bottom): *In 1938, ten . . . in New York City. Library of Congress*

p. 170: *Workers in a . . . stores, October 1948. Library of Congress*

p. 171: *Manuel Estrada Cabrera . . . with open arms. Library of Congress*

p. 172: *Three Mayan children . . . plantations throughout Guatemala. Library of Congress*

p. 177: *Guatemalan president Jacobo . . . by the CIA. Associated Press*

Chapter 17: Sweet Empire

p. 181: *Milton Hershey, the "Chocolate King," in 1903. Hershey Community Archive*

p. 182: *Havana's Paseo del . . . after Kitty's death. State Historical Society of Colorado, Library of Congress*

p. 185 (top): *Cuban plantation workers . . . on a wagon. State Historical Society of Colorado, Library of Congress*

p. 185 (bottom): *Sugar plantation workers . . . boss on horseback. Library of Congress*

p. 187: *Before Milton Hershey's . . . the one above. Library of Congress*

p. 191: *Cuban dictator Gerardo . . . revolted against him. Library of Congress*

p. 192: *Sumner Welles, US . . . November 10, 1938. Library of Congress*

p. 193: *US Army Chief . . . November 11, 1938. Library of Congress*

p. 194: *Major General Craig . . . and their capabilities. Library of Congress*

p. 195: *A hand-painted mural . . . in Havana, Cuba. Library of Congress*

Acknowledgments

This book would not have been possible without the support, guidance, patience, and scholarship of many incredible people.

I am grateful to Koko Tanimoto Kondo for her activism and our friendship. You are this book's inspiration. I would like to thank the Peace Resource Center at Wilmington College, All Souls Unitarian Church, American University's Nuclear Culture Institute, Paul Boyer, Elaine Tyler May, Laura McEnaney, Robert J. Lifton, Greg Mitchell, John Hersey, Norman Cousins, Kiyoshi Tanimoto, Paul Robeson, David Grann, Jack Niedenthal, David Vine, A. Powell Davies, Kenneth Rose, Guy Oakes, Bruce Cumings, Stephen Kinzer, Peter Chapman, Simki Kuznick, Indira Fleet and Jim Rasenberger for your research, writing, and extraordinary talents. This book would not have been possible without your contributions. Nor would it have been possible without the diligence, patience, and expertise of our wonderful editors, Ruta Rimas and Nicole Fiorica.

Though not directly cited in these pages, I would like to express my eternal gratitude to the following people: to my parents, Sharon and Jeffrey Singer, who gave me life and continue to inspire me to pursue excellence. To my wife, Rachel, and our daughter, Evie, who supported me, encouraged me, and consoled me through many months of research, writing, and rewriting. To those who served as my greatest role models, nurtured my intellectual and spiritual development, incubated my love for history, and fostered my commitment to human rights, including Abraham and Estelle Singer, Ida and Sidney Pats, Sheila and Alan Friedman, Nancy and Alan Kirson, Isaac Bormel, Joe "Yakel" Bormel, Florence Litt, Tom Hockstra, Jean Lillquist, Steve "Goldy" Goldsmith, Cathy Butterfield, Leonard Steinhorn and Robert Griffith, Robin White, and the super-naturally talented D. Watkins.

Last but not least, to Peter Kuznick and Oliver Stone, intellectual and cultural powerhouses who have always believed in me, supported me, and pushed me to achieve goals I once thought unimaginable. Working with you continues to be an honor and a privilege.

—E. S.

Index